To Dr. Schmidt

Marin Fitzgerald

THE AIDS INDICTMENT

THE
AIDS
INDICTMENT

Marvin R. Kitzerow Jr.

MRKCO Publishing
Div. of MRKCO Marketing

Published in the United States by MRKCO Publishing
Div. Of MRKCO Marketing

Library of Congress Control Number: 00-090460
International Standard Book Number - 0-9679529-0-5

Text Design Action Press, Fond du Lac, WI

Books are available at your local bookstore or at retail by sending a check or money order for $14.95, including free shipping and handling to MRKCO Marketing; PO Box 32034; Chicago, IL 60632.
Illinois residents, include $1.31 sales tax.
or
by credit card at: _aidsindictment.com_

Books are available at wholesale or for promotion by contacting MRKCO Marketing at PO Box 32034, Chicago, Illinois 60632.
or
Contact the publisher at: _aidsindictment.com_

Over 1000 research scientists, Nobel Prize winners, college professors, physicians and professional persons no longer believe that HIV causes AIDS!

AIDS is not a death sentence and is easily reversed by utilizing alternative health care implementing natural hygiene!

Thousands of HIV positive persons have been surviving AIDS for over sixteen years by refusing all alleged antiviral drugs!

Table of Contents

Dedication

My gratitude and thanks go out to the late T.C. Fry, Dean of Life Science Institute. His dedication to the health and welfare of humanity inspired me to write this book.

Society owes a great deal of gratitude to Dr. Peter Duesberg for his dedication to scientific research excellence and his relentless perseverance against overwhelming opposition and ridicule to educate and change the course of intellect in the true cause of AIDS. Although Dr. Duesberg is paying the price now for his innovative approach, the test of time and self-evident truth will ultimately prevail and the ignorant will see the light.

Special gratitude goes out to Jeremy Selvey, Director of Project AIDS International and the late Mark L. Alampi for the effort that they have expended in their pursuit of truth in AIDS research and the dissemination of information to the masses.

Also recognition should be given to Dr. Harry Haverkos from the National Institute on Drug Abuse and all of the research scientists who have contributed to the study of Nitrite Inhalant Abuse.

Special gratitude goes out to:

Professor Ronald Wood for his efforts in ridding our society of "poppers."

Lisa Loschetter, Amy Plymouth, Lisa Wagner, Matthew Raulston and Cindy Powers for their long, arduous hours spent in transcribing and editing.

Finally, my family and close friends who have supported me during the years I have spent on this project. Thank you!

About The Author

Marvin Kitzerow, Jr. over the past twenty years has engaged in nutritional science research, primarily focusing on the causation of human pathology. Utilizing his knowledge of food chemistry and including the study of gastroenterology (pathology relative to the digestive process), Kitzerow is working to understand and relate the vital role that diet plays in the illnesses of man (Dietary Pathology).

The author is a graduate of The Nutritional Science Program taught at the Life Science Institute in Austin, Texas.

Besides authoring and lecturing in nutritional science, Kitzerow has spent the past ten years in the research associated with the writing of *"The Aids Indictment."*

The opinions expressed in this book are those of the author and do not necessarily reflect those of the publisher, printer, distributors or any point of purchase with regards to this book.

The information in this book is for dissemination of knowledge and should not be construed as giving medical advice. Your choice of health care and my right to express my opinions are protected by the First Amendment to the U.S. Constitution regarding the freedom of speech.

Prospectous

If you do not read this book in it's entirety, you will never know the truth behind the United States AIDS epidemic.

Upon reading this book, you will realize the fact that we have been told only half of the story.

One hundred percent of the first AIDS patients were aggressive abusers of toxic nitrite inhalants and, or IV drugs.

These patients presented Pneumocystis carinii pneumonia (PCP) and, or Kaposis Sarcoma (KS), a questionable cancer, rarely found in otherwise healthy young men.

Thus, the prescribed treatment of chemotherapy, originated out of a knee jerk reaction to KS symptoms, while the PCP patients were also treated with chemotherapy, anticipating they too, would eventually develop KS.

This author contends that prescribing killer, chemo drugs to these already chemically toxic patients, was the true cause of death in these mortality statistics.

Research presents a direct link to KS as a result of chronic, aggressive, abuse of nitrite inhalants, which are referred to as one of the most immunodestructive, cancer causing chemicals known to man. In a very short time frame, all of these chemically toxic patients who were treated with chemo, died of full blown AIDS.

Evidenced by the fact that all these patients died while on chemotherapy, it was very obvious that chemo was a total failure.

When HIV was alleged to be discovered by an American research team headed up by Dr. Robert Gallo, the statement was made that HIV was a direct killer of white blood cells, subsequently explaining the mechanism that causes AIDS.

Now that AIDS was being blamed on a virus, you would not treat a virus with chemotherapy, you would conjure up an alleged antiviral drug, especially since the chemotherapy route was a miserable failure.

Zidovudine (AZT) was a failed chemotherapy that was subjected to early retirement, due to the fact that it was so toxic it caused cancer at any dose.

The pharmaceutical manufacturer Burroughs Wellcome, in a marketing ploy, pulled the failed AZT drug out of mothballs and essentially, just re-classified it as an alleged antiviral drug.

No matter what the drug company called this drug, it was still a chemotherapy drug that destroyed the immune system, and as such, was already a failure. So AZT was destined to failure by its very nature.

Now, over 13 years since AZT was first licensed, more than 400,000 U.S. citizens have died of AIDS. If that is not a record of failure, I don't know what is. Not one life has been saved utilizing aggressive therapy with AZT. Doctors have only prolonged the life and misery of AIDS patients by reducing the daily dose, while slow death is inevitable.

A SUSPECTED TRAGEDY SURFACES

A growing list of scientists no longer believe that HIV is a direct killer of white blood cells (wbcs). They believe that other than an indicator of toxic blood, HIV plays little to no role in causing AIDS.

Over one thousand research scientists, physicians, college professors, Nobel Prize winners and professional persons no longer believe that HIV causes AIDS.

As HIV is being proven everyday not to cause AIDS, the probability arises that hundreds of thousands of otherwise remedial patients have died as a result of chronic abuse of alleged antiviral drugs that were prescribed by their physicians.

Research has also established the fact that problems in manufacturing AIDS test kits may have been responsible for thousands of persons testing false HIV positive who were rushed into killer, antiviral therapy.

People who tested false positive and died of chronic antiviral therapy would obviously present pseudoscientific statistics that aided in misleading scientists into the HIV/AIDS hypothesis in the first place.

4

It is a fact that thousands of HIV positive individuals are surviving over 16 years by not accepting alleged antiviral therapy. Either these people all tested false positive or their HIV status is insignificant. I would challenge the Burroughs/Glaxo Wellcome company to produce one person who has survived with aggressive AZT therapy. I will let you be the judge. If a virus is the cause of AIDS, why does a non-viral or lack of antiviral therapy have the most promising results in saving life?

Please, by all means, reserve your answer until you have read this book.

Introduction

In 1981, five cases of Pnuemocystitis Carini Pneumonia (PCP) were reported to the Center for Disease Control (CDC) in Atlanta, Georgia.[1] Soon to follow, eight cases of a rare cancer, among otherwise healthy young men, diagnosed as Kaposi's Sarcoma (KS), were reported to the Center for Disease Control (CDC).[2] Immediately, within that same year, red flag scrutiny of medical files presented 200 cases of either PCP or KS.[3-5] In retrospect, delayed reporting of homosexual men being diagnosed with KS or PCP, in 1980 would finally surface. All of these cases exhibited a state of greatly diminished immunity with unknown cause.

The unique and common bond that showed up in nearly 100 percent of all these early Acquired Immunodeficiency Syndrome (AIDS) cases is that those AIDS patients were found to have abused volatile nitrite, also known as room odorizers. The few patients who disclaimed nitrite abuse were abusing intravenous drugs.

It is, in my opinion, that chemical abuse was the most blatantly obvious cause of these immune deficient individuals. Due to the scattered and non-relative association of these individuals, a contagious bug or virus seems less likely, at least from my perspective.

Chemical abuse, recreational as well as prescription drugs, and its ability to cause the AIDS related symptoms KS and PCP, were amply recorded in medical literature, long before the AIDS epidemic began. This chemical cause was accepted fact which had absolutely nothing to do with a virus.

It was known as early as 1974, that PCP[9] and KS[10-12] were commonly associated with immunosuppressive drug therapy, commonly prescribed for arthritic patients and transplant recipients in order to prevent tissue or organ rejection. The physician is using powerful drugs to suppress the immune system in order to keep the body from attacking the foreign, transplanted organ. At the same time, the drugs are creating diseases in the patient that is manifesting into a cancer, known as KS. This also weakens the immune system and allows bacterial infection to proliferate in the lungs, thus causing the PCP.

7

Presented is viable medical research, evidence that immuno-suppressive drugs cause the side effects of KS and PCP, the two primary illnesses associated with AIDS. In a study involving 213 young and otherwise healthy homosexual men, all but a couple abused the same drug. All developed the same common illnesses associated with immunosuppressive inhalants.

If volatile nitrites are shown to be immunosuppressive and cancer causing, can one be correct in concluding that volatile nitrite inhalants, when aggressively abused, cause KS and PCP, which are eventually diagnosed as symptoms of AIDS? The obvious cause and effect relationship regarding volatile nitrites and AIDS seems to be a basic exercise in common sense.

Some important and startling conclusions, regarding the abuse of volatile nitrites and their relationship to the AIDS virus, will be revealed in the following chapters with the support and documenta-tion of valid research and case studies. The following facts that will be explored and proven are:

• Volatile nitrite inhalant is one of the most cancer causing immune destructive chemicals known to man.

• By 1974, the practice of inhaling one of the most cancer causing immune destructive chemicals known to man had reached every corner of the gay community and would begin to take hold in the heterosexual community four to five years later.

• AIDS is predominantly caused, or brought on by aggressive abuse of toxic inhalants and chemicals in the form of recreational and specific prescription drugs as well. Aggressive abuse of anti-biotics actually causes symptoms of AIDS.

• The profile of the majority of AIDS patients in the United States will include the abuse of volatile nitrite inhalants, regularly and aggressively, for approximately four to seven years.

• The remainder of AIDS patients are IV drug users. Also included in this category are the innocent AIDS patients, babies born to chemical abusing mothers, hemophiliacs transfused with tainted coagulation factor 8, and seniors being prescribed chronic immunosuppressive drugs. The major contributor to the demise of these sufferers was chemotherapy and AZT treatment, not their human immunovirus (HIV) status.

- Misdiagnosing HIV as the causative factor in AIDS patients has precipitated the life threatening treatment of chemotherapy and AZT, which is subsequently responsible for causing the death of otherwise remedial AIDS patients.

- Prescribing toxic prescription drugs to an already toxic patient is tantamount to murder.

- AIDS is a survivable illness, once the true cause, chemical abuse, is halted and a strict, healthy, dietary, life style is practiced.

- Millions of dollars in medical research, proving that AIDS is caused by chemical abuse (namely volatile nitrites) was thrown out with the discovery of HIV.

- The connection of nitrite abuse and KS, relative to AIDS, was finally realized and room odorizers were quietly banned and deemed an illegal substance by an act of Congress.

February, 1991 was the date in which volatile nitrites, or room odorizers, were no longer allowed to be sold legally.

- Nitrite, room odorizer manufacturers deceptively represented their products as room odorizers while 100 percent of their consumers purchased them for use as illegal drugs for over twenty years.

This book will present documented and validated research, proving that volatile nitrite inhalants are one of the most dangerous substances known to man. Aggressive abuse of inhaling this chemical, approximately over four to seven years, is all that is necessary to initiate AIDS in humans. This leaves HIV as only a fragmented, residual cellular debris, caused by chronic abuse of inhalants and drugs, recreational and prescription.

The reality of an epidemic of abuse of volatile nitrite inhalants occurring exclusively within the gay community, beginning in 1971, shall also be presented. This epidemic is primarily responsible for the majority of AIDS statistics, forming the AIDS epidemic in the United States.

The ban and subsequent removal of nitrite inhalants a.k.a. "Room Odorizers" or "Poppers," will be primarily responsible for the decline in new AIDS cases in the United States and the beginning of the end of the U.S. AIDS epidemic.

9

Indictment

Volatile nitrite inhalants, also known as room odorizers or poppers, were the most obvious cause of AIDS in the majority of all the early gay patients suffering from KS and or PCP. The massive research implicating the capability of nitrites to destroy the immune system and initiate Cancer along with the timely entry of the manufacture and sale of nitrite inhalants into American society, is just part of the case I have put together to form this indictment.

For over twenty years all of the United States consumer protection agencies allowed nitrite room odorizers, one of the most cancer causing, immunodestructive chemicals known to man, to be fraudulently distributed into interstate commerce, as well as within international markets.

From the beginning, nitrite room odorizers were purchased as sexual accessory drugs and not room odorizers. Odorizer manufacturers did not acknowledge that the product was a drug, and this imposed illicit fraud on American society. The room odorizer industry was fully aware of the fact their products were being purchased solely as a drug to augment sexual activity. The room odorizer industry is product liable and responsible for the majority of AIDS statistics, forming the United States AIDS epidemic. They are responsible for epidemics in other countries as well, because the industry has distributed their product worldwide.

All the insurance companies who have financed AIDS treatment, and all the families who have lost a loved one have an avenue to recapture monetary losses in a civil class action law suit. They should be entitled to share in the billions of dollars in profits enjoyed by the room odorizer industry during the past twenty years.

The FDA, CPSC, NIH, CDC and NIDA have known, since 1971, about the deceptive perpetration of the odorizer industry and the actual commercial use of odorizers being drugs. These organizations are to blame for allowing the room odorizer industry to market their death dealing products to children, teenagers, adults, and predominately the homosexual community for over twenty years.

11

A major medical error was made by the NIH and CDC, in exonerating volatile nitrite inhalants and their role in AIDS, due to premature cessation of their government study observing nitrite inhalant abusers.

World renowned researcher, Dr. Peter Duesberg, is on record as claiming that HIV could not possibly cause AIDS, while also maintaining that a chemical abuse is more likely the cause of AIDS. His expertise has been completely ignored by the NIH and CDC since 1987.

Dr. Gallo and the American Research Team who originally claimed to have discovered HIV and later agreed to share the discovery with the French, were the primary players in claiming that HIV caused AIDS. The American Team did their research in a hazardously fast paced manner in order to beat the French team and win the lucrative patent for the HIV blood test.

I believe, that monetary gain was at the forefront of the "rush to pass judgment" on HIV. This monetary motivation was instrumental in misdiagnosing HIV as the cause of AIDS. This misdiagnosis has precipitated the treatment of powerful poisonous drugs, chemo-therapy and AZT, to already toxic patients (who were aggressively abusing nitrite inhalants and or IV drugs), which contributed to the mortality of these individuals.

The misdiagnosis of the HIV virus as the cause of AIDS has given a green light to the nitrite inhalant abusers since 1984 and has set back nitrite and AIDS research over twelve years; subsequently, trying to kill HIV with chemotherapy and AZT is why all of the AIDS patients, who have accepted this traditional medical treatment, have died. It was presented at the 1994 Asian AIDS Conference that 40,000 HIV positive patients who have refused traditional medical treatment with chemotherapy or AZT, are living with HIV and have survived AIDS over sixteen years. This revelation should be compelling enough to realize that chemotherapy and AZT treatment is wrong and HIV is not the cause and only evidence of toxic damage to the bloodstream. As you will read later, I will disclose the path that long-term HIV survivors are taking. HIV positively is not a death sentence, and it is possible to survive AIDS.

If nitrite inhalants were not a problem, why did the Federal Government, by an act of congress, secretively shut down the billion-dollar room odorizer industry without a fight or any news coverage in the media?

Since room odorizers have been deemed illegal, new cases of AIDS have dropped by three percent nationally, as presented in the *Chicago Sun-Times* on February 3, 1995.

Since California had made volatile nitrite products illegal long before the rest of the United States, and due to a comprehensive and aggressive educational program on the danger of nitrite inhalants, the San Francisco Department of Health has predicted that by 1997 the appearance of new AIDS cases would be dropping dramatically.

Intravenous drug abuse, recreational drugs, and aggressive chemical therapies by physicians with immunosuppressive drugs all contribute to immune deficiency; however, these drugs were not exclusive to the gay community as was the use of nitrite inhalants for the first six years of entry into American society.

Common sense dictates that the primary cause of AIDS in 90% of the AIDS cases, being homosexual, is a causative factor, highly restrictive to the gay population. Nitrite inhalants are the only products commonly abused by the majority of homosexual men who maintained a strong exclusivity to these particular products. If nonexclusive causes were responsible for AIDS, the AIDS epidemic would not have remained predominantly in the homosexual community, with homosexuals still comprising approximately 80% of current AIDS statistics.

Now, twelve years after HIV was discovered and put to scientific scrutiny, it has not even come close to demonstrating the devastating effects that develop from aggressive abuse of volatile nitrite inhalants. Nitrite inhalants have been shown to be able to cause all of the thirty AIDS indicator illnesses.

The Federal Government has made commercially manufactured nitrite room odorizers illegal; however, a new product has replaced the old fraudulent scam that was being perpetrated by the room odorizer industry. A product being deceptively represented as a video head cleaner is being sold in almost all adult bookstores. It is impossible to find this product in regular video equipment stores. The fact that video equipment stores do not market this so called "video head cleaner," and the fact that the adult book store customers that purchase this product, do so, with the intent of abusing it as an inhalant drug, indicts the manufacturers of the H & E video head cleaner in the fraudulent distribution of a drug that has not been approved by the United States Federal Drug Administration (FDA).

Do-It International Inc., who manufactures this product, is welcomed to join the list of indictable conspirators in the class action suit, along with every retail store as coconspirators.

A Message From The Author

The preliminary overview is merely a condensed version, highlighting the bare essentials, in order to entice you into wading through the chronology of nitrite inhalant research. I have attempted to write the chronology with a minimum of technical terms in order to provide easy reading for the lay person. Although some of the conclusions are re-visited, once again, in the chronology, it is necessary to read the compendium of research in order to verify my conclusions and become aware of the complete scenario leading up to and the final days of the AIDS epidemic in the United States.

I promise you, that upon reading this book in its entirety, you will understand why AIDS occurred in this period in U.S. history and also why the end of the AIDS epidemic is in sight!

Chapter 1

What is AIDS?

Acquired Immunodeficiency Syndrome (AIDS) is a very understandable illness when explained in pure and simple terms. When the immune system is exhausted and is no longer able to manufacture the primary cells in the body that are responsible for attacking and destroying disease causing organisms, such as bacteria, this is referred to as a deficiency of the immune system.

Syndrome means that it is a mystery why the immune system shuts down, either temporarily or permanently. The human immune system is very resilient. It takes years of chemical abuse to develop a full blown immune disorder. All that remains is for the physician to find out what chemical the patient has been abusing. We, human beings, cause most all of our own illnesses by the life styles we practice.

In nearly, 100 percent, of all full blown AIDS cases in the United States, the patients have been inhaling volatile butyl nitrite inhalants and or injecting IV drugs. The only situations where individuals acquired full blown AIDS, who were not abusing chemicals, were victims of HIV tainted blood product transfusions and babies born to mothers who were abusing chemicals. In these cases, it was the rush to treat these victims with chemotherapy and/or AZT that caused their full blown AIDS and ultimate death, not the HIV contained in the tainted blood products.

In a research study, coming out of the 1994 Asian AIDS Conference, 40,000 HIV positive individuals were found who are beating the AIDS mortality statistics by living with HIV for more than 16 years now. The communality, that connects these individuals together, is the startling fact, that these individuals are not submitting to traditional medical treatment with aggressive chemotherapy or AZT. In many cases, the return to HIV negative status is occurring.

What is vitally important to understand and realize, is the chemical abuse with AZT or chemotherapy was hurting AIDS patients more than their HIV status.   HIV is not the problem with these long term survivors. Their health care providers are treating HIV status only as an indicator and not the cause of AIDS. The change in treatment therapy here, is to minimize chemical insult with drugs and boost the immune system with a healthy diet and lifestyle. In so doing, the rejuvenated immune system is dealing with the HIV.

If you bear with me, I will prove in this book, beyond a shadow of a doubt, that AIDS is a chemical problem and not caused by HIV or any virus, for that matter. The virus associated with AIDS is only a barometer of toxic chemical abuse and not the cause of AIDS. If you concentrate your thought process for a moment, the real proof of whether AIDS is caused by chemicals or viruses lies within which treatment therapy works and which one does not. Believing AIDS is caused by a virus and, subsequently trying to eliminate the virus by killing it with a powerful chemotherapy/AZT drug, has been a miserable failure; whereas, abstaining from chemical abuse is working.

So, it is quite obvious to an open-minded individual that the cause of AIDS is chemical abuse and not the HIV virus. The only hope to survive AIDS is practicing non-toxic health care along with eating a healthy, natural hygiene diet. AIDS patients will never be cured by a physician whose only treatment is chemical. Hundreds of thousands of otherwise remedial AIDS patients have died because they went to a physician instead of stopping their drugs and cleaning up their lifestyle.

In 1983, Drs. Chermann and Montagne, from the Louis Pasteur Institute in France sent a sample of viral tainted blood to the National Institute of Health. The French called the virus that they found in the blood Lymphadenopathy Associated Virus (LAV). A research team, including Dr. Gallo from the NIH, renamed the virus HTLV, later coined HIV and announced to the world that HIV causes AIDS. The fact that HIV causes AIDS was arrived at, in warp speed (less than a year). The speed at which this conclusion was made by the NIH smelled of bad research.

16

Upon receiving the news that LAV, a.k.a. HIV, caused AIDS, Dr. Chermann told a medical conference in Connecticut, only months after Dr. Gallo announced that HIV caused AIDS, that LAV, a.k.a. HIV, could not solely cause AIDS because the virus possessed no poisonous or antagonistic quality and that only chemical abuse could do all the damage that was going on in the bodies of AIDS patients.

Dr. Peter Duesberg, one of the most knowledgeable Virologists in the world, also came to the same conclusion in stating that, "HIV could not even cause the common cold, let alone all the AIDS indicator diseases." Dr. Duesberg injected test animals with HIV and studied the effects of HIV on animals for over two years. Chimpanzees, exposed to HIV, did not develop AIDS up to thirteen years since their exposure.

Ignoring these physicians' warnings to the medical community was a major blunder that the CDC and NIH made. It is plain and simple, "Only through chronic abuse of chemicals, prescription or non-prescription, can AIDS develop in human beings (Kitzerow, Jr. 1988)."

Chapter II

Toxic Poisoning Causes Immune Suppression a.k.a. AIDS

All human beings have an organ called the thymus which is located just behind the heart. The thymus is the most important organ in the body with regards to our ability to fight opportunistic bacterial infection. The thymus is responsible for creating mature T-cells that circulate through the bloodstream, attacking and devouring all microscopic disease causing organisms, such as bacteria. If the thymus is injured to the extent that it is no longer able to create T-cells, bacterial organisms are allowed to grow unchecked, causing disease.

The extreme example, where injury to the thymus caused the extensive reduction in T-cells that allowed pathological organisms to grow, thus causing death, was exhibited by a group of patients who died of AIDS. In the autopsy of 100 percent of these early AIDS patients who were aggressively abusing volatile nitrite inhalants a.k.a. "poppers" a.k.a. "room deodorizers," it was found, that all 100 percent of these inhalant abusers had destroyed their thymus. The cause of death was blamed on AIDS, but the real cause should have been blamed on the substance that destroyed the thymus in these unfortunates in the first place, nitrite inhalants!

Of all the research I have read on the subject of AIDS, this knowledge that chemical abuse causes total shut down of the thymus, is the most important finding in understanding the mystery of what causes the immune system to fail in the progression to AIDS. It is quite obvious that destruction of the thymus is necessary to slow down the T-cell count that is associated with full blown AIDS.

It seems very elementary that tracking down the true cause of AIDS must start by investigating what 85 percent of the AIDS statistics (homosexual men) are ingesting, inhaling or injecting into their bodies that would cause the destruction of the thymus. At the same time, whatever that substance is found to be, it has to be nearly exclusive to homosexual men. To this day, AIDS is still an 85 percent homosexual illness in the United States.

Do viruses, namely HIV, or chemicals or both cause the destruction of the thymus that results in AIDS? If one is found not to be able to cause the atrophy of the thymus, by process of elimination, the real cause of AIDS will surface.

In the compendium of nitrite inhalant research that I have documented it is easy to understand how nitrites are able to cause destruction of the thymus irrefutably. Laboratory research proves nitrite inhalants destroy the thymus, as well as the autopsy findings. The fact that nitrite inhalants are the only chemicals that are nearly exclusively abused by homosexual men adds to the obvious awareness of nitrite inhalants as being the major player in the cause of AIDS in homosexual men. In AIDS patients who develop the symptoms of Kaposi's Sarcoma (KS), it is found that aggressive abuse of nitrite inhalants (NI) is reported by nearly 100 percent.

Nitrite inhalants just happen to be the most toxic and direct insult to the bloodstream. This is why the majority of AIDS patients have abuse of these drugs in their, drug abuse history. NI are said to be the most cancer causing, immune destructive chemicals known to man.

Secondarily toxic by nature are industrial solvent inhalants (ISI) which include glue, petrol, aerosol shoe spray, kerosene, cheap nail polish remover and a whole assortment of volatile sprays.

In third world countries, Kaposi's Sarcoma· is endemic or common in patients suffering from AIDS-like illnesses. It just so happens that an epidemic of ISI abuse began in these countries in the Sixties, as reported in a research monograph titled "Epidemiology of Inhalant Abuse: An International Perspective," which can be ordered from the government printing office.

In industrial nations, nitrite inhalants, a.k.a. "poppers", a.k.a. "room odorizers," are the most common chemicals that are being consumed by chemical abusers, suffering with AIDS.

Inhalants NI, as well as ISI, are the most obvious suspect in the cause of most of the world's AIDS cases. Whereas chronic aggressive abuse of recreational drugs and other IV drugs are able to cause AIDS, they are not the most common in worldwide AIDS statistics!

The medical research community is just finally realizing, that AIDS worldwide, does not occur by one neatly packaged cause. While they still believe HIV is a player in the cause of AIDS, it is now fashionable to discuss other cofactors. The cofactor theory is surfacing because HIV is being found to be a latent nontoxic viral debris lacking sufficient numbers in the bloodstream to cause the once suspected destruction of T-cells.

As I stated earlier, the cause of AIDS must be found to be able to cause atrophy of the thymus. Ten thousand virologists and an annual budget of seven billion dollars of tax payers' money has failed to prove that HIV is toxic enough to even cause the common cold.

"Wake up world!" AIDS is caused by chronic, chemical abuse. The viruses associated with AIDS are only the residual cellular remains of cell death in the bloodstream as a result of toxic chemical poisoning!

These viral remains or debris only show up after years of chemical abuse has begun to take a final toll on the thymus.

All cellular debris and viruses are cleaned up in the bloodstream all our lives. Cells are constantly dying and being recycled by T-cells. Even T-cells have only a five year life expectancy. They die and are subsequently policed up by new T-cells. It is when the thymus is no longer able to produce new T-cells, in abundance, that viruses accumulate in the bloodstream.

From my perspective, I believe that the genesis of all viruses in humans and other animals is due to toxic poisoning of the bloodstream, by poisonous food stuffs and chronic chemical abuse. The only exception is where viral tainted transfusions have taken place or babies have acquired viruses vicariously from their mothers who were abusing chemicals.

In hemophiliacs, transfused with HIV tainted blood products, the detection of HIV prompted toxic killer, anti-viral therapy with chemotherapy, and the worst of all, AZT, which is the true cause of death in these patients as well as babies who received antiviral chemicals. Again, the cause of death in these unfortunate persons was chemical abuse and not their HIV status. Hemophiliacs are also prescribed with a plethora of immune destructive drugs that can be considered as cofactors in their cause of death.

BABIES REVERT TO HIV NEGATIVE

Mothers, who test HIV positive, were aggressively destroying their thymus over four to seven years with chemical abuse and thus developed AIDS symptoms. I believe the antiviral treatment, as well as antibiotic therapy of these mothers, caused full blown AIDS in these patients. However, the babies in the womb of these chemical abusing mothers were only exposed to the mother's drugs for a brief nine months, not enough time to destroy their thymus. After only nine months in the womb, the baby's thymus is still in good shape. Once the mother's toxic blood is replaced, by the baby's, and the baby's thymus recuperates and begins to produce increased numbers of T-cells, eventually the baby will return to HIV negative. This will only happen if the physician is not contributing to immune dysfunction with chemotherapy, AZT or any deceptive cancer drug.

I believe the long time frame that various chronically abused chemicals take to cause atrophy of the thymus is the answer to the mystery of delayed time lapse associated with the progression of AIDS. It is also very understandable that the more toxic the chemical, the more aggressively abused, with the most direct route to the bloodstream, would be at the head of the list in affixing blame in the cause of AIDS. Inhalants are the most toxic, the most abused and are directly absorbed into the bloodstream with IV drugs coming in second!

Many cases of babies returning to HIV negative are surfacing.

MANY AIDS CASES CLAIM NO DRUG ABUSE

A few AIDS statistics claim that they have never abused drugs. This kind of scenario, which is very rare, fuels the virus theory as the cause of AIDS. The chemical/viral dilemma can be partly blamed on the FDA and NIH. The FDA has refused to classify nitrite inhalants, a.k.a. "poppers," a.k.a. "Room odorizers," as drugs. Therefore, after the discovery of HIV in 83/84, AIDS patients whose only primary chemical of abuse was "room odorizers," would answer no to the question of drug abuse! If they did not acquire HIV status from drug abuse, how did they become HIV positive? Their only suspect at this point lies in the sexual transmission of a virus. Ignorance gives way to HIV theory.

I guarantee, that in any case of immune dysfunction where the hard questions are asked under a lie detector if necessary, chemical abuse chronically will be the cause of AIDS. Chemicals that have the potential of causing AIDS are nitrite inhalants, industrial solvent inhalants, IV drugs, all recreational drugs, as well as immuno-suppressive prescription drugs, such as anti-inflammatory drugs used in treating hemophiliacs, bypass surgeries, and arthritis, as well as aggressive abuse of antibiotics, just to name a few.

Evidence is surfacing that thousands of persons may have tested false positive for HIV as a result of faulty HIV test kits. Consequently, if these people were rushed into toxic killer chemotherapy or AZT, and developed full blown AIDS as a result of the toxic effect of their chemo and/or AZT therapy, this would also explain away AIDS cases, who could truthfully claim to not have drug abuse in their history. Faulty HIV testing will be discussed in upcoming chapters.

Another group of AIDS patients who would fall into the category of individuals who would testify that they had never abused recreational drugs including inhalants are the hundreds, maybe thousands, of individuals who suffered from abuse of antibiotics. Whereas persons who fell into the high risk groups (homosexual men having unprotected sex) would engage a physician to prescribe extremely immuneosuppressive antibiotics prophylactically anticipating that they could prevent AIDS symptoms. Actually, these persons along with their doctor created AIDS symptoms due to the deleterious effects of the antibiotics that were being abused. Such examples are Bactrim and Septra. While the manufacturer's directives of these drugs recommend a maximum prescribed duration of up to 14 days, these good doctors were doling out these drug regimens indefinitely or at least until these persons finally got sick. The tragedy here is that these persons were not sick in the first place and when they finally did get sick they blamed their illness on unprotected sex and HIV contagion. The only problem with this thought process is that when most of these persons got better after halting their prophylactic antiobiotic treatment and their AIDS symptoms went away and they tested HIV negative, they went to court. Many cases have been settled out of court.

The serious error in blaming HIV in these cases only falsely fueled the HIV/AIDS frenzy.

AIDS IS NOT NEW

All the AIDS indicator diseases have been described in medical literature for hundreds of years. The early cancer patients in the 40's, 50's and 60's were dying of AIDS, as a result of the aggressive abuse of chemotherapy! It wasn't realized, until thousands of AIDS deaths occurred, that cancer patients cannot tolerate chemotherapy longer than five years, so five years is the immune dysfunction time frame of most chemotherapy drugs. Cancer patients were dying of AIDS and not the cancers they were being treated for.

People, who have cancer and are being treated for it, are expected to die, so society is conditioned to accept thousands of cancer related deaths annually, without question, even though the true cause of death was an AIDS related illness, resulting from chemotherapy, and not the cancer that they were originally being treated for. Oh no! The physician took the credit for curing the cancer; however, the physician killed his patient, ultimately, with chemotherapy!

The first couple of thousand AIDS cases became newsworthy because all these patients were not being treated for cancer with chemotherapy, and yet they were all young otherwise healthy individuals, experiencing the same immunodestructive symptoms that people being treated with chemotherapy were getting. To add to the mystery, all these AIDS patients were homosexual. Something, that this group of individuals was doing, began to cause their deaths at alarming rates. Beginning in 1981, the first 2,000 AIDS patients did not know each other, in most cases, so a contagious organism was highly unlikely. What was proven by the Center for Disease Control, was that nearly 100 percent of the early AIDS patients were all aggressively abusing a relatively brand new chemical of abuse, namely, volatile butyl nitrite inhalant. The fact that these early AIDS patients were also presenting a rare cancer of the lymph nodes called Kaposi's Sarcoma (KS), normally unheard of

24

in otherwise healthy young men, was just one more red flag that called attention to these specific patients.

The practice of inhaling "butyl nitrite," by nearly all of the early AIDS patients, as well as being the most common link to connect all of them, became the most obvious suspect to blame for the demise of these individuals.

All the resources of the Federal Government, and the medical, researchers began investigating the toxic properties of butyl nitrite inhalant as well as initiating a study of the relatively new nitrite inhalant abusers who were not yet sick.

Massive tax payer monies were expended, and the results of the nitrite inhalant research, as evidenced in the chronology of nitrite inhalant research that I have compiled into this book, proved out to indict nitrite inhalants as one of the most toxic cancer causing immune destructive chemicals known to man. The extreme toxicity providing the ability for nitrite inhalant not only to cause the cancer that all the early AIDS patients were experiencing, but also to be able to cause all the 30 indicator illnesses associated with AIDS, was such an open and shut case that it seems only morons would fail to name the practice of inhaling volatile nitrite inhalants as the major player in blaming the cause of AIDS in a group of individuals who were abusing this chemical, especially when nitrite inhalant abuse was the most common connection. To compound the obvious, none of these early AIDS patients were shown to know each other, thus minimizing the possibility of a contagious organism. Study after study, utilizing many independent researchers, made the direct connection between patients developing the common cancer KS who were also abusing, aggressively, volatile nitrite inhalants.

At this point, an intelligent mind would ask itself, what were our astute decision makers thinking about at the National Institute of Health (NIH) and the Centers for Disease Control (CDC) when they did not alert society to the potential hazards of inhaling pure butyl nitrite inhalant. The research connecting KS with the nitrite inhalant abuse was done in the early 80's. It's now 2000 and the CDC, as well as the NIH, has, as of yet, failed to warn the American society of the link between KS and abusing volatile nitrite inhalants.

Research proves, beyond reasonable doubt, that nitrite inhalants cause AIDS as well as KS in humans. The decision makers at the NIH and CDC are just too ignorant to see the writing on the wall.

One of the reasons more education about the nitrite inhalant/AIDS connection is not forthcoming from the CDC and NIH is due to a study done by the Centers for Disease Control (CDC). The CDC observed 2,500 relatively new, nitrite inhalant abusers who were not yet sick for 2½ years. During that time frame these individuals did not develop KS. So the CDC and NIH took the stand that volatile nitrite inhalant does not cause KS in humans. Even though all laboratory research proves otherwise, the CDC utilized this study to ignore the irrefutable lab research and the millions of tax payer money to fund it.

The reason that the nitrite inhalant abusers in this CDC study did not develop KS and subsequently AIDS, was due to the fact that this study was not carried out long enough. This study was done in the early 80's before a profile of the first AIDS patients was available. When a study profile of full blown AIDS patients was finally completed, it was learned that AIDS patients were abusing nitrite inhalants for a minimum of 4 to 6 years before their AIDS showed up. So the CDC study that only lasted 2½ years proved nothing. What it did do, though, was to exonerate the primary cause of AIDS and give the green light to inhalant abusers. I can guarantee that all of the individuals that participated in this CDC study (all 2,500 of them) who went on to continue to abuse nitrite inhalants for the 4-6 year time frame, are all dead. Aggressive abuse of nitrite inhalants was the primary factor in the profile of these AIDS patients.

Many people have abused nitrite inhalants and have not acquired AIDS, because they have not met the necessary criteria to be classified as aggressive abuse which is about 6-7 sniffs a day for 5-6 days per week for 4-6 years straight. This abuse requirement, as well as not understanding it, is what posed the major problem in connecting nitrite inhalant abuse with AIDS, due to the fact that not all people who have abused nitrite inhalants in their lifetime have acquired AIDS.

It is the same scenario that plays out in alcoholism. Not all people who drink alcohol become alcoholics. However, if you abuse alcohol aggressively, you will become an alcoholic and experience the chronic illnesses associated with chronic alcoholism.

In order to support my statement made earlier, that the toxic poisoning of the blood stream by chemicals is able to originate viruses, I would like to call your attention to studies of similar situations where chemical toxicity has been obviously proven to cause viruses in human beings.

If a person receives an organ transplant, their physician will prescribe a powerful anti-rejection drug such as Cyclosporin. After a sufficient length of time, the drug will cause a virus called Cytomegalovirus (CMV) to appear in the blood stream. If the drug is stopped, the CMV goes away. When Cyclosporine is started again, the CMV appears again. What is happening is that the drug is killing an unknown group of cells in the body and fragmenting them into cellular debris namely CMV. This is the same occurrence that goes on when people abuse nitrite inhalants and IV drugs. I believe that HIV virus originates in human beings abusing these chemicals.

Toxic poisoning by aggressive abuse of chemicals, primarily volatile nitrite inhalants and/or specific IV drugs is all that is necessary to cause HIV virus to appear in the blood stream. The ignorant hypothesis by the medical community; that HIV must be dealt with chemically, is the true cause of ultimate death in patients found to be HIV positive.

BENZENE DERIVATIVE LUBRICANTS

In the eleventh hour of the publication of this manuscript, it was brought to my attention that another causative factor with the potential to cause immune dysfunction, has surfaced. Research done by Project AIDS International, under the chairmanship of Jeremy Selvey, suggests that sexual lubricants, containing benzene derivatives are extremely plausible and high up on the totem pole of the list of constituents that are capable of initiating immune dysfunction leading to AIDS.

Reference will soon be made to general inhalants, including glue that children in the early 60's were dying from, in this book. Benzene derivatives, found in paint thinners and solvents and toluene, found in airplane glue, are referred to as aromatic hydro-carbons. These chemicals are widely known for their extremely toxic and poisonous nature.

What was not known until researcher Selvey discovered it, was the fact that a sexual lubricant that entered the homosexual marketplace in 1978 was formulated with benzene derivatives. The

27

product was {Lube}, manufactured by TBM Enterprises in West Hollywood, CA. While {Lube} was highlighted, other brands of anal lubricants utilizing benzene derivatives were found.

Selvey posed the fact that rectal absorption is eight times more efficient than oral ingestion, reminding us that toxins induced rectally by-pass the digestive tract. Given this knowledge, coupled with the known facts of toxic poisoning associated with benzene derivatives, exposed internally, it is very easy to include rectal absorption of toxic chemicals in the already compiled list of chemical agents capable of initiating immune dysfunction leading to AIDS.

What makes an interesting correlation is the fact that nitrite inhalants, as well as these particular lubricants, entered a predominately homosexual market just before AIDS began showing up in 1978/1979.

Just as rectal absorption by-passes the body's protective organs, so do IV drugs and inhalants which directly insult the blood stream and subsequently the thymus which ultimately regulates the body's T-cell count.

Just as the Merck Medical Manual has defined the cause of AIDS from the beginning as being malnutrition, drugs (prescription and recreational) and radiation, Jeremy Selvey's expose' on benzene derived anal lubricants compounds the support for a chemical/AIDS hypothesis. Whereas there is no toxicology study that demonstrates any toxic mechanism of HIV that is capable of initiating any immune dysfunction.

The research paper titled "Aromatic Hydrocarbon Toxins and Their Derivatives As A Non-Viral Cause of Acquired Immune Deficiency Syndrome" by Selvey, J.F.; Alampi, M. L.; Scharffenberg, R.S., 1985, may be found in the soon-to-be published book, "The Secrets Behind HIV and AIDS; Causes-Cures Contradictions and Conspiracies".

It would be bad science to eliminate any one of the fore-mentioned chemical causes of immune dysfunction in light of the toxicology (study of toxic substances and relative treatments) and epidemiology (study of disease frequency and distribution in society), that I am about to present in this book. What I intend to present is that any toxic chemical aggressively abused chronically is capable of immune suppression.

It is obvious that, given all the different AIDS indicator illnesses (30), along with the different immune dysfunction time frames, leading up to full blown AIDS, there are many causes of symptoms leading to immune dysfunction.

Ultimately, though, no matter what caused each and every unique case of immune dysfunction, it was the universal treatment of choice with chemotherapy or AZT that subsequently lead to an AIDS mortality statistic.

Chapter III

Why AIDS at this Period in History?

What the general public is unaware of is the fact that the homosexual community, at large, began abusing one of the most cancer causing, immune-destructive chemicals known to man beginning in 1971, and by 1974, it had reached every corner of the gay community all over the world. From 1971 to 1976, this product was being sold, exclusively, to the homosexual community. For the most part, this chemical has remained, predominately, a consumer product in the homosexual community and explains why the majority of AIDS cases, even to this day, has remained in the homosexual persuasion. The chemical that I am talking about is butyl nitrite, a yellowish liquid, bottled in 3/4 ounce bottles. When inhaled, it relaxes the anal sphincter muscle to permit anal sex and also seems to prolong orgasm, which attracts the smallest segments of the heterosexual community that were attracted to this chemical abuse.

In the chronology of nitrite inhalant research that I have put together in this book, the obvious connection of aggressive abuse of nitrite inhalant over a period of 4-6 years by almost 100 percent of all of the early AIDS patients is made. This 4-6 year exposure to nitrites is a similar time frame that chemotherapy chemicals begin to cause AIDS like illnesses in cancer patients. Chemotherapy drugs do not even come close to the toxic effects of nitrite inhalants as evidenced in my chronology.

Amyl Nitrite was bottled in small glass ampoules, covered with nylon mesh, to allow them to be broken, in order to treat heart

31

patients, for angina pectoris. The popping sound that occurred when these ampoules were broken coined the name poppers.

Poppers were allowed to be sold over the counter from 1963 until 1969, when the FDA reinstated prescription status due to sky rocketing popper sales as a result of abuse of these drugs.

While amyl nitrite was restricted, its second cousin butyl nitrite was not. Clifford Hassing, a homosexual medical student realized the opportunity to make large sums of money by bottling the unrestricted butyl nitrite in small brown bottles by selling them to the homosexual community. In order to do this, without having to get his products through drug scrutiny, he lied to the FDA and the Consumer Products Safety Commission (CPSC) about the true nature of his product. He called his product "locker room" and claimed it was a "room deodorizer", all the while knowing 100 percent of his customers were purchasing "locker room" to inhale as a sexual accessory drug. "Locker room" smelled like stinking sweat socks which should have alerted the FDA and the CPSC that these products were being deceptively marketed. As a result of gullibility, stupidity, and laziness on the part of the FDA and the CPSC, volatile butyl nitrite, one of the most cancer causing immuno-destructive chemicals known to man, was allowed to be fraudulently marketed, all over the world. It was sold wherever homosexual newspapers were published and marketed, for over 20 years.

In 1976, another company headed up by W. Jay Freeser, began broadening the distribution of a similar product, called "Rush" not only to the homosexual market, but also the heterosexual consumers, as well as high school students, to the extent that the National Institute of Drug Abuse (NIDA) reported by 1979, 6 million students had used nitrite inhalants (a.k.a., room odorizers) and in one year NIDA reported a 100 percent increase in abusers to 13 million.

Another major room odorizer manufacturer that I haven't been able to get a lot of information on was a company named Great Lakes Products, headed up by a gentleman named Joseph Miller, located in Indianapolis, Indiana. All in all, eventually, there were approximately thirty various brands of room odorizers being sold through gay publications and adult book stores.

Finally, through efforts of Professor Ron Wood, a Toxicologist in New York and an act of Congress, headed up by Congressman Mel Levine and Henry Waxman, the room odorizer industry was shut down. Tragically, this bane of society was allowed to exist, under the noses of the FDA and the CPSC for over 20 years, until February of 1991, when it became illegal to possess these products.

To understand the magnitude of how extensive the practice of inhaling the most cancer causing, immune destructive chemical known to man, had developed in the homosexual community, over 50 million dollars of this chemical was sold in New York and San Francisco alone in one year.

If all the room odorizer manufacturers in the United States were subpoenaed into court and forced to submit their product distribution records, you would find a direct connection and a template that would accurately match the concentration of AIDS cases throughout the United States.

I believe that by itself, aggressive abuse of volatile nitrite inhalant over a period of four to six years, is all that is necessary to cause AIDS in human beings. In early CDC questionnaires, many AIDS patients verified the fact that nitrite inhalant, a.k.a., room odorizers, was the only chemical that they abused while a very few individuals claimed to have abused IV drugs only. Basically, what is easily understood is that toxic insult of the blood stream directly, by either IV drugs or nitrite inhalant, aggressively for a long enough period, are both capable of causing abusers to acquire AIDS as their reward.

If volatile nitrite inhalant is the major player in the cause of AIDS, once these products have been banned, one would expect to see, brand new, AIDS cases beginning to decline. This is precisely what is happening. Brand new AIDS cases have been dropping by 3 to 6 percent since 1991 when room odorizers were made illegal by an act of Congress. Due to the successful educational program alerting the gay community in San Francisco to the nitrite/AIDS connection, the San Francisco Department of Public Health predicted years ago that by 1997, new AIDS cases would be dropping to an all time low. This is what is happening in San Francisco, the second largest state with regards to AIDS statistics.

Since we know that it takes 4 to 7 years of toxic insult of the blood stream, by nitrite inhalant, to develop full blown AIDS, if you factor an average of 6 years, added to 1991, the year that room odorizers were taken off the shelves, one would expect to see new AIDS cases to be dropping around 1996-97. Guess what? They are nationally!!

The AIDS epidemic in the United States started 7 years, on average, after the year 1974, when room odorizers had reached every corner of the homosexual community. Now, six years, on average, since room odorizers have been taken off the market, AIDS is beginning to decline. It's blatantly obvious that aggressive abuse of nitrite inhalant is the major cause of AIDS, not a virus, not even HIV.

The room odorizer (volatile nitrite inhalant) era in the United States and for that matter, the world, has existed without the general public at large even knowing what was going on. Through the smoke screen of false propaganda, blaming AIDS on a virus, namely HIV, the public's attention has been diverted away from the true cause of AIDS.

Many people would have immediately ceased the practice of inhaling butyl nitrite, a.k.a., room odorizers in the early 80's had the CDC alerted the public, as to what was known about nitrite inhalants and AIDS. Many deaths would have been averted.

Volatile nitrite inhalant, aggressively abused over a 4 to 6 year period, is all that is necessary to subdue the immune system. In some individuals, it may take longer, depending on how otherwise healthy they are. The sum total of all the acts of poisoning the blood stream by, all chemicals as well as nicotine, caffeine, alcohol, all contribute to the length of time it takes to weaken the immune system to the degree that a diagnosis of AIDS presents itself.

While 100 percent of all the first full blown AIDS patients who developed Kaposi's Sarcoma (KS) were inhaling butyl nitrite aggressively over 4 to 6 years, only a few claimed IV drugs to be their only chemical of abuse. It is highly probable and more than likely that any very toxic chemical, abused aggressively, over a long enough period of time, will cause AIDS in human beings and other animals. All over the world, toxic inhalants are being abused. For example, children in Brazil, who are suffering from AIDS related complex (ARC), are inhaling cheap nail polish remover and aerosol shoe spray. The fumes of industrial solvents are a favorite choice of inhalant abusers in Africa. So, when one asks what do AIDS patients in the U.S. have in common with African AIDS, the answer is inhalant abuse. I believe that while IV drugs as well as aggressive abuse of any toxic chemical is sufficient to cause AIDS, nitrite inhalants are the primary cause of AIDS in the United States.

First of all, AIDS statistics, for the most part have remained primarily in the homosexual community. Even to this day heterosexual numbers still only comprise around 10 percent. Something that the homosexual community is doing on a semi-exclusive level is causing them to acquire AIDS. Also, what causes AIDS in these individuals has to be relatively new since AIDS is new. The only new chemical of abuse that has been practiced predominately by the homosexual community since 1971 is the act of sniffing the most cancer causing, immune destructive chemical known to man, volatile nitrite inhalant, a.k.a. "poppers," "room odorizers," "rush," "locker room," etc. Aggressive nitrite inhalant abuse is an obvious cause of AIDS.

In order to fully understand why the AIDS epidemic has taken place in American society, at this period of time, a person needs to observe the total picture.

1963

The FDA allowed poppers to be sold "over the counter" which established a foundation of nitrite inhalant abusers.

1969

The FDA reinstated prescription requirements to poppers due to skyrocketing sales and obvious abuse by the homosexual community (poppers were formulated with "amyl nitrite").

1971

The FDA and CPSC allowed Clifford Hassing in California to substitute butyl nitrite in place of amyl nitrite and subsequently bottle pure butyl nitrite and sell it to the homosexual community under the disguise of a room odorizer.

1974

By 1974 the gay community at large began abusing nitrite inhalants. It takes 4 to 6 years of aggressive abuse of nitrite inhalant to develop full blown AIDS. This was evidenced by the fact that AIDS cases began showing up in 1979 to 1981 which is around the 4 to 6 years after nitrite inhalant became popular.

1980's

Early investigation by the CDC indicted, but had not yet found guilty, the practice of abusing nitrite inhalants as the cause of the development of a rare cancer called Kaposi's Sarcoma (KS) in AIDS patients.

An early CDC study of nitrite inhalant abusers who were not yet sick failed to present KS in a 2 1/2 year study. Nitrite inhalants were falsely exonerated as the cause of KS, due to the premature cessation of this study. It was realized, many years later, that the early AIDS patients with KS were probably abusing nitrites for at least 4 years before KS showed up. This lack of understanding and failure to acknowledge nitrite inhalant abuse as a cause of AIDS is what I refer to as an unfortunate research error that failed to shut down the AIDS epidemic in the early stages. Whereas the pseudo-scientific theory that HIV causes AIDS, only led research down the wrong road and is responsible for the deaths of thousands of otherwise remedial AIDS patients. Sixteen years of failure in treating HIV and AIDS patients should be testimonial enough that the HIV theory and subsequent treatment for HIV is dead wrong.

1981

In 1981, approximately 7 years after the year that poppers were established as having reached every corner of the gay community (1974), the first AIDS cases began to show up. These cases, presented symptoms of Kaposis Sarcoma (KS), a rare cancer not found in young Americans. These chemically toxic patients were treated with aggressive chemotherapy which their weakened immune systems could not tolerate. Consequently, the first AIDS mortality statistics occurred. This author believes that chemo-therapy is what these patients died from.

1984

Dr. Robert C. Gallo, at the National Institutes of Health, claimed that the human immunodeficiency virus (HIV) was a direct killer of human white blood cells (WBCS), subsequently explaining how HIV is alleged to cause AIDS. His theory of HIV, being a direct killer of WBCS has never been duplicated in any scientific research by anyone else. Therefore, the foundation supporting HIV as a direct killer of WBCS and the cause of AIDS, is without support.

1985

As a result of extensive education in the homosexual community on the awareness of nitrite inhalant's possible role in causing Kaposi's Sarcoma (KS), the gay community began to abstain from inhalant abuse. I believe this to be the turning point in popper abuse which presented the slowing down of homosexual KS statistics.

1987

Burroughs Welcome Ltd., a pharmaceutical company, claimed to have developed an antiviral drug, AZT from a toxic, failed cancer drug and licensed it to be prescribed to patients for a virus that has never been proven by anyone, to have the toxic ability to cause AIDS. This author believes that antiviral drugs, namely AZT, replaced the chemotherapy drugs that were the cause of death, in the first AIDS patients, as the primary cause of death in AIDS patients since 1987, up until now.

1997

In 1997, 6 years after poppers were banned in the United States, brand new AIDS cases began dropping by 6 percent, the obvious connection between the history of nitrite inhalant abuse in the United States relative to the similar time frame that it takes to develop full blown AIDS, should be easily arrived at.

Why AIDS occurred in our society in this period of time is due to greed and irresponsibility in the individuals who manufactured street versions of poppers in the first place, and gullibility, stupidity and laziness on the part of the FDA and CPSC for allowing these products into society in the second place.

Thirdly, the research error blaming HIV as the cause of AIDS and coming in forth, the ignorance and gullibility of the physicians who have been killing their patients with alleged antiviral drugs based on the unproven theory that HIV is toxic enough to cause AIDS in humans.

Chapter IV

AIDS Tests Found Unreliable!

What if you were tested for HIV antibodies and the tests were inaccurate, presenting a false, positive HIV finding?

Needless to say, your life would turn upside down!

Naturally your doctor would start you on AZT!

There would be a 100% chance of your dying, in two to six years, depending on whether you were taking 1,500 or 500 MG of AZT per day, respectfully, as evidenced by AIDS mortality statistics. It is very obvious that 500-1,500 MG of AZT per day will kill a healthy person in two to six years.

Wouldn't it be tragic if you died from a medical treatment for a virus that you never had based on a false HIV antibody test? That is precisely what has probably happened to hundreds or possibly thousands of unfortunate persons misdiagnosed with faulty HIV antibody tests.

The Wall Street Journal article and "Statement of Fact" on the following pages were provided by Project AIDS International with permission to publish.

For those who believe that AIDS is caused, purely by chemical abuse, such as myself, people with AIDS who have claimed to have absolutely no chemical use, history, including poppers, are a puzzlement to the chemical/AIDS theory. False HIV antibody tests would obviously clear up this mystery.

The HIV establishment has been supporting their HIV/AIDS theory, while at the same time, discrediting the chemical/AIDS theory with the fact that there exists HIV, antibody, positive, persons who express having no chemical abuse history. False, antibody positive tests, shoot down one of the major arguments in favor of the HIV theory.

Now, that I think of it, I posed the idea that Magic Johnson may have presented an HIV antibody positive test as a result of abusing poppers. Now, the possibility prevails that maybe Magic was a victim of a false positive test.

Wondering how many misdiagnosed HIV positive persons were aggressively prescribed with AIDS drugs and ultimately died, is a haunting thought.

FDA Uncovers Flaws in Abbott Labs' Diagnostic Devices, Including AIDS Kits

©WALL STREET JOURNAL
Chicago Bureau
Health/11-January-1995
Page B8
by Thomas M. Burton

The Food and Drug Administration has uncovered a wide range of flaws in Abbott Laboratories' quality-assurance procedures used in assembling medical-diagnostic products, including kits to test for hepatitis and AIDS.

The FDA findings have lead the agency to hold up approval of some new medical diagnostic devices made at the company's suburban Chicago manufacturing plants, which are among Abbott's major production facilities. FDA conclusions focus on what senior agency officials term a "looseness" in Abbott's quality-control methods that can potentially lead to inaccuracies in diagnostic test results.

FDA officials plan to re-inspect the Abbott facilities in the next few weeks to see if the shortcomings highlighted in recent correspondence have been remedied. Many deficiencies turned up during a July 1994 inspection visit, or even date back to an inspection in February.

In composite trading on the New York Stock Exchange, Abbott fell 50 cents to $31.25.

The federal agency's findings have come as something of a shock to Abbott, based in North Chicago, Ill., because its flagship medical-diagnostic division has made it the world leader in producing diagnostic products for hospitals, blood banks and doctor's offices. The division makes up about one-quarter of the company's $8 billion in annual sales. People familiar with the events say Abbott has, for the first time in memory, cut back its diagnostic personnel force by as many as 100 people or more, in part to compensate for costs related to the FDA findings. Abbott declined to discuss specific FDA concerns. But, it said regulatory issues had "no unusual impact" on the diagnostic business in 1994 and that Abbott "continuously address" FDA concerns.

The blood-test kits at issue are used by blood banks to ensure that hepatitis and the AIDS virus don't contaminate blood donations used in surgery and transfusions; the tests are also used by physicians to test individual patients. While many specific FDA findings focus on those tests, other criticisms are more general and apply to diagnostic-equipment manufacturing across the board, senior FDA officials said.

Some production lots of the blood tests produced larger-than-normal numbers of so-called false positive results, according to interviews with FDA officials and FDA documents obtained under the federal Freedom of Information Act. False positives, a phenomenon also sometimes called "nonspecificity," mean that a test "detects" virus when none is present.

There have been a large number of complaints on non-specificity" in Abbott diagnostic test kits, according to a memorandum of an Aug. 1994 meeting between Abbott and the FDA.

The American Red Cross, a major buyer of Abbott's hepatitis and AIDS kits, saw an increase in false positives during the first half of 1994, said Jacquelyn Fredrick, head of Red Cross testing laboratories. She said this necessitated redoing those tests or, in the case of a repeated positive result, discarding the blood.

In response to the FDA findings, Abbott has begun to institute a global plan covering the plants in suburban Chicago and others in Dallas and Santa Clara, Calif.

Some of the FDA's criticisms concern how the company checks to see that the millions of tiny plastic beads used in millions of blood test kits are properly coated with a protein during manufacturing.

When used by hospitals and blood banks, the protein-coated beads are doused with an enzyme-antibody mixture also contained in the kit. A few drops of blood serum or plasma also are placed on the bead, whose yellow-orange color changes if hepatitis or AIDS virus are present.

The FDA criticized quality-assurance procedures used to ensure every bead is uniformly coated. Improper coating in only a few beads could lead to incorrect results, the FDA said. Senior FDA aides said one concern was that Abbott didn't check enough beads in enough production lots. In an Oct. 11 letter to Abbott, the FDA's acting compliance director for biological products, James C. Simmons said the company's methods "failed to verify that there was uniform coating" of beads in the Abbott test kit known as HIVAB.

The agency also found Abbott's efforts "inadequate" in checking the coating of beads for the Auszyme hepatitis B test kit. Mr. Simmons also criticized Abbott for "failure to adequately investigate and follow up device failures." Including one with its HTLV-1 Leukemia test.

— END OF ARTICLE —

STATEMENT OF FACT

The United States Centers for Disease Control and Prevention (CDC), under the direction of the Department of Health and Human Services (HHS) states unequivocally that the "AIDS tests" –e.g.: Enzyme Linked Immunosorbent Assay [ELISA] and Western Blot [WB] confirmatory-which are tests searching for alleged specific antibodies to the Human Immunodeficiency Virus (HIV)-are, by CDC's definition 99.97% accurate in identifying alleged HIV specific antibody.

In fact, as demonstrated by studies conducted by other scientists such as Dr. Eleni Papodopulos-Eleopulos of the Department of Emergency Medicine at the University of Perth Medical Centre in Australia, neither test is specific in its identification of HIV antibody. There is a minimum of a 40% chance that the antibody tests specified will result in a false positive reaction.

Based on the CDC's 1994 HIV/AIDS Surveillance Report for the period of July, 1993 to June, 1994 the cumulative "reported" cases of HIV seroprevalence (i.e.: HIV+ asymptomatic) are 62,443. This is what is reported by "confidential" test sites in the 26 states required to report, and does not take into account either the anonymous test sites, nor those state's numbers that are not required to be reported.

Using the **minimal** number presented by the CDC of 62,443, and taking into account that at least 40% would have a false positive result, approximately 24,977 people have been wrongly diagnosed as being HIV+.

While being told that you are HIV+ is a different experience for each person, there are several similarities that certainly warrant numerous causes of action. First and foremost, you are being told that you have an "inevitably fatal disease" when, in fact, you don't. This usually results in the new "patient" taking actions that the average "healthy person" would not contemplate, to wit: cashing in life insurance policies, aborting children, divorce, suicide, loss of income or job due to clinical depression, following the "prescribed treatment avenue" of taking numerous immunosuppressive prescription drugs when no illness is present, resulting in the patient becoming sick due to the effects of the drugs, suffering social stigmas, and loss of one's sense of personal worth, *ad infin item.*

42

Project AIDS, International (a division of People's International Health Project-a nonprofit, public benefit organization) realizes that financial compensation will not bring back those who have died, nor will it fully compensate those who have suffered so much needless mental anguish, but we feel that this monumental action will help to guide AIDS research into other more viable areas of both causation(s) and treatments and the legal action will derail the current mindset of HIV/AIDS.

There is at least one case in Florida where an award of $600,000.00 was received based on a woman who was wrongly diagnosed with HIV, put on standard treatments, and two years later tested negative to HIV.

Chapter V

Why AIDS All Over the World?

Because AIDS is caused by chemical abuse, it is easy to see how this disease can manifest itself anywhere in the world. No society, on this planet, is free of chemical abuse of one form or another.

In Brazil, thousands of young children are suffering from AIDS related complex (ARC), as a result of abusing inhalants, such as nail polish remover, kerosene, aerosol shoe spray, shoemaker's glue, gasoline, acetone, etc.

In Africa, in reading of the epidemiology of inhalant abuse in Nigeria, it was stated that "there is hardly any drug that is not abused by Nigerians." Inhalants of abuse, in Africa, include shoe polish, exhaust fumes, glue, gasoline, paint thinner, and lighter fluid, just to highlight a few.

The aforementioned countries are highlighted to emphasize a point that I would like to make. Outside of the United States, African countries and Brazil reported the highest numbers of AIDS statistics to the World Health Organization in April, 1992. It is also not mere coincidence that these countries also present a correlating picture of chemical abuse.

It should be noted that inhalants which are abused in third world countries are more evenly abused along both genders, especially in Africa and Brazil. This is why AIDS cases in these countries are also reflective of the same gender lines of inhalant abusers, unlike industrialized countries where "room odorizers," a.k.a. "poppers," a.k.a. volatile nitrite inhalants have been distributed to predominantly the gay community, the concentration of AIDS cases also remains predominantly in the male homosexual community.

Nitrite inhalants are a homosexual chemical of abuse, mainly used to facilitate anal sex, whereas industrial solvent inhalants, are a pauper's chemical of abuse that takes the place of, for example, alcohol that is not affordable to the average third world citizen in search of a cheap high.

In the United States, only a few heterosexuals have discovered, not only where to find "poppers," because they are hard to find for a straight person, but also the fact that these inhalants also seem to prolong orgasm. This is why heterosexual AIDS cases still, to this day, only approximate about 3 percent of the U.S. AIDS statistics.

In Amsterdam, in 1988, I observed volatile nitrite inhalants, a.k.a. "poppers," a.k.a. "room odorizers" being sold on every street corner. It is not purely coincidental that Amsterdam presents the most AIDS cases of all the cities in the Netherlands.

It is so obvious, to an open mind, that chemical abuse causes AIDS throughout the world. It is the medical personnel who have been brainwashed into thinking that beasties and gremlins, namely HIV, cause illness in man.

Last, but not least, it is important to include malnutrition as a contributing factor in immune dysfunction, especially in third world countries. The primary causes of immune disorders, described in the medical Bible, namely the Merck Manual, as far back as 1952 and beyond, are malnutrition, drug abuse (prescription and recreational as well as chemotherapy), and radiation.

It should also be known that AIDS statistics in Africa, according to anyone who thoroughly investigates the actual situation there, finds that the AIDS statistics are greatly exaggerated and misrepresented. Many cases, where malnutrition and starvation prevail, are being blamed on HIV without proper testing.

It has been described, where people have died in traumatic situations, such as automobile accidents and have been added to AIDS statistics. There is monetary motive to inflate AIDS statistics, due to big money that is funneled into third world countries in a direct relationship to AIDS statistics by AIDS organizations in the industrialized nations.

46

It is also highly probable that HIV/AIDS antibody testing, in the past, may have been as much as 40% inaccurate, causing false positives to add to already inflated AIDS numbers. Research done by Dr. Eleni Papodopulos of the Department of Emergency Medicine at the University of Perth Medical Center in Australia has concluded that the antibody tests, Enzyme Linked Immunosorbent Assay (ELISA) and the Western Blot (WB) have been found to be as much as 40% inaccurate! So if testing in Australia has been found faulty, we can only imagine what the testing accuracy is in Africa.

Lawsuits in the United States are being settled where people have been wrongly diagnosed with HIV utilizing the ELISA and WB tests and subsequently, were started on AIDS treatment, while upon re-testing were found to be HIV negative. The people have gone to court and have won substantial settlements. How many people have been wrongly diagnosed and died of chemotherapy or AZT? That's a scary thought.

It is in the best interest of HIV/AIDS propagandists who are fueling HIV/AIDS hysteria to fan the flames with inflated worldwide statistics, especially since the U.S. AIDS epidemic has peaked and is presently dwindling.

Chapter VI

SMON....
The AIDS Rehearsal

Long before the U.S. AIDS epidemic, said to have been established in 1981, there was a similar epidemic that had begun in Japan in the middle 1950's. Evidenced by the fact, that little knowledge of this major epidemic is known in the United States, it is very clear that the medical establishment has done a good job of covering up this embarrassing episode.

Essentially, this epidemic was the result of physicians prescribing a drug for common stomach disorders that was later proven to cause intestinal problems, internal bleeding, diarrhea, nerve damage, blindness and in many thousands of cases, death.

The SMON epidemic was given its acronym by researchers attending a general meeting of the Japanese society of internal medicine in 1964. The letters stand for Subacute-Myelo-Optico-Neuropathy, based on the symptoms of nerve damage and blindness.

The Japanese ministry of health disbursed grant money and commissioned a group of virologists to search for a suspected viral pathogen as their target. During this research period, it was observed that a great number of SMON patients had been prescribed with diarrhea-fighting drugs, enterovioform and emaform, which called attention to these drugs. However, the scientists, working on SMON, were primarily virologists, obsessed with the search of a virus and subsequently over looked this chemical connection. Besides who would suspect that people were dying at the hands of medical doctors! Could that possibly happen!

49

Anyhow, three years of research failed to discover a viral connection to SMON, and the project ended.

Meanwhile, the disease was escalating to epidemic proportions and the Japanese reinstated the war on SMON, in 1969. Once again, the search for a SMON virus ended in failure. However, unlike the first commission, only comprising of virologists, this new group included a pharmacologist, Dr. H. Beppu, who revisited the SMON/chemical connection. By investigating the same drugs that the original research group over-looked in 1964, he discovered that entro-vioform and emaform were actually separate brand names for a chemical named clioquinol and that this drug killed the experimental mice that he tested this drug on.

To sum this up, clioquinol was indited as the cause of the SMON epidemic. Consequently, thousands of lawsuits were initiated against the pharmaceutical company CIBA-GEIGY and the physicians that prescribed these drugs to their patients.

When clioquinol was banned in Japan, the SMON epidemic abruptly ended.

Years of wasted time chasing a virus by obsessed virologists occurred while thousands of people died at the hands of their physicians who were prescribing toxic killer drugs. Today, ladies and gentlemen, that is exactly what is going on regarding the present day AIDS epidemic. Scientists, in charge at the government level, who are formulating government AIDS medical policy, are inundated with viral obsession.

In spite of failure to save one patient with so-called anti-viral drugs for over 21 years, the National Institute of Health/CDC continues to disseminate the failed hypothesis of a virus (HIV), as the cause of AIDS and subsequent prescribing of toxic killer chemotherapeutic drugs disguised as anti-viral drugs.

All the DNA chain interrupters, touted as anti-viral drugs, are systemic killers that eventually cause total collapse of the immune system without any possibility of surviving.

While every patient who is taking chemotherapy, AZT, as well as the most recent "drug cocktails" is dying sooner or later, the patients who are refusing this so called anti-viral therapy, are surviving longer than any other HIV positive patients to date. Today, these long term non-progressors are considered to be living indefinitely. The longest survivors are utilizing the least amount of drugs. I don't know how much clearer anyone has to have it explained to them.

AIDS is a chemical problem that has nothing to do with a virus.

Chapter VII

Why Treating AIDS Patients Chemically is Not the Answer

Full blown AIDS, as I have already stated, is caused as a result of chemical exhaustion of the thymus organ and ultimately the complete immune system. So prescribing dangerous and toxic drugs like chemotherapy and AZT is like throwing gasoline on a fire. The fact that 100 percent of all AIDS patients that have been treated with aggressive chemotherapy, in the early years of AIDS, and 600 to 1,200 milligrams (mg) of AZT daily have all died, should be testimonial to the obvious. Chemical abuse therapy for the AIDS patient is dead wrong.

In the early years, AIDS patients who were treated with chemotherapy lived only 2-3 years. So the obvious awareness of the failure of chemotherapy prevailed.

AZT was a failed cancer drug that caused bone marrow hemorrhaging and thus was sitting on a back shelf when it was brought out of early retirement to fight the HIV virus, in AIDS patients. The original dose of 1,200 milligrams (mg) a day permitted the patient to live for only 2-3 years, not much better than chemotherapy. Then the dosage was cut in half to 600 milligrams a day. Now, the patients were still dying; however, 5-6 years was the new life expectancy.

On August 10, 1994, on CBS television, Dr. Bob Arnot reported on a study out of the 1994 Asian AIDS Conference that had reported the fact that there were over 40,000 long term AIDS survivors living with HIV for over 10-12 years. Huh?

The life expectancy of an AIDS patient who goes to a physician for traditional medical treatment with AZT is only 5-6 years. How are the AIDS patients in the aforementioned study, living with HIV for over 12 years.

It is very simple and basic. They have all refused traditional, medical treatment with AZT. They have halted their chemical abuse and are eating a healthy diet and living a healthy life style. Many of the HIV positive individuals in this group have also returned to HIV negative status.

If you, the reader, are paying attention, you should be aware of the obvious in that if you're treated with 1,200 milligrams of AZT and you only live for 2-3 years, and then the dosage is cut in half to 600 milligrams of AZT, your life expectancy doubles. When you cut out the AZT all together and you can begin to live over 12 years and even in some cases, return to HIV negative status by not taking AZT at all...Don't you see, that the treatment was the real cause of death and not the HIV virus?

Ryan White may have received a tainted blood transfusion, but what really killed Ryan White was the treatment that was imposed upon him.

Kimberly Bergalis did not acquire HIV and subsequently AIDS from her dentist. As Kimberly stated on national television, on the Oprah Winfrey show, she was plagued with upper respiratory illnesses all her life. Kimberly, possibly, acquired AIDS from a lifetime of aggressive abuse of antibiotics or possibly she could have been one of the 13 million school children who were abusing nitrite inhalants in the 70's and 80's that NIDA reported on, in 1979 and 1980.

I believe Magic Johnson acquired his HIV status while abusing nitrite inhalants and his subsequent return to HIV negative status is due to his abstaining from that practice and living a healthy life style. I find it highly unlikely that Magic Johnson's physician found a powerful drug that eradicated the HIV from his blood stream. Talk to me Magic. Call me if you like. Magic may also be one of thousands who tested false positive and never had HIV in the first place.

In 100 percent of all full blown AIDS patients whose illnesses developed spontaneously, aggressive abuse of chemicals singularly or in concert, is the cause. Thus chemical poisoning and exhaustion of the immune system causes AIDS. Therefore, further treatment of AIDS chemically only serves ultimately to destroy the patient's immune system, leaving the treatment, as the true cause of death, in otherwise recoverable AIDS patients.   This is why chemical therapy is not the answer to treating already immune compromised individuals.

In blood transfused recipients of HIV, hemophiliacs and infants born to HIV positive mothers, the aggressive rush to chemotherapy and/or AZT was not only responsible for the development of an AIDS diagnosis, but ultimately the cause of death, initially, with the pneumonia that developed only being the secondary cause.

Medical Internists have failed to save lives with chemotherapy and AZT. Now protease inhibitors, as well as the drug cocktail regimens, are proving to be failures. There will never be a success-ful chemical treatment for someone experiencing AIDS. Also, early intervention with killer drugs based on an HIV antibody test is diabolical and life threatening.

The tragic error in blaming AIDS on a scape goat, namely the HIV virus, only serves to choose the wrong therapy in dealing with AIDS. AIDS is a chemical problem and not a viral problem. The HIV virus only serves as an indicator of toxic, chemical damage to blood and not the cause of AIDS. Therefore, treating an AIDS patient with aggressive use of chemicals is only medical genocide!

"AIDS drug AZT fails test completely"

© NEW YORK TIMES – February 14, 1995

WASHINGTON – In a major surprise, the drug AZT – now the standard treatment for children infected by the AIDS virus – proved so ineffective in halting disease progression that federal officials have called off part of a large study involving it.

AZT, or zidovudine, also had unexpectedly high rates of adverse side effects in children, like bleeding and biochemical abnormalities, officials said Monday.

The long-term study, begun in August 1991, involved 839 children initially aged 3 months to 18 years, who were treated in 62 hospitals. The children were divided at random into three groups; one that received AZT, one that received didanosine, or ddI, and a third that received a combination AZT and ddI.

The study was intended to continue until the last child recruited had completed two years of therapy. But an independent committee monitoring the trial recommended that the AZT part of the study be halted because AZT alone was unexpectedly proving to be the least effective of the three therapies.

Federal officials agreed and halted the AZT treatment February 6. Children receiving AZT alone had more rapid rates of disease progression, AIDS-related infections, impaired neurological development and death.

The findings clearly caught health officials by surprise. AZT is widely considered the drug of choice in treating HIV-infected children and adults.

###END OF ARTICLE###

Chapter VIII

A Chronology of Nitrite Inhalant Research

Amyl nitrite was first used therapeutically to relieve angina pectoris (Burton, et al 1867)[13]. Amyl nitrite is a relatively unstable liquid, found to relieve the symptoms of patients suffering from angina pectoris, a severe pain and constriction around the heart. This pain was caused by an insufficient supply of blood to the heart. Upon inhalation, the amyl nitrite vapor would indirectly stimulate the heart to work harder, thus allowing a recovery from the insufficiency.

Amyl nitrite was originally packaged in glass ampoules surrounded by a protective mesh. This mesh would prevent the scattering of glass because the ampoules, literally, had to be broken when needed. When an ampoule was broken, a popping sound would result. This is where the street name poppers is derived from.

1897

Butyl nitrite was compared to amyl nitrite and was found to have the same properties made from similar chemicals. Both products had similar effects on animals as well as on humans. Amyl nitrite was so similar to butyl nitrite that butyl nitrite was considered an acceptable alternative or substitute in the manufacturing of poppers for the treatment of angina (Burton, et al, 1897)[14].

[This last paragraph is enhanced because of its importance. The direct relation and similarity of the two chemicals pose an important fact. They can both be primarily used as direct drug substitutes. As a result, they were fraudulently marketed as a product that is actually a pharmaceutical. Through deceptive marketing, nitrite odorizer manufacturers avoid drug regulation laws.]

As far back as 1897, medical science was aware of the identical chemical effects on the human body by either amyl or butyl nitrite. When the FDA claims that butyl nitrite does not fall under their authority, as a regulated drug, one would have to raise one's eyebrows and fall back on a popular cliche—,"Stupid is as stupid does."

1937

The administration of nitrites can produce oxygen starvation of vital organs, and the pooling of blood in the arms and legs (Wilkens et al, 1937)[15]. This is the earliest description in medical literature of a condition known as methemoglobenemia. The word is frightening to the lay person, however easy or difficult to pronounce. It simply describes the inability of the red blood cells to support and transfer oxygen. In most cases this occurs as a result of massive, toxic insult to the blood stream. When a substance like amyl or butyl nitrite is inhaled, a reaction occurs causing the heart to pump extremely fast. This causes a rush of greatly expended oxygen to the brain which produces a temporary feeling of euphoria. The more oxygen received, the more euphoric the feeling. However, the increase in oxygen to the brain causes a decrease of oxygen throughout the rest of the body. It takes time to replenish the loss of oxygen, and it's during this recuperation period that the damage occurs. This lack of oxygen causes damage to brain cells, as well as to red blood cells, turning blood a rusty, brown color. If an excessive quantity of nitrite vapor or liquid is consumed, it can result in death from heart failure, if not attended to immediately.

I will refer to methemoglobinemia from time to time because I feel it will benefit the reader to have a basic knowledge of the consequences that inhaling volatile nitrite can cause. This is one of the lesser complications that can occur. Any simpleminded human being should be able to rationalize the fact that the chronic abuse of toxic substances causes great harm to one's health.

1942

Inhaled nitrites can produce profound methemoglobinemia which is a toxic insult to the blood forming organs that causes red blood cells to become incapable to support oxygen (Darling, 1942).[16]

1944

The above findings were also confirmed by researcher Lester (Lester, D. 1944)[17].

1948

Nitrites have long been known to be capable of producing the disease methemoglobinemia (Finch, C. 1948)[18].

1956

Magee and Barnes were the first researchers to report on the phenomena, whereby, exposure to nitrites formed compounds known as nitrosamines. These compounds were able to initiate cancer (Magee et al, 1956)[19].

This cancer being referred to is the very cancer soon to be associated with Kaposi's Sarcoma. This type is the cancer being presented by most all the early AIDS patients. It is not merely coincidental that the only common, aggressive chemical abuse by nearly 100 percent of these AIDS sufferers was nitrite inhalant or poppers.

1958

Multimedia sources, in the late 50's and early 60's, alerted society to the awareness of serious physiological damage, as well as death that has occurred as a result of inhalation of toxic substances. Thousands of cases of mortality statistics involving children, teenagers, and adults who voluntarily inhaled toxic substances are in the literature. One must recall the children who died from sniffing glue. There is absolutely no reason whatsoever to list inhalants that are harmful to humans and animals, for 100 percent of all chemical vapors on Earth are destructive to living cells in human beings and other animals.

It is the mindless and dimwitted position, commonly espoused by the medical, scientific community that a study of each and every chemical inhalant is needed to prove inhalant toxicity. This mentality is the primary source of questionable doubt, coupled with the lack of serious education on toxic inhalants, as well as all chemical abuse in the early educational system that is responsible for the ignorance that precipitates substance abuse. It is the responsibility of both the medical and scientific communities to sufficiently inform and shake up the educational system regarding the seriousness of substance abuse. Education should come in early grades to prevent this abuse. Also, it seems that parents are ignorant with regards to inhalant abuse and substance abuse in general. This lack of knowledge is so rampant that there must be a national, adult, education program developed to assist parents in raising their children to avoid substance abuse.

[The brief exposure to the dangerous aspects of inhalants in the 1950's and 1960's would soon be forgotten. Hundreds and thousands of predominantly homosexual men and eventually heterosexual children, teenagers, and adults would begin to practice the inhalation of volatile nitrite, one of the most potent immunodestructive cancer causing chemicals known to man.]

1960

In 1960, the family owned England based pharmaceutical giant, Burroughs Welcome, held the exclusive patent on amyl nitrite poppers, which were being used as an inhalant to speed up the heart of patients suffering from angina. The company applied to the FDA in this year to have amyl nitrite's restrictive prescription status removed. The FDA granted their petition, and poppers became available as overthecounter drugs in September of 1960. For nine years, during this unrestricted period which prevailed, popper abusers began to grow in great numbers. The sale of poppers skyrocketed abnormally. This alerted the FDA that this substance was being abused at that time.

1963

The existing popper abuse that prevailed in 1963 would not be written in medical research literature until 1978 (Israelstam) [20]. The majority of poppers were being used for the augmentation of sexual performance, specifically for the prevention of premature ejaculation and the relaxation of the anal sphincter muscle (rectum) to permit anal intercourse. This explains the skyrocketing use by the homosexual community.

Current experiments with mice demonstrated the speed at which nitrite inhalants cause internal damage sufficient enough to cause death within ten to twenty minutes (Sutton, 1963)[21].

1964

In 1964, researcher Lubell established the actual reason behind the abnormal increase in the sales of nitrite inhalants. Lubell found that these drugs were primarily being used as sexual accessory drugs (Lubell et al, 1964)[22].

This was some of the earliest testimony regarding the excessive use of amyl nitrite inhalants which prompted the pharmaceutical industry and the FDA to begin reinstating poppers back to restrictive, prescription status which will take the FDA five years to accomplish.

As far back as 1964, the FDA was well aware of the widespread abuse of nitrite inhalants being used as drugs of euphoria. Later on, the FDA avoided their responsibility in regulating volatile nitrite inhalants that would be deceptively sold as room odorizers. The FDA invoked an attitude of ignorance, gullibility and stupidity in dealing with the room odorizer industry.

1969

Finally, five years after the FDA began to reinstate prescription status to poppers, as a result of testimony established in 1964, (Lubell, 1964)[22] these abused nitrite inhalants were reclassified as prescription drugs. Unfortunately, the long time frame in which poppers went unregulated, precipitated a snowballing group of nitrite, abusing consumers, which continued in spite of the FDA regulation. Prescription status only constricted supply to an already created monster that would leave a wide open door for an entrepreneur to enter with an underground replacement.

The mindboggling, bewildering, as well as frustrating scenario that is about to unravel, not only will amaze you, but you will find hard to believe.

The need to manufacture and distribute a substitute inhalant in a black market structure was completely unnecessary. Due to clever deception and outright lying by nitrite inhalant manufacturers, coupled with the ignorance, gullibility, and laziness of the various consumer protection agencies, nitrite inhalant products would soon be available, exclusively, to the homosexual community by a legal, yet underground distribution program. All this occured under the very noses of the Consumer Protection Agencies, the FDA and the CPSC, that are mandated to protect society from these types of harmful substances.

Mounting, documented, evidence continues to elucidate that the majority of nitrite inhalants are purchased for sexual augmentation and aphrodisiac stimulation (Louria, 1970)[24]. Volatile nitrites were being inhaled to enhance sexual exhilaration (Pearlman, 1970)[25].

According to the Journal of the American Medical Association, 1970 was the year that street versions of the prescription drug amyl nitrite became available.

There may have been a few small entries into the market, but the largest manufacturer and distributor that I found information on, didn't begin to market his product until 1971. These street versions, in order to circumvent drug laws, utilized the acceptable alternate chemical for poppers established in 1897, butyl nitrite. Even though these almost pure nitrite products were deceptively called room odorizers, the word of mouth advertising in the tightly knit homosexual community along with printed exposure in gay newspapers and magazines, utilizing subtle advertising like (hit) "Take a Hit Today;" (brute) "Natural Brute will Bring Out the Best in You;" (climax) "Share Man's Ultimate Climax with a Friend;" and "Danger: Excessive Use May Cause Euphoria," the true and only use of these ostensibly marketed room odorizers became known to the street smart substance abuser.

The only people who were fooled, were the fools in the United States Consumer Protection Agencies who allowed these products onto interstate/world wide commerce in the first place. The term fool may be harsh. However, these persons are either "fools founded on ignorance or conspirators based on knowledge" (Kitzerow, 1996).

Due to the greatly reduced supply of poppers, caused by the reinstatement of prescription status by the FDA, the awareness of a wide open market began to appear to various individuals in 1969. One such person was a homosexual medical student by the name of Clifford Hassing in Los Angeles. Hassing had become aware of the identical comparison of butyl nitrite (BN) to its restricted cousin amyl nitrite being used in poppers, and that BN was unregulated.

One would expect that if an upstart, medical student could come to the conclusion that amyl nitrite and butyl nitrite were essentially the same chemicals, the FDA would possess the same logical connective thought process. Wrong! The FDA took the ignorant position that butyl nitrites do not fit the definition of a food, drug, or cosmetic as specified by the Federal Food, Drug, and Cosmetic Act from which the FDA derives its regulatory authority. Therefore, these drugs are not regulated by the FDA. That is precisely how FDA left it. Even after being involved in the five year process that it took the FDA to reinstate poppers to a prescription drug, due to massive abuse, the FDA did not feel it necessary to implement a plan that would regulate butyl nitrite. Only one year prior the Journal of the American Medical Association (Pearlman, 1970) warned of street versions of poppers being manufactured and sold. Still, this did not phase the FDA.

Thus, Clifford Hassing packaged almost pure butyl nitrite in small brown bottles approximately .3 to .4 oz. each, formed a company, West American Industries, and began deceptively marketing his product as a room odorizer called "Locker Room," so named from the offensive smell, similar to used sweat socks, that butyl nitrite takes on. This fact in its own right should be a subtle, but obvious, red flag to anyone suspecting that "Locker Room," or any bottled nitrite compound, is not being sold as a bonafide air freshener. Any human being who believes that nitrite room odorizers are actually sold as air freshener...I don't even have to finish that statement. I am embarrassed to even be associated with the same species of animal on this planet who is so God dammed stupid to even consider believing the foolish ploy of the room odorizer industry. I am not sure of the testing or qualification methods, if any, Hassing's product had to pass. Evidently not many, because he managed to get his product past the Consumer Product Safety Commission as well as the FDA.

For five years, "Locker Room" was exclusively sold to the homosexual community, by mail order, through semi-underground gay newspapers and magazines, as well as all over the world, wherever the gay population and nitrite room odorizer advertising managed to reach. They were also sold in gay bookstores, bathhouses, and night clubs, as well as being sprayed like pesticides over the dance floors at discotheques.

For five years, "Locker Room" was sold, unchallenged, by competition until 1976, when a competitor would enter the market and compete for their slice of the most debilitating, death-causing, commercially sold product of the century. The fact that the homosexual community was the exclusive target of West American Industrie's, "Locker Room" is precisely the reason why AIDS hit the homosexual community first, and subsequently, began taking its toll prior to gaining momentum in the heterosexual arena. I will present a graph, later, showing a parallel between elevated AIDS statistics and the relatively delayed entry of a company notorious for serving the heterosexual, nitrite, room odorizer consumers.

Clifford Hassing had the nerve to submit his deceptively marketed product to the U.S. Patent Office. The real appreciation of how ridiculous this move was will soon come into view as you, the reader, realize that Hassing and all the future odorizer manufactures were actually packaging slow death in a bottle. The act of trying to patent such a product is unbelievable. Somehow, considering the level of intelligence of which the Consumer Protection agencies will deal with these deceptive marketing companies, I would not be surprised if Hassing had gotten a patent on his death potion. Under the patent process there must have been some kind of requirement to submit a formula or some type of chemical analysis, which permitted the patent office to scrutinize this product and at least smell this so called air freshener. The least that one would expect to happen is an investigation of a company that is attempting to patent an air freshener that stinks. O.K., so maybe I'm expecting the impossible of our patent office in hoping, per chance, that there might be a sharp enough processor that would become aware of this perpetration. The patent office must have smelled a rat or they even possibly opened the bottle, because Hassing's patent was rejected.

Hassing wanted to keep his nitrite inhalant exclusively available to the gay community in order to avoid unwanted legal exposure, and, of course, he wanted to prevent competition. It would only be a matter of time until competition would rear up and stick out its ugly head.

Many companies would get on the bandwagon by entering the nitrite room odorizer market with their own fraudulently marketed product. The variety of inhalants were marketed under the following trade names:

Aroma of Man	Jac Aroma
Bang	Jock
Ban Apple Gas	Krypt Tonight
Black Jack	Liquid Increase
Blast	Lockeraroma
Bolt	Locker Room
Bullet	L.R.
Cat's Meow	Mama Poppers
Climax	Mama Poppers Old Fashioned Fragrance
Discorama	OZ
Dr. Bananas	Rush
Guruaroma	Ruth
Hardware	Satan's Scent
Heart On	Shot Gun
Highball	The Blues
High Baller	Toilet Water

For the next twenty years, under the watchful eye of all of the United States Consumer Protection Agencies, odorizers would be fraudulently entered into interstate, international, and worldwide commerce. This was just the beginning of this all-American tragedy.

Had any one of the commissioners in any one of the United States Consumer Protection Agencies during the years 1970 to 1991, commissioned a basically simple consumer market survey of nitrite room odorizers, they would have ascertained that all of these odorizers were being purchased for the sole purpose of altering mind and body function. This would therefore establish these consumer products to be defined as drugs. As such, these drugs would have had to have been submitted to the Food and Drug Administration for approval, and they would have been taken off of the market. If the simple task of completing a market survey was accomplished, a major catastrophe could have been avoided.

The verbiage as stated in the definition of a drug is as follows:

Drugs are "articles other than food intended to affect the structure or any function of the body of man or other animals."

"Intent may be shown by the circumstances that the article is, with the knowledge of such persons or their representatives, offered and used for a purpose for which it is neither labeled nor advertised."

The intent section, I understand to mean, that if the end use should be shown to be a drug, no matter what the manufacturer calls his product, it is still a drug by definition. "For, if a substance cannot be ultimately defined by the most common use that consumers are found to be using it for, then fraudulently deceptive perpetrations will prevail and society will be all the worse off" (Kitzerow, Jr. 1996).

Primarily, I feel that the FDA was in the best position to determine that nitrite room odorizers were drugs, and had they done their job, this industry would never have gotten started. By the end of this documentation, you will become aware of the serious error in judgment that the FDA made in not stepping in and putting a halt to the manufacture and sale of nitrite room odorizers.

1972

Beginning in the late 1960's and into the early 1970's, rumors began to surface that nitrite inhalants were being abused by both sexes in an attempt to augment the physical pleasure of sexual intercourse (Everett, G., 1972).[26]

Purchasing volatile nitrites for the specific purpose of inhaling them as a sexual aphrodisiac was reinforced. (Gay, et al, 1972)[27]

1973

Reports of depressed immunity in various animal species after inhalation of nitrogen dioxide was presented. (Fenter et al, 1973)[28] Nitrogen dioxide has been shown to cause the same type of pathology as volatile nitrite.

As far back as 1973, the inhalation of nitrite substances began to surface as the cause of depression of the immune system. It should be noted that nitrogen dioxide is not even as toxic as amyl or butyl nitrite.

1974

The year 1974 is established as the year in which the practice of inhaling nitrites sky rocketed. It is referred to as the year of the "popper craze" (Mayer, 1983)[35].

A virus, known as cytomegalovirus (CMV), Kaposi's Sarcoma (KS) and pnuemocystis, Carinii Pneumonia (PCP) are all the major symptoms directly associated with the early AIDS patients, and also commonly occur in high frequencies directly related to immuno-suppressive, anti-inflammatory, anti-rejection drugs utilized in organ and tissue transplantation (Walter, 1974)[9]. Here is obvious evidence that chemicals which suppress or interrupt the immune system's ability to fight off bacterial or protozoa organisms that cause the diseases PCP, KS, and CMV do so without HIV being present. (At this point in time HIV had not yet been discovered, I am just illustrating a point.) Also, CMV viruses, associated with suppressive drug therapy given to transplant recipients, went away after the drug therapy was stopped. This is further proof that the drugs were responsible for these viruses and ailments and not HIV.

This researcher believes that all viruses originate in humans and other animals as a result of toxic insult of the blood stream from chemicals, which may be prescription or non-prescription, taken into the body by inhalation, ingestion, or injection.

The mysterious virus, known as cytomegalovirus or CMV, mentioned previously, is one illness that indicates the presence of AIDS. With this in mind, you can begin to understand that a virus associated with AIDS will appear as a result of prescription drug therapy and then will miraculously disappear when the drugs are stopped. It should be easy to realize the blatantly obvious connection between chemicals and the origin of viruses. At this point, I just want to open your mind and further elaborate on viral origin later.

In 1974 the Los Angeles Police Department arrested bookstore owners for the sale and distribution of inhalants, marketed in small bottles. The apparent use of these products, coupled with the exhibited intelligence of the Los Angeles Police Dept. (LAPD), prompted their move to arrest the proprietors.

However, when the search for intelligent regulatory literature in the drug abuse regulations files was done by the California State's Attorneys Office, they could find none. Current regulatory literature only dealt with amyl nitrite and not butyl nitrite, which was being sold by the book store owners. Consequently, the legal process ended. (Reed, 1974)[36]

1975

Nitrite inhalants were found to enhance sexual performance and orgasm. Some users stated that they were no longer able to function sexually without the use of nitrites. (Everett, 1975)[37]

A more widespread pattern of nitrite odorizer use was associated with overt sexual activities including prolonged penile erection and relaxation of rectal sphincter tone, thus facilitating anal intercourse. (Labataille, 1975)[38]

This study is one of the earliest statements connecting the degree of sexual activity with a proportional amount of nitrite room odorizer use. This eventually precipitated the theory in some early researcher's minds that the more odorizer use, the more sex partners. This study laid the ground work for the pseudoscientific theory that AIDS must be a sexually transmitted disease. This theory was a plausible consideration, but the researchers who totally accepted the sexual transmission of a contagious organism, completely ignoring the increase of nitrite exposure, would be doing improper science in vacating further nitrite study in pursuit of a contagious organism. This is exactly what will happen when HIV is discovered in 1984.

An amazing observation of mine is the fact that as HIV is discovered, medical science and AIDS statistics will not associate any ailment caused as a result of aggressive abuse of the most Cancer causing immune destructive inhalant known to man. (In most cases early AIDS patients were abusing nitrites for over six years.)

1976

The National Institute of Drug Abuse recorded 13 emergency room admissions due to nitrite inhalant abuse along with another 84 related complications associated with inhalation of volatile nitrite (NIDA, 1976).

In 1976, the formation of a new company intent on manufacturing their own version of nitrite room odorizers appeared. Pacific Western Distributing Company, or PWD, headed up by chairman W. Jay Freezer, under the subsidiary of Pharmex Ltd., entered interstate, international world wide commerce with their room odorizer version named "Rush." The name itself was a subtle advertisement in its own right that this product was not a room odorizer(Reed, 1979).[36]

Pacific Western began such a broadening distribution of their product that it became available in record stores, pharmacies, magazines, gay and standard newspapers, straight night clubs, adult book stores and porn shops. Until PWD entered the market, room odorizers were mainly being marketed to the gay community by Clifford Hassing's company, West American Industries or WAI. With this larger more encompassing market distribution, new consumers were being introduced to nitrite room odorizers. Children, teenagers and heterosexual adults began abusing nitrites as the FDA continued to look the other way.

Also in 1976, no sooner than PWD got into the market, a complaint regarding "Rush" involving a young student in Marine County California attracted the California State Health Department. Dr. Alan Slagle, a pharmacist in the department, said the complaint, "Just sort of vanished!"

Back in 1971, when Clifford Hassing failed to acquire exclusive rights to control distribution of room odorizers as a result of his failed patent attempt, he voiced his fear that competitors would cause unwanted attention to nitrite room odorizers. As PWD entered the market, Hassing's prediction and worst nightmare came to fruition. Pacific Western Distributing originally called their product "Rush". However, in an attempt to capitalize on the already familiar market established by Hassing's product called "Locker Room", PWD added a room odorizer named "L.R." to their product line. To this Hassing cried foul and spent thousands of dollars in a court battle, arguing that "L.R." was a parasite of Hassing's, "Locker Room". The pitiful irony here is that these two human parasites were arguing over who was going to sell the largest quantity of the most immune destructive substance commercially being distributed to society for retail sale.

As a result, Pacific Western began to grow at warp speed and in a very short period captured approximately 60% of the market. Even the *Wall Street Journal* took notice of Pacific Western's accelerated growth.

In scientific literature, as well as documentation contained within the World Health Organization's database, it is fact that inhalation of toxic substances is evidenced all over the world. Abuse of harmful chemicals surfaces in almost every culture on this planet. Most recently, inhalant abuse worldwide was the focal point of an international conference held in Mexico in 1976.

Serious concerns were brought to light regarding the abuse of toxic inhalants by children and adults in countries such as: Africa, Native America, Australia, Aborigine, Japan, Canada, Europe, Latin America, Puerto Rico, Mexico and the United States, just to name a few.

In Brazil, thousands of young children are suffering from AIDS related illnesses as a result of inhaling aerosol shoe spray and nail polish remover. It is not surprising that HIV transmission plays little to no role in these immune deficiency cases. These children are not homosexual, nor do they possess needles to transmit the HIV. Most importantly, a majority of these young children are not sexually active.

1977

Resulting from an accidental fire and subsequent injury, and stemming from nitrite vapors catching fire from a nearby candle, the Consumer Product Safety Commission (CPSC) was alerted to the hazards of nitrite inhalants.

The pros and cons of labeling verses banning nitrite room odorizers were discussed by the CPSC staff and recorded in a memo from Perez to Schmeltzer on July 11, 1977. (CPSC Memo, 1977) This CPSC staff discussion is a formal notice that they were aware of nitrite abuse as far back as 1977, and were aware that these products were primarily purchased as drugs. What more did an intelligent body of individuals whose mandate it is to protect society from harmful consumer products need to act in banning these products from interstate commerce?

This CPSC discussion, under Commissioner Goyan, ended without any action being taken due to a question of jurisdiction. The CPSC felt that the room odorizer product was a drug and as such, fell under the scrutiny of the FDA. When asked by the CPSC to define this as a drug, the FDA came to an unbelievable decision. They blindly accepted the manufacturer's deceptive label of room odorizer on this volatile chemical, and as a result, the FDA refused to classify them as drugs. Their determination was that this was a consumer product. The FDA's gullible and ignorant determination regarding odorizers therefore bounced the ball back into the CPSC's court.

This appalling jurisdiction dispute would carry on for thirteen years, during which a toxicology professor, Dr. Ron Wood, would

70

submit petition after petition to ban the sale of room odorizers. Meanwhile, the mainstream public, especially gay men, would go on inhaling this destructive chemical until an act of Congress would finally ban the sale of this dangerous killer drug.

Pacific Western's aggressive marketing scheme again got them into trouble, due to the deceptive and obviously bold connotation used in the words they selected to describe the benefits of their product ,"purity, power, and potency".

In December of 1977, the Superior Court of the state of California filed a suit basically stating that Pacific Western was marketing "Rush" not as the liquid incense it was labeled to be, but as an aphrodisiac drug as its ads implied. The disposition of the case would not come down until January 1978 (Reed, 1979).[36]

Volatile nitrite inhalants were found to cause dizziness, headaches, rapid heart beat, inadequate blood flow to the brain, fainting, general decrease in blood pressure, increased eye pressure and loss of oxygen in the blood stream (Bruckner, 1979)[39].

With all these deleterious effects on the body, it is amazing that anyone with medical training could come to the conclusion that organ damage is not occurring, let alone the massive destruction going on in the delicate environment of the blood stream, as well as within the lymphatic system. In expecting a black and white, flagrantly obvious cause of AIDS, such as blaming the development of AIDS on a common scapegoat, such as a virus, the medical community is ignoring and underestimating the overall systemic trauma that inhaling a toxic substance, such as volatile nitrite, can inflict on the human immune system. Not to come across as redundant, but I must point out, once again, that knowing prescription immunosuppressive drugs commonly cause PCP and KS, should bring one to see the obvious connection of volatile nitrites with the development of AIDS. This seems highly pragmatic and logical. I feel that a researcher, ignoring the obvious in search of a less logical path, like a virus, is basically obsessed with viral theory in general.

At this chronological period within this research, 1977, HIV has not yet been discovered. All research, up to 1984, is going to indict and find guilty nitrite inhalant and immunodestructive drugs as the cause of AIDS. Then, in 1984, the discovery of HIV will destroy all the logical thought processes and expensive research already completed. I am going to jump ahead in a "chronological time warp." I am going to let you in on a little inside information. It is now the year 2000, sixteen years since HIV was discovered. The general public is not aware of the major problems that researchers are having, trying to connect HIV with most of the AIDS indictor illnesses, whereas the return to immunosuppressive chemicals is looking more promising every day. So pay close attention to the nitrite research that I am accumulating as we move along. I implore you to keep an open mind. Self-evident truth always survives the true test of time.

Nitrite room odorizers were included in a hazardous inhalant compendium (Couri, 1977)[40]. This adds to the already existing list of overwhelming evidence being established by authoritative experts, supporting the fact that nitrite room odorizers are used as drugs.

1978

It was estimated that in New York city alone, the sale of nitrite inhalants had reached more than 100,000 bottles a week, at a cost of fifty million dollars a year to predominantly the homosexual community in 1978. A guide to homosexual love-making asserted that by 1974, use of nitrite inhalants had passed into every corner of gay life. As stated earlier, these products were being used, for the relaxation of the anal sphincter muscle, to facilitate anal intercourse, prolonging orgasm, stimulating music appreciation and enhancing meditation (Sigell, 1978)[41].

The FDA is still buying the lie that room odorizer manufacturers are selling these products to be used as air fresheners.

It is a fact that the toxic effects of inhaled volatile nitrites include the following: light headed feeling, weakness, nausea, defective muscular coordination, delirium, headache, fainting, profound low heart rate, skin flushing, increased ocular pressure, lung irritation with the potential to cause Cancer. Users stated they could no longer perform sexually without use of these drugs (Sigell, 1978)[41].

Reports of depression of cellular immunity in various animal species after inhalation of nitrogen dioxide, have been found to cause similar pathology to volatile nitrites (Maigetter, 1978)[42].

In 1978, *The American Journal of Psychiatry* contained an article which presented the potential for Cancer to develop from the interaction of nitrite and normal residing nitrogen compounds in the human body, similar to the already proven Cancer caused from sodium nitrite used in meat preservatives (*American Journal of Psychology*, 1978).

In 1978, prompted by research proving that nitrites cause Cancer by combining with components in the human body forming highly dangerous carcinogens called nitrosamides and nitrosamines, the FDA regulated nitrites as food preservatives in meat. Who doesn't remember the press coverage surrounding allowable nitrites in bacon and other meats?

If you remember Magee and Barnes (1956) had also proven that nitrites caused Cancer; it only took the FDA twenty-two years to enact a program to protect society from these cancer causing nitrites.

Finally, on January 6, 1978, a verdict in the case of California vs. Freezer and PWD, which began in December of 1977, came forth. The judge declared "Rush" to be a drug that was not approved" (Reed, 1979).[36]   Not only had a states attorney publicly acknowledged that "Rush" was being sold for the purpose of being inhaled as an aphrodisiac (constituting the definition of a drug), we now have a formal court official, a judge, formally announcing that the volatile nitrite inhalant was in fact a drug that was not approved by the FDA. This is all that should have been necessary in order for the FDA to initiate an investigation and remove these products from worldwide commerce. The FDA could have been a hero, as far back as 1978, by saving society from these death delivering drugs, instead; they chose to do nothing. Even after the judge declared Freezer's products to be drugs; the judge granted him a full hearing to defend his case. In his defense, Freezer cited a research paper done by Nickerson (1978) which Pacific West Distributing Company's (parent company), Pharmex Ltd. privately financed.

The room odorizer industry has lied, from the beginning, by stating to the FDA and CPSC that their products were intended to be used as room odorizers because no one was purchasing these products for the purpose of freshening the air. Also, any research tracking the harmful effects of inhaling the minimal concentration of nitrite that one might come in contact with from minute quantities being dispersed in an open room, would be totally irrelevant in ascertaining the harmful effects one would experience by direct inhalation.

73

The research paper done by Nickerson[45] was based on the lie, being perpetrated by the odorizer industry. By ignoring the real truth, evidenced by a massive accumulation of research, contrary to manufactures claims, the real reason consumers were purchasing room odorizers was for use as a drug. The good doctors in the Nickerson study only contributed to the big lie.

The research team, headed up by Mark Nickerson, stated in the beginning of their paper entitled, "Isobutyl Nitrite and Related Compounds," (Nickerson 1978)[45], that commercially bottled volatile nitrite was primarily used as a room odorizer. To this day, there is absolutely no unbiased study elucidating room odorizers being used as air fresheners, where as all the studies, other than Nickerson's (1978), found in scientific literature, have proven beyond a reasonable doubt that all consumers of room odorizers purchased them to get high and enhance sex.

This researcher believes that the room odorizer industry, in general, is guilty of the most harmful deception ever imposed on mankind, and Nickerson's bastardized study only aided in that disastrous deception. Had Nickerson done responsible research, the room odorizer industry would have been stopped in their tracks. The industry would also not have won their court cases and the AIDS epidemic would never have begun.

As a result of the Nickerson paper and other arguments on the California vs. Freezer court case, an unbelievable turn of events culminated out of the trial. Freezer was allowed to substitute an almost identical formula and was allowed to continue to sell volatile nitrite inhalant under a new name, "Bolt." The search for intelligence on this planet was, definitely, not to begin in that San Francisco court room on that day! If morons can achieve high positions in the judicial system, this was a shining example.

If I was to take any jury of twelve reasonable thinking humans and make them aware of this seriously dangerous deception that the room odorizer industry was engaged in, I have no doubt in my mind that all would find these companies guilty of fraudulent entry into the international commerce of a hazardous substance.

The shameful tragedy is that the court evidenced their awareness of this deception by the disclosing the original finding, that "Rush" was a drug that had not been approved by the FDA. Changing the bottle and formula did not change the reason why consumers were purchasing these products.

74

Sufficient research, establishing the real purpose for which volatile nitrite room odorizers were being purchased go back as far as 1970. (Loria 1972; Pearlman 1970; Everett 1972; Gay and Shepard 1972; and Labataille 1975). In all, ninety-eight emergency room admissions, strictly resulting from inhaling room odorizers, were recorded by NIDA in 1976. All research studies proved beyond a doubt that these products were being purchased as drugs. There is no research testifying to the fact that anyone in history has ever purchased a nitrite room odorizer to be used as an air freshener.

The odorizer industry had lots of money available to influence research, government agencies, and public opinion, as was evidenced by their success with the California Department of Health.

Almost immediately after Freezer beat California's attempt to ban his product in January, 1978, the state of Connecticut filed a suit to ban "Rush" and all similar products, citing cases where children were abusing the inhalant. Connecticut concluded that mere label restrictions forbidding the sale to minors would not be enough, and that a total ban was their only recourse. Judge Robert Stator heard the case.

Freezer and legal counsel used their classic diversionary lie that implied that "Rush" was intended to be used as a room odorizer, and when used as directed, posed no harm even to children. Again, Freezer referred to the "bastard study" by Nickerson (Nickerson et al 1978).

The state of Connecticut upheld the ban on products, formulated from butyl nitrite, which was formally stated in the original Connecticut petition; however, Freezer's product ,"Rush," was reformulated with Isobutyl nitrite, a close relative of butyl nitrite. Remember, in the state of California, Freezer was forced to change his formula and was allowed to continue to manufacture and sell his death potions. Because of the discrepancy in the chemical terms, the state of Connecticut gave in and once again Freezer slithered out from under the grip of the legal system, a result of a ridiculous technicality. Deja vu! Court room idiocy rears its ugly head once again. At this point, my being dumbfounded doesn't even approach the disgust I felt when I learned of the disposition of the Connecticut case. "Rush" and "Locker Room" were allowed to return to the marketplace in Connecticut.

Within the past decade, organic nitrite preparations have become popular drugs of abuse among homosexual men and in the discotheque crowd (Mc Clung et al 1978)[46].

Inhalation of volatile nitrites is used for increased sexual stimulation (Dimijian et al 1978)[43]. Researchers reported, in retrospect of their findings in 1963, that the inhalation of nitrites enhanced sexual stimulation, heightened libido, prevented premature ejaculation, increased the volume of the ejaculate, and promoted orgasm intensity and length (Israelstam 1978)[44].

Out of the one hundred and fifty patients suffering from PCP or KS, nearly all were found to be abusing nitrite inhalants, reporting three to six exposures per occasion with from one to four occasions per week.

W. Jay Freezer of the Pacific Western division of Pharmex LTD., stated that an estimated twelve million bottles of room odorizers were sold between 1978 and 1983 (Nickerson 1978)[45].

Kaposi's Sarcoma or KS, has been reported to occur in patients approximately five years from the beginning of therapy, utilizing immunosuppressive drugs such as corticosteroids (Klepp 1978)[10], (Gange 1978).

It is noted that PCP is found to be directly associated with immunosuppressive drugs. Also, the most common Cancer found in AIDS patients, KS, is also shown to be relative to drug therapy. It should be obvious that drug use has a high potential to cause PCP as well as KS all by themselves, without having to involve a virus.

1979

By 1979, over five million people in the United States, alone, were found to be using volatile nitrite inhalants more than once a week (Mayer, 1983)[35].

Subjecting mice to various types of butyl nitrites proved to have consistent lethal potencies when given by various routs resulting in methemoglobinemia, liver damage and death (Maickel 1979)[47].

Nitrites are nitrites, and all are toxic in similar ways to humans and animals. Slightly altering a nitrite will not alleviate the potential harm incurred from inhaling them (Kitzerow 1996).

Confirmation of depressed immunity after chronic inhalation of nitrogen dioxide (NO2) occurs in various animal species.

Inhalation of volatile nitrites has been found to cause similar immune deficiencies to those exhibited after exposure to nitrogen dioxide (NO2) (Holt 1979)[48].

The Drug Abuse Warning Network (DAWN) reported that in 1979 approximately 11.1 percent of the high school seniors in a national study admitted to having abused volatile nitrites. In questioning individuals, specifically regarding the abuse of the nitrite room odorizer "Locker Room," it was found that 3.1 percent of children aged from 12-17, 5.1 percent of young adults aged 18 to 25, and 0.6 percent of adults aged 26 and older have used this drug(Johnson 1979)[49].

(Reed 1979)[36], In the gay life magazine which is internationally known as *Christopher Street,* staff writer, David Reed opens his report on the volatile nitrite explosion by correlating the use of room odorizers to flexing one's heart or "Pumping Gold." According to Reed, odorizer manufacturers boasted that they were selling twenty million dollars a year to an estimated five million regular abusers. Reed goes on to estimate the manufacturer's cost of making the product at approximately fifty cents a bottle, and notes that it was marked up to as high as ten dollars. In abhorrent sympathy of this marketing rape of these poor chemical users, Reed comes to their rescue by referring his readers to a source for making their own "bath tub" version of the recipe. This somewhat underground reporting, on the subject of room odorizers, assisted manufacturers in educating their potential customers in the actual and suggested use of their product and not the implied use that the manufacturers used to sneak this product into interstate commerce. Again, the only people gullible enough to believe the odorizer lie was the consumer protection agencies that allowed this product on the market in the first place.

Underground cultural periodicals like *Christopher Street* and other gay print, as well as the "grapevine," were all coconspirators in catapulting the abuse of what would soon come to be known as the most "cancer causing, immune destroying, substance known to man," prior to AZT, that is. Hopefully, a lesson will be learned as a result of the AIDS tragedy. This would be that may no man, who has love of their fellow man, ever educate or encourage anyone to inhale, ingest or inject any chemical substance. All humans who would encourage such abuse will some day have to stand and face their creator, and may He have mercy on their souls.

It has been written that the body is a temple. Violating that temple is not tolerated by the Creator, and ultimately the violator assumes total responsibility for their actions on the day of judgment.

The gay community is notorious for living in the fast lane, regarding the use of drugs. It is unfortunate that the tight communication network that is prevalent within their community worked against them, in that they began teaching one another the practice of inhaling volatile nitrites. Each and every person who actively promoted nitrite abuse can assume a portion of the blame for the AIDS epidemic and the self annihilation of thousands of their friends and loved ones. Fortunately, for the heterosexual community, the mainstream media printed very little about nitrite inhalant use. In fact, the nitrite era for the most part, has come and gone, and still, today, most of the general public has not even heard of room odorizers or volatile nitrite inhalants. What is amazing is the fact that the nitrite era managed to exist in the U.S. for more than 20 years, and the majority of American citizens don't have the foggiest notion of what had transpired. This is especially ironic during a time when a secret, one time sexcapade of a public official, can become world knowledge.

The gay community was exposed to nitrite inhalants years ahead of the heterosexual community, and more notably, this is the reason why heterosexual AIDS cases took much longer to begin showing up in medical literature. The heterosexual community's lack knowledge regarding nitrite abuse, is exactly the reason why heterosexual AIDS statistics have remained in the less than ten percent category, and will never amount to more than that. This is due to the decline of AIDS statistics that will begin showing up in 1997, which shall be explained in the following pages.

On two separate occasions, a 25 year old man had to be treated in an emergency room for excessive abuse of volatile nitrite inhalant. Due to the methemoglobinemia associated with nitrite abuse, the patient was actually turning gray, due to insufficient oxygen in the blood (Horne, 1975)[51]. One would think that a person would learn a lesson from being treated once in an emergency situation, let alone twice. It is this sort of mentality that seems to be common in all substance abusers. The search for the high, while being ignorant to the ultimate price, has led many unsuspecting adventurers into the abyss from which very few escape.

In April, 1979, the National Institute on Drug Abuse (NIDA), issued a press release, commonly referred to as a"NIDA Capsule,"

78

which publicly acknowledged the awareness of the FDA, Consumer Product and Safety Commission (CPSC), and NIDA as to the extent that nitrites or room odorizers, were being purchased by U.S. consumers as drugs to be abused. The following release, printed verbatim, is a self indictment, proving that none of these consumer protection organizations performed in a capacity that was in the foremost interest of American society (NIDA, 1979)[52].

NIDA Capsule:

Butyl Nitrite

Butyl nitrite, packaged in small bottles, under a variety of names such as "Locker Room," "Rush," "Jacaroma," and "Bullet," is the key ingredient in room odorizers. Abused by inhalation, butyl nitrite is an organic chemical which produces a high, lasting from a few seconds to a minute. It, reportedly, causes the user to experience a slow down in time and intensification of feelings. Since the nitrite high is so short, users tend to inhale repeatedly during each sniffing episode.

The National Institute on Drug Abuse estimates that about seven million Americans have experimented with or are chronic users of inhalant products. How much of this use involves room odorizers is not yet known.

Room odorizers are usually sold by drug and paraphernalia stores (head shops), street vendors, or record stores. Some news reports estimate that they accounted for twenty million dollars in U.S. sales last year, or about five million bottles.

Scientific studies have shown that butyl nitrite temporarily dilates the blood vessels, causing the heart to beat harder and faster, to fill the expanded vessels with blood. Immediate effects include a rapid heartbeat, flushed face and lowered blood pressure. What often follows is a headache and sometimes nausea, vomiting, or dizziness.

The long-term effects of inhaling nitrites are not yet known. Because of the effects on the heart, there is the risk that over time, the cardiovascular system may become impaired. Inhaling nitrites could, therefore, be fatal to persons with cardiovascular disease. Another potential long-term effect may be interference with the red blood cells' vital oxygen carrying function. Because nitrites are solvents that break down the protective fatty layer surrounding the liver and brain cells, prolonged use may be linked to hepatitis and brain hemorrhage.

Butyl nitrite has not yet been found to cause physical dependence. However, in some users, tolerance (the need to constantly increase use to achieve the effect obtained with the original smaller dose), has appeared within a few weeks.

As mentioned earlier, the street name for room odorizers is poppers. The name originated with amyl nitrite, a heart stimulant pharmacologically similar to butyl nitrite, once commonly prescribed for angina patients. Amyl nitrite comes in little glass vials that make a popping sound when broken.

Because room odorizers are neither advertised nor sold as drugs, and since they comply with federal labeling regulations, their use to date is legal and difficult to control. Many U.S. communities, however, are trying to ban or limit sales to adults. Georgia and Connecticut have put controls on odorizer sales; Houston, Texas has banned their sale to minors. Several Federal Government agencies, the Food and Drug Administration, the Consumer Product Safety Commission and the National Institute on Drug Abuse are closely monitoring use patterns and health implications.

This release is a tersely blatant exposé, in which extensive internal trauma occurs when nitrites are inhaled. The knowledge of how extensive this abusive behavior was occurring in society was obvious. (Lubell, et al 1964), (Louria, 1970), (Pearlman, 1970), (Everett 1972), (Gay, 1972), (Labataille, 1975), (Sigell, 1978). In many cases, these research papers, describing sales in the millions, were more than mere news stories. This research was also conducted by highly credible scientists. Whoever wrote the NIDA press release was either grossly ignorant of the true numbers, or they were attempting to gloss over a serious societal problem. The fact that individual states were moving to ban these products from interstate commerce while the FDA, CPSC, and NIDA were "Continuing to monitor," clearly shows a serious problem existed with all of these agencies in 1979.

Nitrite abusers were found to experience nasal irritation, nausea, and temporary loss of erection as a result of overuse. (Lowry, 1979)[53] Similar effects of nitrite inhalants have already been established as far back as 1937 (1937, Wilkins)[15], (1944, Lester)[17], (1948, Finch)[18], (1963, Sutton).[21]

1980

The similarity that exists between Isobutyl nitrite, butyl nitrite and amyl nitrite with their effects on the human body are revisited. The similar toxic effects were established in 1897 (1897, Burton).

"The toxic effects of nitrite inhalation include rapid flushing of the face, pulsation in the head, cyanosis, confusion, vertigo, motor unrest, weakness, yellow vision, hypertension, soft thready pulse, and fainting. Prolonged inhalation of amyl nitrite has resulted in death due to respiratory failure. The use of volatile nitrites to enhance sexual performance and pleasure can result in syncope and death by cardiovascular collapse." (Haley, 1980)[54]

An excellent report on the toxic effects of abused inhalant mixtures appeared in 1980 (Pryor, et al 1980)[55]. The incidence of deliberate use by homosexual men has been greater than that of heterosexual men (Lowry, 1980).[56] The means of distribution and availability of nitrite room odorizers, being predominantly used in the homosexual community, is evidenced by the majority of hospital visits associated with nitrite inhalant abuse by primarily gay men.

Interactions of nitrites and mouse skin lipids (fats) have been shown to produce potentially carcinogenic substances. Cholesterol reacts with nitrite to form nitrosamines and or nitrosamides, which have been shown to be carcinogenic (Mirvish, 1980)[57].

The rare cancer, known as KS, which was showing up in otherwise healthy young homosexual men who were found to be commonly abusing volatile nitrite inhalants, rekindled the interest in nitrites and their potential to initiate Cancer. It was not so long ago that nitrites and their role as carcinogens were proven. In 1956 Magee and Barnes found, as did the Cancer research done in 1978, that when used in meat preservatives nitrites caused Cancer. They have dealt with the major concerns over nitrites and now, while scientists are "beating the same dead horse," homosexual men by the thousands are inhaling almost pure nitrite. This is incredible.

In October 1980, NIDA issues another press release capsule. In only one year, their estimate of Americans who have risked death or trauma by inhalants, has jumped from seven million to thirteen million. In 1979, 140 people died from abusing inhalants. The capsule reiterates the early statistics on high school students in which over 500,000 inhalant abusers were reported to have used inhalants as recently as one month prior to the survey. Georgia, Connecticut, Houston, Texas, Maryland and Tennessee have moved to either restrict or ban nitrite room odorizers. What is NIDA doing? They are researching the health consequences of inhalant abuse, and they are attempting to discover methods to prevent and treat that abuse (NIDA, 1980)[58]. They are researching the health consequences of inhalant abuse. People are dying! In one year, there was an increase of six million people inhaling these substances, which have already been proven to cause damage to the nervous system, liver, kidneys, blood and bone marrow, as well as death from heart failure. It is time for NIDA researchers to take off their lab coats and march their bodies to every regulatory, law making body in Washington to sound an alert. The abnormal increase of six million inhalant abusers, in one year, was obviously caused by the room odorizer industry. What are the researchers at NIDA doing about this? Is NIDA going to alert the law makers and shut down the room odorizer manufacturers? Not a chance! They are getting in line to receive grant money for AIDS research.

On November 12, 1980, Ronald W. Wood, Ph.D. Assistant Professor of Toxicology at the University of Rochester's School of Medicine and Dentistry, and also a world renowned authority in the field of toxicology, petitioned the U.S. Consumer Product and Safety Commission to enact more stringent packaging and warning labels on nitrite room odorizers, primarily to include the words "toxic after inhalation."

For over ten years, with the funding and support from NIDA, Professor Wood studied the harmful effects of inhalant abuse. In 1976, he attended the International Conference in Mexico City. At this conference, the problem of inhalant abuse world-wide, became readily apparent.

The abuse of inhalants in the U.S. is a major problem, and time constraints have prompted Professor Wood to look beyond the study of this nitrite inhalant abuse that was obviously going on with room odorizer products. It was apparent to him that these products had absolutely no constructive value to society, and he was confident that it would only be a very brief time before the authorities would remove them from interstate commerce.

Due to the length of time it takes to do proper research, he assumed the room odorizer industry would have been long gone, before his nitrite research was complete. For a prudent thinker like

Professor Wood, this was a logical assumption. Little did Professor Wood know that there would be no prudent thinkers at the FDA or CPSC for the next 14 years to step up and challenge the room odorizer industry.

The haste in Professor Wood's attempt to enforce stringent labeling and packaging was prompted by the numerous recorded deaths, attributed to nitrite inhalant abuse and the immediate need to maximize damage control to society until the expected removal of room odorizers would take place.

1981

On September 9, 1981, the CPSC voted to deny professor Wood's petition with a formal letter of response, finally drafted on February 10, 1982. Not bad, considering professor Wood's petition was presented in November of 1980.

The CPSC, in denying the petition, stated, that present warning labels were adequate, and special packaging was not indicated, since there was no substantial data in regards to injuries incurred by children under five years old.

The CPSC replied that, "The commission is unaware of demonstrated human toxicity associated with inhalation of room odorizers containing alkyl nitrites, and no substantial injury data is associated with their inhalation." This is quoted directly from the formal letter of response.

Both amyl and Isobutyl nitrite were found to be direct mutagens. A mutagen is any agent that is capable of causing genetic mutations, which is the first step in the genesis of Cancer. Take note that mutagens primarily include chemicals, medicines, and radiation, not viruses such as HIV. The National Cancer Institute has been unsuccessfully attempting to blame the cause of Cancer on viruses for many decades (Quinto et al, 1980)[59]. Cancer is caused when normal cells that are living in a harmonious environment are subjected to toxins that alter that environment. Sporadic numbers of cellular debris, also known as viruses found in the human body, are not sufficient enough to alter an environment to cause mutation. Therefore, viruses do not cause Cancer (Kitzerow 1996). Researcher Quinto goes on to call attention to this relatively new class of chemical mutagenic agents (volatile nitrites) and the potential risk of Cancer from abuse of these substances (Quinto et al, 1980)[59].

A reference was also made to the recent increase of volatile nitrite availability over the past five years on the American market. It is estimated, by the companies that manufacture nitrite room odorizers, that over five million people have used their product.

Quinto makes a warning statement in saying, "The accusation of mutagenicity of these compounds urgently calls for a more thorough inquiry into the oncogenesis (ability to initiate tumors) risks to which millions of users of this drug may be exposed" (Quinto et al, 1980)[59].

Bogovski and Bogovski tested 290 nitrite compounds and their potential to induce Cancer. The results revealed that 252 out of 290 nitrite compounds, or 87% were potentially carcinogenic (Bogovski, 1981).[60]

The death of a thirty year old black male was attributed to oral ingestion of Isobutyl nitrite room odorizers. He suffered fatal methemoglobinemia (Dixon, 1981).[61]

Also, patients who repeatedly inhaled volatile nitrites developed crusty lesions around their nose and lip, which subsequently cleared up after cessation of the practice (Fisher 1981).[62]

Two male homosexual patients who had inhaled two bottles of volatile nitrite room odorizer labeled "Locker Room", experienced excessive irritation of the skin, trachea and bronchial area, which developed into trachea bronchitis. Associated coughing, fever expectoration of blood from the mouth, larynx, trachea bronchi and lungs was observed. Flushing of the skin, as well as, breathing insufficiency, due to an accumulation of infectious secretions in the air passageways, were also patient symptoms of excessive volatile nitrite abuse (Covalla, 1981).[63]

Pilot questionnaires in 1981, revealed that volatile nitrite inhalants were used by nearly all homosexual patients diagnosed with AIDS (CDC 1981).

People who believe in the HIV hypothesis in regards to the cause of AIDS, would like you to believe that all of these patients, who were actually abusing this highly immune depressing, Cancer-causing inhalant, simultaneously came into contact with an AIDS infected person. Subsequently, this person passed HIV on. They feel that the nitrite abuse has nothing to do with the development of AIDS in these patients.

Australian physicians reported in the Medical Journal of Australia in 1981, that two cases associated with inhaling volatile nitrites were observed to have suffered extreme destruction of red blood cells and were also diagnosed as having Heinz body hemolytic anemia. This was added to the list of physical devastation caused by nitrite inhalant abuse. In the two cases, both male patients had inhaled amyl nitrite regularly over a three months period, with excessive exposure of up to twenty sniffs per occasion. Thorough testing ruled out everything as the cause of AIDS except nitrites. The patients were informed of the hazards nitrite inhalants posed and were advised to return in one month. Both patients abstained from nitrite abuse and consequently their blood disorders cleared up upon re-testing.

Prolonged nitrite inhalant abuse causes damage to the blood forming organs, and also can be the cause of the blood disorder as well as an enlarged spleen (Romeril et al, 1981).[64] One of the functions of the spleen is to filter non-functioning red blood cells and other adverse particulate from the blood stream. An enlarged spleen is a result of excessive damage occurring in the blood stream.

The aforementioned Australian report establishes the fact that nitrite sales and abuse have occurred around the world, and, to what extent will not be known until the room odorizer manufacturers are subpoenaed into a court of law.

As one becomes more aware that the cause of AIDS is brought on by chemical inhalant abuse and as one realizes that room odorizers were being marketed world wide, it should be fairly easy to understand how AIDS could occur simultaneously in other countries.

If one believes aids is caused by a virus, which takes from seven to ten years to develop into full blown AIDS, and has to be established by a common inter-relative association between individuals, then the HIV theory seems less plausible than the chemical abuse theory. Not only is the HIV theory less plausible, it is truly difficult to explain how AIDS appeared almost simultaneously all over the world given the slow pace in which HIV develops within AIDS patients.

In 1981 the state of Maryland's Department of Health surveyed 101 inhalant abusers. The results revealed that butyl nitrite was the most widely abused inhalant.[65]

"Patients with acute acquired methemoglobinemia can present a confusing picture and follow a rapidly fatal course. This is especially true in cases in which adequate history is unavailable. We have recently seen three cases of methemoglobinemia secondary to ingesting or inhaling the contents of an over the counter room odorizer containing Isobutyl nitrite. We wish to alert the health community of this health hazard" (Hamilton 1981).[65]

In one case, a thirty year old man was found lethargic on a park bench. He was seen earlier at a discotheque and had a little brown bottle in his possession. The patient died of cardiopulmonary arrest, associated with oxygen starvation of the blood, caused from nitrite abuse (Shesser et al, 1981).[66]

A copy-cat inhalant product was found advertised in *High Times* (July 1981, page 23), which contained a local anesthetic called procaine HCL. The ad stated the following: "Like the real thing! If inhaled or ingested may cause stimulation, excitement, or other toxic reaction. Not intended for drug use." The product was labeled as "Rock Crystal Incense." This is one more example of the fraudulent entry of a hazardous substance into interstate commerce with no constructive purpose.

Unless strict laws with stiff penalties are enacted to deal with fraudulent marketing of dangerous chemicals, society is subject to a never ending supply of parasites that lure society into the abuse of harmful substances.

Volatile nitrites have the potential to initiate the Cancer Kaposi's Sarcoma (Digovana, 1981).[67]

Of the first five homosexual men with AIDS reported to the CDC, all had aggressively abused nitrite inhalants, and only one had abused IV drugs. It is important to know that only two of these men were promiscuous (CDC 1981).[67]

If one believes that AIDS is caused by a contagious organism such as a virus, a pattern of close association of the early AIDS patients should have been easily observed. Contact between all of the early AIDS patients was non-existent to rare at best. Even when tracing the sexual partners of HIV positive sufferers today, the lack of the majority of their former partners acquiring HIV status, presents serious problems with the viral, contagion theory. Magic Johnson, who admits to having many past sexual partners (over

100), has not had one case come forward to sue for his millions in accrued wealth for passing HIV to them. I believe Johnson was possibly abusing volatile nitrite inhalants.

Kaposi's Sarcoma (KS) is an important manifestation of AIDS. It is the most common Cancer reported among AIDS patients, and its occurrence among gay men in New York and California was one of the earliest harbingers of the AIDS pandemic.

As a result of the common practice of excessive nitrite inhalant abuse by all of the very first full blown AIDS patients diagnosed, nitrite inhalants or NI were investigated as a possible cause of AIDS. In early 1981 pilot questionnaires, CDC researchers found that nearly all homosexual men with AIDS were heavy abusers of NI. An additional survey of 420 patients in New York , San Francisco and Atlanta, found that over 86% of the homosexual patients were abusing NI over a period of 5 years (CDC 1981).[68]

A fact from this study, that I would like draw attention to, is the similar time frame of over five years of NI abuse resulting in AIDS. It is also well known, that the destruction of the immune system occurs, in patients on immunosuppressive chemotherapy after five years. It is highly reasonable to assume an otherwise healthy individual would experience an immune dysfunction, time frame or IDTF relative to how toxic the substance abused was and how often it was being abused, as well as the duration of abuse. Early chemotherapy patients died of AIDS illnesses as a result of this drug treatment, and not from the Cancer that they were being treated for. Nitrite inhalants should and must be considered to be the most Cancer causing immunodestructive chemicals known to man! Common knowledge of this fact would mean that only a moron would refuse to consider the connection between steady and prolonged nitrite abuse and development of Cancer and immune deficiencies otherwise known as AIDS.

I believe that it takes a minimum of four years, to a maximum of seven years, depending on the frequency of exposure to volatile nitrite on a daily basis, as well as the amount of days in a month, in which the nitrite is abused, coupled with the persistency of months of abuse within a year, to develop immune dysfunction from NI abuse. One must also take into consideration the relative health of an individual and the sum total of all their chemical abuse habits in order to establish each person's own unique IDTF. The IDTF will be different for each individual.

It is important to know that not all U.S. AIDS patients abuse NI, just as not all AIDS patients develop KS. Those AIDS patients not abusing NI were found in most cases to be abusing IV drugs. It was also discovered that in Brazil, children suffering from AIDS related complex, were abusing cheap nail polish remover and aerosol shoe spray. Therefore, it should be apparent that AIDS can result from habitual chemical abuse. Early in the AIDS epidemic, nitrite inhaling, homosexual men were studied. The study lasted less than three years. All of these men were being treated for sexually transmitted diseases and immune deficiencies, but had not developed KS. I believe these individuals had not reached the necessary time frame of four years or more of nitrite abuse. Possibly these individuals might not have been abusing frequently enough to develop KS, as did nearly all of the first AIDS patients. As a result of these individuals not developing KS, in the short duration of this CDC study, NI's were exonerated as a plausible cause of AIDS. The time frame of four to seven year duration in the development of AIDS related KS was not known in 1981. I believe a major research error was made in this study due to a lack of information. Now that this point has been made, I think it's time to re-think NI and its relative causation of AIDS. The growing evidence which indicates that nitrite abuse is the main cause of AIDS, will be exposed in the following pages.

It will soon be shown that the timely entry of AIDS into American society directly correlates with the beginning of this new chemical of abuse, NI also known as room odorizers, available primarily to the homosexual community. Beginning in 1971, NI's popularity steadily increased, and by 1974 it had reached every corner of the homosexual community. This is six years prior to the time that AIDS cases began to appear in medical literature, precisely the IDTF being associated with nitrite abuse. Also, it is not purely coincidental that the same approximate six year period parallels the entry of heterosexual AIDS cases, appearing in medical literature. With the entry of Jay W. Freezer's company, and subsequent distribution to the heterosexual community, in 1976, (allowing a couple of years to develop momentum, add six years), one would expect heterosexual AIDS cases to appear approximately around 1984 to 1985, which is about the time that heterosexual cases did begin to show up.

In a paper published in the New England Journal of Medicine, researcher D.T. Durach asks, "What do young Africans, elderly Americans, kidney transplant recipients and homosexual men have in common? The answer is Kaposi's Sarcoma, a tumor that is found in these diverse groups for reasons that we do not understand." Another question looking for an answer is, why is AIDS apparently new, since both viruses and homosexuality are as old as history?

"Some new factor may have distorted the host/parasite relation. So-called, recreational drugs are one possibility. They are widely used in the large cities where most of these cases have occurred, and the only patients in the series reported in this issue, who were not homosexual, were drug users...perhaps one or more of these recreational drugs is an immunosuppressive agent. The leading candidates are the nitrites, which are now commonly inhaled to intensify orgasm..." (Durach et al, 1981).[69]

The toxic property of the prescription drug amyl nitrite has been known for years. Butyl nitrite has identically the same pharmacological toxicity's and comprises the very ingredients of "Rush," "Locker Room," and all of the street varieties of nitrite inhalants, which prompted the early researchers to begin to suspect nitrites as a primary player in causing AIDS in gay men or as a cofactor (Durach et al, 1981).[69]

In the text above, Durach touched on the reason why homo-sexual men are obviously developing KS. Due to their voracious appetite for nitrites, along with the mounting evidence illustrating the serious implications associated with abusing these killer chemicals, it is only a matter of simple deductive reasoning why they do develop KS.

As to what homosexuals, the elderly, kidney transplant recipients, and young Africans have in common besides KS is the fact that all of these people presenting AIDS symptoms can trace the origin of their KS to substance abuse, either prescription or non-prescription. Under close scrutinization, any person who develops full blown AIDS will present a history of chronic chemical abuse, either prescription or non-prescription.

The elderly are being subjected to highly dangerous antibiotics, arthritis and chemotherapy drugs, as well as radiation, all of which can cause identical symptoms of AIDS. Besides having the availability of volatile nitrites in larger cities, Africans have thousands of years of experience in exotic substance abuse. According to statistics most of the AIDS patients in Africa include people in the upper social economic areas, which have greater access to toxic inhalants and other substances. There is also high level medical information that indicates AIDS positive test results can be faulty, due to the excessive malaria viruses that are common in Africa. It is not that the tests are inaccurate, it is more likely that massive malaria viral debris may be similar in chemical nature. Without an electron microscope visual, the HIV test is only a chemical test.

Nitrite room odorizer products are so toxic that relatively small increments of increased doses can easily result in death (Wood, 1981)[70].

On June 17, 1981, Professor Ron Wood writes a letter in support of his petition (HP 81-2; dated 12 Nov. 1980). The letter was addressed to Sheldon D. Butts, Deputy Secretary of the U.S. Consumer Product Safety Commission in Washington, D.C.

I refer to a statement in professor Wood's letter that eloquently states, in a profound and terse manner, the real crux of the problem to yet another top official, who would not assist in the elimination of the hazardous nitrite room odorizers from interstate commerce.

In his petition Dr. Wood states,"The outrageous situation of agents widely employed for substance abuse, yet ostensibly marketed for other purposes, exists because of the explicit structure of the law. Butyl nitrite containing products are, but one example; powdered "incense products" have been recently introduced that are marketed under trade names that are synonyms for cocaine which contain phenylpropanolamine, caffeine, and benzocaine. Laetrile could indeed be similarly marketed with impunity. This offends our sensibility because of its flagrant contravention of the intent of the law. Without amendment of the Controlled Substances Act or the Federal Hazardous Substances Act, this situation will continue."

It is now almost seven months since professor Wood petitioned the CPSC to enforce more stringent labeling and packaging requirements involving nitrite room odorizers, without disposition.

In December of 1981, a major semi-underground gay publication, *The New York Native,* began to alert the homosexual community that volatile nitrite inhalants, such as "Rush," "Locker Room," etc.., may be associated with the development of KS in homosexual AIDS patients. The article opened with the eyeopening title of "Do Poppers Cause Cancer?" This attention getting article was the first to begin an awareness of the connection between NI abuse and AIDS related Cancer.

Many gay publications would soon pick up on the KS nitrite connection and would be primarily responsible for the decline in volatile nitrite inhalant abuse and subsequent reduction of KS in the gay community. Upcoming research will substantiate a drop in KS statistics beginning around 1984 to 1986. During these years, as you will see, a multitude of research will leave no doubt in anyone's mind that volatile nitrites can cause KS. The gay community is a closely knit group, as a whole, and coupled with their exclusive network of periodicals, massive nitrite research would be very carefully watched and reported on, while the mainstream multi-media would ignore such vital research even to this day. Ask most any "in tune" gay male and, he will acknowledge the awareness of the nitrite/KS connection. On the other hand, the heterosexual community doesn't have the slightest conception of what is meant by the nitrite/KS association. This discrepancy of knowledge is the fundamental reason for the flip flop in the percentage growth in AIDS statistics, which exhibited an increase in heterosexual cases and reflected a stabilizing pattern in the number of homosexual cases, which begins to show up in 1986.

Remember Professor Ronald Wood's petition, submitted to the CPSC on November 12, 1980, for the purpose of enforcing more stringent labeling and packaging of nitrite room odorizers? Finally, on February 10, 1982, almost a year and a half later, Professor Wood was notified by the CPSC that his petition (HP 81-2) was denied.

In a letter to Professor Wood, stating the justification for CPSC's denial of the petition sent from Sadye E. Dunn, secretary at the CPSC, the following was communicated:

"The commission is unaware of demonstrated human toxicity associated with inhalation of room odorizers containing alkyl nitrites, and no substantial injury data is associated with their inhalation. The federal hazardous substances act, administered by the commission, already requires labels that warn consumers of hazards of inhalation, and the commission has found no basis for requiring such labeling for the room odorizers. Never-the-less, the compliance staff will continue to recommend to manufacturers that they include a warning to avoid prolonged breathing of the vapor."

"The commission notes that there are relatively few documented injuries to children under five years of age from ingestion of the room odorizers, even though approximately ten million of them are sold every year. Since special packaging is designed primarily to protect children under five, the commission does not believe that a packaging requirement for room odorizers containing alkynitrites is justified."

Even though adults were spilling room odorizers on themselves, causing harmful chemical burns, as well as fires, due to spillage and their relatively flammable nature, the CPSC didn't feel that a packaging requirement was necessary. Special packaging requirements usually are implemented to protect little babies and not adults. In this particular application, the adults needed more protection than the youngsters.

Obviously, the commission was not aware of the seriousness of the matter that they were dealing with. Their response was excessively frivolous, in contrast to the effort that the highly credentialed Professor Wood put into the petition, as well as the time it took for the commission to respond, that being fifteen months.

The real eyebrow raiser was the fact that the CPSC was not aware of the toxicity to humans and substantial injury data associated with nitrite room odorizer inhalation.

The need for a few informed and concerned individuals within the CPSC, as well as all of the consumer protection agencies, is obvious and vitally important where street drugs are concerned. What will be proven, very shortly, is that volatile nitrites are the major factors within the majority of AIDS cases in the United States. The leisurely attitude exhibited by all the U.S. consumer protection agencies regarding nitrite room odorizers, over the past twenty years will prove to be a contributing factor in the AIDS epidemic.

The original discussion in 1977 by the CPSC regarding room odorizers, is going to come back and haunt this governmental body, along with the FDA, who refused to define room odorizers as drugs from the very beginning.

1982

Organic nitrites, including amyl and butyl are all mutagenic (Cancer causing) according to the Ames test. Nitrites form nitrous compounds and are so deadly that they are able to induce Cancer in only one dose! Researcher Jorgenson stated, "These are among the most potent known chemical carcinogens to animals! We therefore find it appropriate to suggest that amyl and butyl nitrite may cause KS in homosexual men!" (Jorgensen et al, 1982)[71].

Volatile nitrites have the potential to suppress the immune system and induce KS in humans. Amyl nitrite may be a contributing cofactor to AIDS in the homosexual population (Goedert, 1982)[72].

Marmer and his research team exposed cells to amyl nitrite vapor resulting in cellular abnormalities. Based on their research, a conclusion was made and read as follows: "These abnormalities can help in explaining the role of amyl nitrite cellular toxicity in immunosuppressed male homosexuals!" (Marmer et al, 1982)[73]

In a study of twenty homosexual patients with KS, all were found to be nitrite users. In fact, nitrite inhalants were the only chemicals these individuals were abusing. Multivariate analysis indicated the use of amyl nitrite was an independent and statistically significant risk factor for KS.

An alarming fact came out in this study. Many persons told of passive exposure to nitrite inhalants that were dispersed over the dance floors at discos. (Marmor, 1982)

In 1982, the Marmor Research team reported a significant association between the use of nitrite, sexual activity and the development of AIDS. Their research acknowledged that KS patients had more sexual encounters on the whole, but they did not imply as to what the significance of their observation meant. Early theories suggested that possibly an undiscovered, sexually transmitted virus was the cause of AIDS; therefore, it was assumed that the more sexual encounters one had, the better the chance of acquiring this mysterious entity. Most of these theories came out of abstract reasoning in the midst of blatant volatile nitrite abuse, not only indicting but proving guilty, nitrite room odorizers, as the primary cause of AIDS related KS.

Nitrite room odorizers were purchased by 100 percent of all consumers as a sexual accessory drug. It stands to reason, given the fact that volatile nitrites are able to cause KS, the more sexually active a person is, the more chemical this person uses and subsequently, the sooner the individual will develop AIDS related KS. Also, if this person adds cigarettes, alcohol, and other drugs to their abusive habits, this will accelerate the diagnosis without having come in contact with a transmitted virus. The more obvious conclusion is that viruses are caused by toxic chemicals. Blaming AIDS on a virus says that anyone can abuse the most Cancer causing substance without any repercussion. Also, in the Marmor study, the relationship between the twenty nitrite abusers was not established. The only communality shared by this group of AIDS/KS patients was their nitrite abuse and not the fact that they had unprotected sex or used dirty needles.

The CDC Task Force, in a survey of 420 male patients attending clinics in New York, San Francisco, and Atlanta, found 86.4 percent (242 of 279) homosexual and bisexual men as well as 14.9 percent (21 of 141) heterosexual men, reported using nitrite inhalants for over five years prior to diagnosis. It was found that nitrite abuse frequency correlated with the number of sex partners (CDC Task Force, 1982)[75].

This observation, connecting frequency of sex partners with nitrite abuse, was one of the original revelations that would play a future role in associating a transmissible organism as the cause of AIDS. A researcher, who has a narrow-minded view that all diseases are caused by transmittable organisms would automatically assume AIDS to be a sexually transmitted disease. Researchers with this narrow mind set usually have a hard time connecting the symptoms of disease to chemical abuse, including prescription drugs that doctors regularly dispense. I, on the other hand, take a more contemporary approach to the connection as many other researchers do. Since nitrite inhalants are known to cause devastation to the body, including immune suppression as well as Cancer, nitrite abuse, in it's own right, can originate and promote AIDS. Given the fact that nitrite inhalants are used to enhance sexual gratification, a person with a strong sex drive would obviously abuse greater quantities of volatile nitrite. In this scenario, individuals abusing similar chemicals would understandably develop similar illnesses without any of these individuals having to come in contact with one another, passing a contagious virus. Taking this scenario a step farther, I believe that almost all viruses found in the human body are the residue of fragmented cells, due to toxic insult of the blood stream by chemical abuse of illegal, as well as prescription drugs, such as nitrite room odorizers, marijuana, alcohol, heroin, anti-inflammatories, chemotherapy and AZT, just to name a few.

Lowry reported in the *Journal of Psychoactive Drugs* that he conservatively estimated approximately 250 million recreational doses of volatile nitrites were consumed by 1982 in the United States (Lowry, 1982).[76]

This study compounds the already enormous list of documentation establishing that nitrite room odorizers are actually drugs and not the deceptive category of room odorizers that the manufacturers claim.

An article by Roger Maickel, printed in the January 1982 edition of *Moneysworth,* addressed passive exposure of volatile nitrites at discos. The major headline which opened the article read: "Users of Disco Drug Die of Its Delight." With a byline of Chicago— it continued stating the following: "Butyl nitrite, a legal, but potentially lethal substance, used to enhance sexual pleasure, and drive disco dancers to ecstatic frenzy, is creating a new type of hazard, a toxicologist warns."

"If you get enough of it in your body, the chances of saving you are zero," says Purdue University Professor, Roger Maickel about the chemical marketed variously as "Rush," "Locker Room," "Climax," and "Discorama." "You may be an unwitting victim," Maickel also adds. It has been reported that these compounds are sprayed over disco floors to excite dancers.

"Some government agency ought to take a stand before there is a spate of deaths that could have been avoided," Maickel asserts.

On April 19, 1982, Professor Wood contacted Administrator Anne Gorsuch of the Environmental Protection Agency in a petition letter requesting that nitrite room odorizers be banned. It was addressed to Anne Gorsuch that these products be banned. The beginning of the petition read as follows:

"Under section 21 of the Toxic Substances Control Act, I am petitioning you to issue a rule under section G(a)(2)(A) prohibiting the distribution of alkyl nitrites in consumer products. In their current pattern of commercial distribution, alkyl nitrites pose an unreasonable risk of injury to health because of their intoxicating abuse potential and other toxic effects including death. These materials are marketed, ostensibly, as room odorizers or liquid incense products, even though they have an aroma vaguely reminiscent of dirty sweat socks; hence, such trade names, "Locker Room," or "Aroma of Men." They are available in small containers (10 ml) through the mail and from boutiques, head shops and adult book stores. Abuse potential is an intrinsic pharmacological property of chemicals. The pleasurable consequences of acute exposure are such, that increases the probability of repeated exposure. In the absence of such properties, chemicals do not maintain ingestion or inhalation. Alkyl nitrites are widely abused by inhalation by high school children. The National Institute on Drug Abuse estimates that in 1980, 11.1 percent of all high school seniors (1% = 30,000 seniors) reported in 1980 have experimented with amyl or butyl nitrite."

The petition goes on to list the internal physiological damage to the body, that can occur resulting from inhalant abuse. Included in the petition was a letter of high interest and concern from Congressman Henry Waxman, Chairman of the Subcommittee on Health and the Environment, as well as nine additional legislators and scientists supporting Professor Wood's petition. Their names and titles follow:

Chairman Leo C. Zeferetti of the U.S. House of Representatives, Select Committee on Narcotics Abuse and Control; Senator Gordon J. Humphrey, from the United States Senate Committee on Labor and Human Resources; Congressman Frank Horton, U.S. Representative of the 34th District of New York; Senator Alphonse D'Amato of New York; Congressman Barber B. Conable Jr. representing the 35th District of New York; Joyce Nalepka, Associate Director of the National Federation of Parents for Drug Free Youth; Ellen K. Silbergeld, Ph.D., Chief Toxic Scientist for the Environmental Defense Fund; Director William Pollin, MD of the National Institute on Drug Abuse; Dr. Louis Lasagna MD, Chairman of the NAS-NRC committee on substance abuse and habitual behavior.

They all wrote EPA Administrator, Anne McGill Gorsuch, with their individual pleas to the EPA to do the right thing by removing these dangerous substances from the market and mouths of our children teens and adult abusers. In other words, they pleaded for these products, which have no positive value whatsoever, to be removed from interstate commerce.

Evidently these legislators and scientists carried little weight in this matter because the EPA denied Professor Wood's petition. In a long-winded response citing bureaucratic red tape to sidestep the decision to ban odorizers, they passed the buck back to the Consumer Product Safety Commission and blamed the CPSC for not banning these products in the first place. There, I have to agree with the EPA. Had the FDA done their job and defined nitrite room odorizers as the drugs they actually were and still are, the EPA would not have had to waste their time. Remember, the FDA was asked in 1977 and again in 1980 to classify nitrite room odorizers as drugs.

The pharmaceutical industry is required to spend millions in order to get a new drug on the market. All the room odorizer industry had to invest in order to get their drug into society was a little time to make fools out of the United States Consumer Protection Agencies, especially the FDA. The formal EPA denial is found in the Federal Register; Volume 47, No. 146, Thursday 23 July, 1982. Regardless of the outcome, I have to commend Professor Wood for his persistence and valiant efforts.

CPSC Petition Sept. 3 1982

On September 3, 1982, Professor Wood's dedication to public health and welfare prompted him to resubmit a petition, requesting the CPSC to ban room odorizers containing volatile nitrite and to declare them as hazardous substances. Also, he demanded that the CPSC prohibit their distribution in interstate commerce.

Petition HP 82-1 alleges that room odorizers containing volatile nitrites are toxic, hazardous substances, and that inhalation of these substances can cause substantial personal injury and illnesses in the form of a behavioral disorder, specifically a substance abuse disorder, which increases the probability of repeated exposure to volatile nitrites.

On October 18, 1982, Gabriel G. Nahas, Ph.D., a professor at the college of physicians and surgeons at Columbia University, wrote a letter to the Consumer Product Safety Commission regarding volatile nitrites. In the letter he states, "It is now, well apparent that amyl nitrite, in addition to the abuse potential and acute behavioral impairment it produces, may have grave chronic effects as a result of the in vivo (in the living body) production of nitrosamines. The public has the right to be protected against such toxic substances, so widely used, and the petition addressed by Professor Wood should be very seriously and promptly examined by your commission."

On August 17, 1983, the CPSC will deny Professor Wood's petition, due to the ongoing jurisdictional dispute. The CPSC claims the FDA is responsible for regulating consumer products being used as drugs. I agree and I think, by now, you will also agree. Everyone knows these products were being used as drugs, but the FDA refused to classify these products as drugs from the very beginning. Now the CPSC is right back were they started, at the FDA, and it only took six years from the original discussion at the CPSC in 1977.

Once more, Professor Wood's unrelenting dedication and alarming call to protect society would fall on deaf ears.

The seemingly perpetual followup phone calls and letters, too numerous to list, coupled with the time Professor Wood had invested, continues to amaze this researcher, as I'm sure it did Professor Wood. I feel Professor Wood's efforts are Nobel Prize quality.

Nitrite use by Homosexuals in England

Alerted that inhaled nitrites might play a role in AIDS, researcher T.J. McManus in London, England interviewed 250 homosexual patients at St. Mary's Hospital. His researchers found that 86% had inhaled nitrites over the previous five years. This finding was nearly identical to the 86% of nitrite abusing homosexuals in the U.S. CDC study in 1981 and 1982. The study concluded that obvious similarities in recreational habits exists between homosexuals in England as well as in the U.S. (McManus, 1982)[77].

Now, there is documentation available of hundreds of homosexuals in the U.S., Amsterdam, England and Australia all inhaling nitrites and all being treated for AIDS-like illnesses within the same relative time span. If AIDS was spread from individual to individual via transmission of a virus, then the "Johnny Appleseed" person who started it all had to move pretty quickly to infect thousands of people on four continents, especially when infecting them all at around the same approximate time. The only possible way a major disease can appear, in thousands of individuals, at the same time all over the world, is if these people were exposed to the same cause, at the same time, and not the arduous, time consuming process, that a one-on-one transfer of a virus pathogen would take. A simultaneous blanket of chemical abuse is a much more logical cause of immune deficiency than the viral cause theory.

In gay men who do not yet have AIDS, nitrite usage is correlated with the immunological abnormalities similar to those found in AIDS patients. (Goedert, 1982)[78]

This study also refers to the trendy, long term use of volatile nitrites as a sexual stimulant and to the direct association between immunodeficiency disorders, the progression of Pneumocystis Carinii Pneumonia, Kaposi's Sarcoma and Hyperinfection with a common virus, Cytomegalovirus. The unsurprising and widely known connection between immunosuppressive drug therapy and organ transplant recipients with the expression of cytomegalovirus, is also referred to. The primary AIDS illnesses of KS and PCP, and even cytomegalovirus expression, is able to be induced as a result of simple chemical insult to the blood stream, whether that chemical is a prescription anti-rejection drug, anti-biotic, chemotherapy, recreational drug IV drug or an exotic, toxic substance as well as a nitrite inhalant. This should be an obvious conclusion, that is surfacing in the minds of most logical thinking persons. I personally believe that radiation also results in the cellular breakdown or fragmentation that can cause a virus to appear in a patient who did not, previous to radiation therapy, exhibit such a virus. I also feel that radiation, coupled with chemotherapy treatment for cervical Cancer, may play a major role in the appearance of viruses in female patients. All of these chemicals have the ability of destroying the immune system.

In court proceedings, odorizer manufacturers would play games with words by claiming that "Their products were room odorizers that were not meant to be inhaled, and when used properly, no harmful effects would be experienced. " They also cited the incomplete study that correlated nitrite exposure with a person passing gas in the Superdome, which obviously would fail to present any immediate adversity.

For over two years, until true results of these studies were printed, the odorizer industry, as well all gay publications, claimed that volatile nitrite inhalants were safe based on these incomplete studies. This misled the public and caused immeasurable damage to proper nitrite inhalant education.

Dr. Vincent Quagliarello did an extensive investigation of the known available research associated with acquired immune deficiency syndrome. The most probable cause of AIDS centered around an amyl nitrite/drug hypothesis. References cited, also included studies showing a depressed T-cell count in opium addicts (Quagliarello, 1982)[80].

1983

One hundred percent of the animal species used in research, 39 total, developed Cancer after repeated exposure to nitrite compounds. No species tested was resistant to its Cancer causing effects (Prussman 1983)[81].

The immunosuppressive effects of Isobutyl nitrite on human blood leukocytes, in-vitro, (culture dish) was established. Two hours of nitrite exposure to human lymphocytes in culture was all that was necessary to induce immunosuppression and Cancer. Nitrite abuse also was found to inhibit interferon A and B which potentially contributes to disease susceptibility.

Passive exposure at homosexual discotheques was common place. Laboratory evidence supports the fact that volatile nitrite inhalants can cause immunology damage after only one dose.

Researcher Hersh stated, "We speculated that these immuno-suppressive effects, combined with the ability of nitrites to convert amines to nitrosamines, may be related to the development of opportunistic infections and Kaposi's Sarcoma in homosexuals, who use this agent. These in vitro studies strongly suggest that inhalant nitrites may indeed be dangerous, and their use should be condemned by those physicians who treat patients who use the drugs regularly" (Hersh, 1983)[82].

I have to pause here for a moment, because the last sentence of the aforementioned study struck a nerve. This doctor was warning physicians to inform patients abusing nitrites of their hazardous capabilities. I feel it was his duty to warn the public at large, especially those who contemplate the use of drugs such as teenagers. Could it be, that researchers are so self-elevated that they are above the task of picking up a phone and calling the proper authorities to alert the public? In this book, I have listed 81 studies let alone approximately 20 or 30 more, that I have come across, not to mention the plethora, that I haven't even seen yet. Usually an average of four doctors or other professionals work on these studies. Simple multiplication would calculate around 440 doctors or professional people that have hands on knowledge of the seriousness of this deadly nitrite inhalation epidemic. If one were to add in all the physicians who read all the medical articles about this epidemic, then we would have thousands of physicians and researchers who are aware of nitrite room odorizer abuse done by millions of Americans as well as the immeasurable numbers of people around the world.

Only one lone researcher, Dr. Ron Wood, petitioned the United States Consumer Protection Agencies for over ten years to ban this deadly product. He got nowhere. This does not say much for the scientific community as well as our government agencies. In my opinion, they are a disgrace to the human race. This is fair warning to the medical community which is guilty of not informing the American public and the entire world of the dangerous practice of inhaling volatile nitrites. There is not one doctor or medical researcher in the whole United States except for Professor Ron Wood who can say they did their part to educate and inform the greater American public on nitrite toxicity while attempting to stop the odorizer industry completely.

The public owes Professor Wood a debt of gratitude for his part in getting nitrite room odorizers banned. Nobel Prizes have been awarded for a lot more frivolous reasons, and it would be a good gesture on behalf of the medical community to make up for the years that they sat around collecting research money and did nothing to warn the public. I just hope when society finds out what has been going on for the past twenty years that they contain themselves and refrain from social upheaval. That includes everyone in all consumer protection agencies including the CDC, EPA, DEA, and especially the FDA during the years from 1977 to 1991. In this book, we are only in the chronological year of 1983. Professor Wood will not accomplish the banning of nitrite room odorizers until 1991.

Cellular cytotoxicity (poisoning of living cells) was demonstrated due to nitrite exposure, as well as, decreases in immune cells and altered cell structures, otherwise known as Cancer. Conclusion: "These abnormalities can help in explaining the role of amyl nitrite cellular cyto-toxicity in immunosuppressed male homosexuals" (Jacobs 1983)[83].

Daily exposures of nitrite inhalation, in only five days, caused progressive immunosuppression in mice. The researchers report, "This data suggests that nitrites may have a primary or contributory role in AIDS" (Neefe, 1983)[84].

101

Utah Bans Room Odorizers

In the 1983 general session, the state legislature of Utah moved to enact a law banning the manufacture, sale, and possession of all nitrite room odorizers, as well as any chemical inhalant product used for the expressed purpose of altering the physiological state of the body. The bill took affect on May 10, 1983.

The insight, intelligence and ability to work efficiently and expeditiously for the common protection of the residents of Utah, as evidenced by their swift action, in dealing with the deadly nitrite room odorizer industry, is in keeping with the highest tradition of work ethic and perseverance. The good men and women that worked on this law are deserving of the highest compliment possible.

The state of Utah accomplished their goal in a very short period. It will take the FDA and CPSC over a decade to reach the same conclusion.

The AP news story dated May 10, 1983 reported the following: Salt Lake City (AP)—Shops and bars removed butyl nitrite—a chemical inhalant that gives a short, fast high—from their shelves as a new state law took effect today banning its use as an intoxicant. Abuse of the substance, officials say is not widespread, but it is growing among teens who are looking for a less costly alternative to marijuana and other drugs.

"It's a fringe thing. We really haven't worried about it too much, but we will," said detective Dave Bishop of the Salt Lake City Police Department's narcotic division.

He also stated, "The substance is popular among homosexuals and is sold in gay magazines under the names "Rush," and "Locker Room."

The product is marketed as a room odorizer, but users claim that when inhaled, butyl nitrite causes a brief, light-headed feeling that intensifies discotheque music and heightens sexual pleasure.

The new law makes the sale or use of butyl nitrite, as an inhalant, a class B misdemeanor, with a maximum penalty of six months in jail and a $500 fine. It does not ban its use in industrial products. The chemical is used in scientific research, such as in the evaluation of rocket fuels.

102

"The main purpose of the law," said sponsor Olene Walker, a state representative, "is to prevent widespread use among high school students."

Dr. Harry Gibbons, Director of the Salt Lake City County Health Department stated, "It could lead to the use of other inhalants. It's not as bad as cocaine, but a person could become physiologically dependent on it."

Butyl nitrite and related Isobutyl nitrite came into the drug scene in 1969 after another similar compound, amyl nitrite, was made a prescription drug. When amyl nitrite was restricted, entrepreneurs saw a market for a similar but legal chemical.

This paragraph is again, public acknowledgment of one chemical in a product used as a drug being substituted for another product to be used as a drug, while the manufacturer ostensibly claims his product to be an air freshener. This is a deception, a lie, and the fraudulent entry of a hazardous substance into interstate and international commerce. This perpetration demands just penalties to fit the seriousness of the crime! Is the FDA doing anything about this? But of course not.

In a 1983, United States Government memorandum between Elliot Foutes of the ECCCS and Moira McNamara from Health Sciences, a sales history of volatile nitrite, was the subject.

Manufacturers' distributors like Pharmex LTD., in 1979, along with other industry sources, were asked for assistance in compiling the following data.

Table A

Estimated Industry Sales of Room Odorizers Containing Butyl Nitrite or Isobutyl Nitrite from 1973 to 1982.

Year	# Units(millions)	Retail value (millions)
1973	.9	4.5
1974	1.2	6.0
1975	1.5	7.5
1976	2.5	12.5
1977	4.0	20.0
1978B	4.4	22.2
1979B	4.8	24.2
1980B	5.3	26.6
1981B	5.9	29.3
1982B	6.4	32.2
1983D	7.0	35.0
1984D	7.7	38.5
1985D	8.2	41.0
1986D	9.0	45.0
1987D	9.9	49.5
1988D	10.8	54.0
1989D	11.8	59.0
1990D	12.9	64.5

114,200,000 – units - $571,000,000

B. Based on an estimated 10% yearly growth

C. Based on an average retail unit value of $5

D. This author's extension up to 1991 being the year of federal banning of the product.

These statistics are as credible as the sources that produced them, and considering the type of people who would engage in this violation of society that the room odorizer manufacturers and distributors were perpetrating, I would assume that their willingness to give the Federal Government accurate statistics was highly unlikely. They, more than likely, greatly underreported their statistics.

On September 9, 1983, the CDC published a brief entry in the *Monthly Mortality Weekly Review*, reporting on the continuing study that I referred to earlier, as prematurely released in the medical journal on December 1982. In this research it was reported that mice were exposed to Isobutyl nitrite at multiple levels of exposure for 13 to 18 weeks. The preliminary conclusion made by researchers was that, "None of the animals exposed to ISBN shows any evidence of immunotoxic reactions" (CDC 1983)[85].

Even though the researchers will admit, upon final publication in 1985, that the exposure levels used were minimal, at best in this study, and did not duplicate the heavy, direct exposure experienced by an inhalant abuser, the results, this incomplete study presented, were still used within an informative pamphlet, irresponsibly disassociating volatile nitrite inhalants and AIDS. This misleading pamphlet was titled, "What Gay and Homosexual Men Should Know about AIDS" and it somewhat exonerated volatile nitrite inhalant and poppers as a cause of AIDS. This pamphlet was tantamount to giving a green light for nitrite abuse. The error in publishing this pamphlet, based on this 1983 MMWR report, will become very apparent as the book progresses. The irony here is that by 1983, people were developing and dying from AIDS while having a definite connection to volatile nitrite abuse. Instead of warning or an outright notice to stop abusing these hazardous chemicals, the pamphlet gave the impression that there was very little to worry about in regards to nitrite exposure.

Remember the petition to ban room odorizers submitted by Professor Ronald Wood to.-the CPSC on September 3, 1982. Finally on August 17, 1983, almost a full year later, the CPSC decision that came down was one more disappointment for Professor Wood. The CPSC claimed these odorizer products did not fall under their jurisdiction because they were being used as drugs. A meeting would be set for February 2nd, 1984 to discuss jurisdiction.

Six more months will prevail while gays, heterosexuals, young children and teenagers inhale one of the most cancer causing, immune destructive chemicals known to man, while our high level officials, in all of the Consumer Protection Agencies, continue to pass the buck and avoid their regulatory responsibilities.

In 1983, a French research team reported that they had isolated a virus they referred to as a T-Lymphotropic retrovirus, from a patient at risk for Acquired Immune Deficiency Syndrome (ATDS) (Barre-Sinoussi, 1993).[86] This French team referred to their new found virus as Lymphonadeopathy associated virus (LAV). It would later be revealed to be the exact, same virus that Dr. Robert Gallo, from the National institutes of Health, would, a year later, name HIV and would claim the full credit for discovering the. organism that caused AIDS, The French team cried foul in regards to Dr. Gallo's claim and a legal dispute ensued.

1984

Finally, at the CSPC meeting on February 2, 1984, which was held to discuss the question of jurisdiction regarding odorizer products, it was elucidated that room odorizers had widespread use to induce pharmacological effects of the human body, associating them with drugs. However, because the manufacturer, calls his product, deceptively a room odorizer, a quandary arises which is elaborated on by Commissioner Stuart Statler. Statler states, "There have been newspaper reports about butyl nitrites for the past ten years. When I was on the Senate Investigating Committee, we looked into this matter. It's clear, whatever the manufacturers claim their products are, there is empirical evidence in this case that shows otherwise." Also surfacing during this discussion was the fact that Peter Preuss, Associate Director of Health Sciences, had a high level discussion with the bureau of Drugs at the FDA. He referred to this person only as Chuck and claimed that the room odorizer problem is not within their jurisdiction, and therefore, did hot have to deal with it.

The awareness of the room odorizer deception, evidenced by Commissioner Statler and Director Pruess, by their remarks at this high level CPSC meeting, is just one more acknowledgment of Federal officials ignoring the obvious scam being perpetrated by the "room odorizer industry".

The American population is experiencing thousand's of. "AIDS-like illnesses as well as deaths related to the common practice of inhaling volatile nitrite room odorizers and if the regulation of these dangerous products is not in the jurisdiction of the CPSC or the FDA, who is left to protect society from this genocide occurring in this country?

Continuing on at the February 2nd CPSC meeting, in the discussion regarding Professor Wood's petition to ban room

106

odorizers, six federal agencies: The Consumer Product Safety Commission (CPSC), the Drug Enforcement Agency (DEA), the Environmental Protection Agency (EPA), the Food and Drug Administration (FDA), the National Institute of Drug Abuse (NIDA) and the Occupational Safety and Health Administration (OSHA), convened to resolve the jurisdictional issue raised by Professor Wood's petition.

At this meeting it was decided that the problem of volatile nitrite abuse was not appropriately addressed by the statutes administered by the CPSC, EPA, NIDA, FDA or OSHA. These agencies would make a formal analysis to determine if volatile nitrites warrant regulation under the Controlled Substances Act. The DEA would consult with the Department of justice to determine if volatile nitrites can be included in new legislation which addresses drug or substance abuse.

Professor Wood's petition, again, was denied. Evidently all of the information included in the petition was not substantial enough to warrant a ban on the sale of nitrite room odorizers.

Now, hold on for just one minute. This is 1984 and the overwhelming evidence indicting the dangers of volatile nitrite abuse that was already in the medical literature, was common knowledge to at least three of the agencies attending this meeting: The FDA, NIDA and the CPSC. The FDA: originally reinstated poppers back to prescription status in 1969. NIDA presented two Capsules in 1979 and, 1980 elaborating on popper abuse. The CPSC by their own statements were aware of the criminally fraudulent perpetration going on in the nitrite room odorizer industry. What input did these agencies provide at this meeting? Did they just sit on their thumbs and say nothing? Evidently they did!

To use a familiar cliché these entrusted persons were making a "federal case" out of a simple matter. Had the FDA used a little "common sense" and classified nitrite room odoriziers as drugs, the matter would have come to an abrupt end.

Isobutyl nitrite was found to suppress natural killer cells of the immune system, the type that normally protects the body from opportunistic infections. The researchers state, that this finding would lead homosexual men who inhale volatile nitrite, into being susceptible to opportunistic infection and Kaposi's Sarcoma. The result of these studies indicate that immunosuppressive symptoms should be added to the other reasons why Isobutyl nitrite should not be accessible to the general public (Lotzva, 1984).

In studying butyl nitrite it was reported that this substance was mutagenic (able to alter genetic cell structure), and therefore, the probability of being carcinogenic, is very likely. (Osterloh 1984)[88].

Volatile Nitrite was Found to Induce Immunosuppression. Researcher, Kenneth Mayer, in reference to studies done by Newell (1984)[91], concludes that nitrites could be significantly immuno-suppressive as well as having the capability of converting to nitrosamines resulting in Cancer. These are plausible statements that are not deflated by the discovery of HIV. Sufficient concern has been raised about nitrites to warrant unequivocal disapproval of the use of these drugs at this time! (Mayer, 1984)[89].

Volatile nitrites known as poppers or snappers caused chemical burns on the bodies of homosexual men using these products (Fisher, 1984)[90].

The New York State Division of Substance Abuse Services found that six percent of the 1.3 million (78,000) 7th to 12th grade students surveyed admitted to purchasing volatile nitrites which were ostensibly being sold as a room odorizer for the sole purpose of getting high. The students referred to the smell of these room odorizers as resembling foul smelling, sweat socks (New York State Division of Substance Abuse Services, 1984).

The aforementioned formally supports the definition of room odorizers as actual drugs, based on the truth, established by the real, end, use, by all of the consumers who purchase this product. It is hard to believe that the FDA would actually believe consumers purchased this product for the purpose of adding odor to rooms, instead of getting high, especially when its odor resembled smelly socks. This does not say a lot for the FDA. The toxic, immuno-suppressive effects of volatile nitrites, along with their possible relationship to Kaposi's Sarcoma is furthermore established in this study. There is also an emphasis on the deadly nitrosamines and nitrosamides, which are formed when various common substances come into contact with nitrites such as other drugs, chemicals, artificial sweeteners, pain killers etc. (Newell, 1984)[91].

In the 1984 edition of *The New York Native,* about three years after their first bomb, alerting the gay community to the association of volatile nitrite inhalants and AIDS related Kaposi's Sarcoma, the magazine created a frenzy with their article headlined, "Poppers, the Writing is on the Wall." This article increased an awareness of nitrite research implicating room odorizers with KS.

This article was the launching pad for a gay multimedia blitz. This blitz more than likely contributed to the decline in nitrite room odorizer use in the gay community and the subsequent decline in gay patients suffering from KS in the mid-1980's. During the mid-1980's, there was a leveling off of new homosexual AIDS case percentages, while the uneducated heterosexual percentages of new AIDS cases began to rise.

On April 23, 1984, at a Washington, D.C. Press Conference the Secretary of Health and Human Service, Margaret M. Heckler, announced to the world that the probable cause of AIDS had been found. She was accompanied by National Institute of Health researcher, Dr. Robert Gallo, who graciously accepted the credit for having discovered the evasive pathogen known as HTLV 3, a variant of a known Cancer virus. Secretary Heckler's famous announcement was quoted as follows: "Today I am proud to announce that the arrow of funds, medical personnel, research, and experimentation which the Department of Health and Human Services and it's allies around the world, have aimed and fired at the disease AIDS, has hit the target...the probable cause of AIDS has been found-a variant of a known human Cancer virus, called HTLV 3." **History should record this statement, as a major blow to AIDS research and thus instrumental in quelling the already mounting evidence implicating chemical abuse, primarily volatile nitrite abuse, as the leading cause of the AIDS epidemic**. Secretary Heckler's statement would just barely be uttered before the cry "foul" would be heard clear across the Atlantic. The French research team at the Pasteur Institute in Paris which included Drs. F. Barre-Sinoussi, J.C. Chermann, and Luc Montagne, claimed to have discovered the same virus over a year earlier. The French team referred to their virus as Lymphonadeopathy Associated Virus (LAV). The two viruses would later be proven to be identical. Even though the French were given the credit in the scientific community, for being the first to discover the virus, an agreement to equally share the credit would be decided by the parties involved. Less than one year after Dr. Gallo alleged that he discovered HIV, his team had already published four papers in an expedient manner blaming HIV as the sole cause of AIDS (*Science,* May, 1984)[92]. Considering the lead time involved in getting a national magazine to press, I conclude that Dr. Gallo and his team moved at warp speed, which is uncommon within scientific research.

In the above statement, I underlined a very important and significant remark. Margaret Heckler admitted, that up until Dr. Gallo claimed that HIV was the sole cause of AIDS by directly killing white blood cells (WBCS), all the accumulating scientific evidence was indicting <u>chemical abuse, primarily Nitrite inhalant abuse as the leading cause of AIDS</u>. So, when HIV is proven, not to be a direct killer of WBCS, as Dr. Gallo said it was, and even worse than that, HIV is proven to be not toxic enough to cause the common cold.... Where does that leave us? We are back at "square one" indicting chronic chemical abuse, with Nitrite inhalants in the lead. It should also be noted, here, that no other scientific paper, authored by any scientist, will demonstrate that HIV is toxic enough to cause any one of the thirty known, AIDS indicator illnesses. The true cause of the majority of AID's deaths is going to be found to be the prescribed universal treatment of choice with toxic killer, chemotherapeutic drugs and AZT for a virus (HIV) that has never been proven by scientific paper, other than Dr. Gallos, to be able to cause AIDS.

Researchers around the world found Dr. Gallo's theories inconclusive, and were even more skeptical when chimpanzees, that were injected with HIV, did not contract AIDS. Given the length of time that we know full blown AIDS takes to develop, (four to seven years,) it would be tantamount to bad science to be able to unequivocally blame HIV as the cause of AIDS in less than a year's time.

As you are witnessing, in the years and millions of dollars being spent on the obvious cause of epidemic AIDS, (nitrite inhalants) scientific research takes sometimes decades to come to conclusions. Yet Dr. Gallo was able to, seemingly overnight, "in a single bound and faster than a speeding bullet", reach amazing conclusions and get it all published in less than a year! Wow, I'm impressed!

It should be noted that the patent for the HIV test is paying off in millions, which is at the root of the real haste in blaming HIV. When history finally proves that HIV is actually harmless, as research to be done by Dr. Peter Duesberg at the University of California at Berkely in 1987 will show, the error of blaming HIV as the cause of AIDS will become apparently obvious. The blaring truth will become self-evident that medical science has funneled billions of dollars down an HIV rat hole. The awareness that years of precious, wasted time, chasing a harmless residual protein debris (HIV virus), caused by abusing chemicals, primarily nitrite inhalants, will add to the travesty. For over twenty years, the Federal Government will allow volatile nitrite inhalants to be abused, while it chased beasts and gremlins (HIV).

As a result, children, young adults, the gay community, as well as a substantial number of heterosexual adults, were led to believe that they could go on inhaling one of the most immune suppressing drugs of our time, and not to worry, just use condoms or clean needles to prevent the transmission of HIV.

I aim to warn the medical community that they have the theory of viral pathology completely backwards. "Viruses are merely fragmented residual particles accumulating in the blood stream of humans or animals subjected to toxic substances injected, ingested, or inhaled (Kitzerow, 1991) Although viruses are able to be passed to one another, animal or human, through body fluids or transfusion products, they are an effect and not a cause of pathology. Viruses, that spontaneously occur in humans (meaning not massively transfused) do so because the person temporarily or permanently shocks or destroys an organ called the thymus with aggressive abuse of chemicals (physician prescribed or self induced). The thymus produces the scavengers (white blood cells or T-cells) that devour and free the blood stream of residual cellular debris also known as viruses. Therefore, viruses are harmless as is HIV and in AIDS, chemical abuse, history will present, as the true and only cause of AIDS (Kitzerow, 1991).

Dr. J.C. Chermann, one of the members of the French Team, at the Pasteur Institute in Paris who first discovered the virus LAV, a.k.a. HIV, gave a lecture at Sloan Kettering Memorial Hospital in New York City on the 22nd of May, 1984. This lecture was less than a month after the press conference where Dr. Gallo's team announced that HIV causes AIDS. Dr. Chermann stated that the LAV virus, a.k.a. HIV virus alone would not be sufficient enough to stimulate T-cell counts, necessary in the development of full blown AIDS. In other words, LAV, a.k.a. HIV, is not antagonistic enough to cause AIDS. The repeated use of drugs, poppers or both would be more likely to play a more important role in antagonizing the T-cell production. Infrequent exposure to LAV/HIV could not solely cause full blown AIDS.

This is a very important point for you, the reader, to understand what was just stated. Dr. Chermann, who was a member of the actual team who discovered LAV/HIV a full year before the American team, consequently giving them a year's head start on testing LAV/HIV, was saying that neither LAV nor HIV could cause AIDS by itself.

I would like to remind you that we already know that immuno-suppressive drugs, prescribed long term, to transplant recipients (Cyclosporine, as well as, Prednisone) can cause the illnesses pneumocystis carini pneumonia and Kaposi's Sarcoma without HIV being present. Surely by now, given what you know about volatile nitrite inhalants and their cancer causing capabilities, if used long enough, (four to six years, five to seven days a week, four to five sniffs a day,) you should be able to see how someone would destroy their immune system. HIV suddenly starts to appear in a different light, especially finding out from a highly reputable scientist that HIV itself can't cause AIDS. Could HIV be a fragmented cellular debris caused by poisonous chemicals, and just an earmark of AIDS, and not the cause?

In a letter from Dr. Mark Novitch, Acting Commissioner of the FDA to Carlton E. Turner, Special Assistant to the President for Drug Abuse Policy, on April 18, 1984, Dr. Novitch states, "The public health service is currently conducting research to investigate chronic effects of butyl nitrite."

Currently? The FDA was aware of nitrite problems since 1969. Extreme adverse effects of short term inhalation of nitrites have been shown in medical literature since 1937[15], and as you, the reader, are privy to the massive effects of nitrite inhalation in scientific literature by 1984, one would have to wonder just how out of touch with reality the public health service and the FDA really are.

Dr. Novitch goes on to say: "We believe that there currently is little evidence of an acute large-scale public health problem. However, efforts to reduce usage would be a wise precautionary measure.

Little evidence! This second sentence answered my reality question and the profound statement about efforts to reduce usage, would tend to profess a flicker of hope that the FDA was coming to life, However, it would take about another four years before laws to ban nitrite room odorizers would be enacted, and the FDA will play very little part in the ban.

In the study of possible causes of AIDS/KS, observations seem to elucidate the fact that nitrites play more of a role in AIDS than an infectious organism. If the cause of AIDS/KS is an infectious organism such as a virus, one would expect that the organism that causes KS would be passed through blood transfusions. However, recipients of blood from donors who were diagnosed with AIDS related Kaposi's Sarcoma have never acquired KS. Obviously the KS causing agent is not a blood borne transmitted agent (Curran, 1984).[93]

Another observation reported in the American Journal of Medicine is there is no consistent pattern of KS transmission among groups of homosexual men linked by sexual contact. Therefore, it is clear that the KS cofactor is not sexually transmitted (Averbach, 1984).[94] There is no documented evidence that the KS cofactor is sexually transmitted.

The most logical and obvious cause of KS is toxic chemical abuse with nitrite inhalant in the lead, along with IV drugs, certain prescription and other chronically abused recreational chemicals coming in second, third, and fourth respectfully.

At this time, I am going to prematurely enter into this scenario some personal observations for you to ponder, which pokes holes in the hypotheses that AIDS is sexually transmitted. I had a very close friend who was one of the most notorious womanizers I know. The man's name was Richard and he had heavily abused nitrite inhalants for over four years. From the time Richard was diagnosed with HIV to full blown AIDS, to coma and death, the whole process took less than a couple of months. Richard had an aggressive sex life with two women that he had been married to with only a 30 day separation between marriages. Also, during his life with both of his wives, he had a stable of over an estimated forty women on the side. It has been, well over, four years now since Richard died, and not one, of approximately forty women, including his two wives, has tested positive for HIV.

Magic Johnson claimed to be extremely active sexually, and yet not one of his premarital sex capades has come forward to try and sue him for transmitting HIV to them.

Paul Michael Glaser is still HIV negative. His wife acquired her HIV four years before she realized she was HIV positive. If AIDS was sexually transmitted surely during four years of marital relations, Mr. Glaser would have acquired HIV status.

It is easily proven that HIV is transmitted in genital fluids, saliva and sperm. But does that transmission go on to progress into AIDS? This researcher believes it doesn't. I believe, that if a person has a healthy immune system and is free of drug abuse, including inhalants, and chronic use of prescribed immunosuppressive drugs, they can not develop AIDS, even after having sex with an infected partner.   In other words, HIV is totally irrelevant, as some very important researchers, that I will soon disclose, have already proven.   HIV cannot cause KS, as well as any of the indicator illnesses associated with AIDS.

I truly believe, if it were possible to do general surveys on television, thousands of similar situations where patients who were diagnosed with HIV and did not pass AIDS on to their sexual partners, would surface.   Since HIV was discovered in 1984, medical investigators quit asking questions relative to nitrite abuse. So when lovers, gay or straight, both abusing nitrites or drugs, develop AIDS, it's automatically blamed on sexual transmittance, due to medical establishment brainwashing without questioning inhalant abuse.   Even when asked, most people don't associate nitrites as drugs because the FDA has avoided classifying them as drugs.   Now, 24 years after the FDA allowed these drugs into interstate commerce, they are surely not about to open the Pandora's Box and allow nitrite inhalants to be viewed as the cause of the AIDS epidemic.

1985

In 1985, researchers (Newell 1985)[95] assembled a chronological table of volatile nitrite availability and use:

1859	Flushing of the skin with amyl nitrite described.
1867	Therapeutic use of amyl nitrite for angina pectoris.
1880	Buytl nitrite investigated but not used clinically.
1960	Amyl nitrite prescription requirement eliminated by the FDA.
1960	Amyl nitrite popper sales skyrocketed.
1963	First report of recreational use.
1969	Amyl nitrite prescription requirement reinstated by FDA.
1970	Street brands of butyl and Isobutyl nitrite available JAMA reports use for sexual augmentation.
1974	Popper craze said to have reached every corner of gay life.
1976	50 million sales per year in one city.
1977	Nitrites permeate gay life.

1978	Three cases of KS/PCP found in retrospect (4 years after the popper craze).
1979	Over 5 million people used once per week. 19 cases of KS/PCP found in retrospect (5 years after the popper craze).
1980	56 cases of KS/PCP reported (6 years after the popper craze).
1981	Nitrite use suspected associated with KS/PCP (7 years after the popper craze.)

In the above table, the immune dysfunction time frame of nitrite inhalant abuse, relative to the progression of full-blown AIDS (4 to 7 years) is very obviously demonstrated. It was 4 to 7 years, respectfully, from the time that poppers, a.k.a. nitrite inhalants became popular, relative to the years that the first AIDS case began showing up in the medical literature (1978 to 1981). The AIDS epidemic in the United States is directly associated with the timely entry of the brand new abuse of nitrite inhalant in American society, predominately the homosexual community. Aggressive abuse of nitrite inhalant for 4 to 7 years is all that is necessary to initiate AIDS (Kitzerow, 1997).

In a study of 31 homosexual men with AIDS, 29 asymptotic homosexual men were compared in order to identify risk factors for developing AIDS.

The study showed that abuse of nitrite inhalants was the most significant risk factor for the progression to AIDS along with a dose response factor. The patients abusing the greatest quantity of nitrite inhalants also exhibited the greatest risk of developing AIDS.

The researchers state, "We believe there are several compelling reasons for considering nitrite inhalation a possible casual factor for development of AIDS and KS/OI. (opportunistic infections) These are, (a) volatile nitrites used as recreational drugs have been shown to be immunosuppressive both in vitro (culture dish) and in vivo (internally); (b) metabolic properties of n-nitroso compounds produce mutagens, teratogen and carcinogens; (c) of 290 N-nitroso compounds, 252 (87%) are carcinogenic; (d) of 39 different animal species, none is known to be resistant; (e) N-Nitroso compounds are among the most highly potent chemical carcinogens for animals (f) there use is extremely common among male homosexuals; and (g) a definite dose-response relationship was shown by both (Marmor et al, 1982)[74] and us (Newell, 1985).[96]

Finally, in 1985, researchers (Lewis et al, 1985)[97] and (Lynch et al, 1985)[98] published the research papers that I referred to as being misleading and incomplete when they were prematurely utilized to give the impression that volatile nitrite inhalants were not a cause of the immune deficiencies associated with AIDS. (Referring to the article in the Medical Journal News 1982 pp. 14 and later in the ("83" MMWR)[85]. This study exposed mice to volatile nitrite at concentrations and durations that did not prove to show immune depression. The concentrations and durations or both were the inadequate factors in this study and not the chemical, for many studies done later at concentrations and durations more resembling the practice of nitrite abusers would go on to prove immune depression. Although immune depression was not elucidated by Lewis and Lynch, extensive damage to bronchial tissue was evidenced and more important the thymus organs in all nitrite exposed mice, were decreased significantly in size.

The thymus is the most important organ in the body of man when the subject of immunity is discussed. The thymus is responsible for the production of the white blood cell known as the T-Cell. The T-Cell is the major immune fighting cell that fights off opportunistic infections. Toxic insult of the bloodstream, by nitrite inhalant, subsequently causes the deterioration of the thymus organ. As the thymus organ deteriorates, so does the number of new T-cells. This researcher believes it is the destruction of the thymus that causes the notorious reduction in T-cells that classifies a patient as having AIDS and not a numbers game where as HIV outnumbers T-Cells and causes T-Cell numbers to drop. As the thymus is destroyed, so is the immune system.

Any toxic substance directly inhaled or injected into the blood-stream will cause eventual destruction of the thymus. Autopsies of early AIDS patients abusing nitrites were found to have atrophied thymus organs in 100 percent of the cases examined.

Forty-two homosexual men with generalized Lympho-nadeopathy (disease of the lymph nodes) commonly found in patients prior to being diagnosed with AIDS related Kaposi's Sarcoma (KS), were studied at Mt. Sinai School of Medicine for 4 1/2 years. One hundred percent of these patients abused nitrites. The patients using the greatest quantities of nitrites developed KS. Twenty-nine percent developed AIDS, 8 with KS. The frequency of sexual encounters paralleled with KS statistics, easily forming the conclusion that "promiscuity might therefore be regarded as a marker for the use of poppers, rather than the reverse statement. (Mathur-Wagh, 1984, 1985)[99-100].

One hundred percent of room odorizers are purchased primarily to be used to augment sexual activity, therefore, it stands to reason that the more sexually active a person is the more nitrites they would be abusing.

W. Jay Freezer, Chairman of the Pacific Western Distributing Company, the room odorizer manufacturing company formed in 1976, died from AIDS related complications on March 27, 1985.

An appropriate eulogy to Freezer's mortality could be simply stated as, "He lived by the sword, so he died by the sword." As this researcher believes, that hundreds of thousands of people have died from Freezer's product, it only seems divine justice that he would meet the same demise.

On April 15, 1985, a case control study of a comparison of homosexual men who were classified antibody positive to LAV/HTLV-III and diagnosed with AIDS, and a group of gay men who were not yet sick, was presented at the CDC AIDS Conference in Atlanta. The degree of nitrite inhalant abuse was the most relevant risk factor observed in the development of AIDS and the progression to Kaposi's Sarcoma. (Osmond, 1985)[101].

Research done at the National Jewish Center for immunology and respiratory medicine in Denver adds to the mounting evidence that volatile nitrite abuse increases the risk of being diagnosed with AIDS. Mice, in three different groups, were exposed to the nitrite inhalant, also known as Rush, daily, every other day, and twice a week. These mice developed a decreased number of immune cells and consequently became susceptible to mycobacterium intra-cellular tuberculosis and subsequently died. These very organisms are implicated as one of the primary culprits affecting people who die of AIDS. However, mice not exposed to Rush, were exposed to the same bacteria and presented recognizably fewer illness and less mortality statistics. The degree of immune system damage was found to be directly related to the relative exposure of the nitrite inhalant, "Rush". In conclusion, the researchers stated "We believe our findings establish that inhaling Isobutyl nitrite should be considered dangerous to homosexuals and others at high risk for developing AIDS" (Gangadharam, et al, 1985)[102].

Not to belittle these hard working researchers, but the wording in their warning, as is typical in other similar statements, seems to be referring to "high risk" individuals only, as if there are humans and other animals, who are not at risk of inhaling volatile nitrite. Here these intelligent doctors have just proven that inhaling volatile nitrite has caused immunosuppression sufficient to cause death from opportunistic bacterial infection, identically resembling the same pattern in which thousands of gay men are dying (almost 100 percent of whom were found inhaling the very chemical they just proved can vicariously cause death) and their warning includes only gay men and others at high risk. Common sense and logic should have surfaced in all of these researchers, long before 1985, that nitrite inhalant is sufficient to cause death in all human and animal life. Had all of the nitrite researchers taken their heads out of the clouds and warned all society of the perils of inhaling nitrites, the AIDS epidemic would have been slowed down before the hetero-sexual community began abusing this killer drug. My bewilderment and amazement at the stupidity surfacing amongst "Our nations finest" is becoming evident by my lack of restraint in expletive use and for that I apologize but you see, I am very "pissed off" and by now you should be developing a head of steam.

It is December of 1994, as I am writing this entry. The medical establishment has still abstained from formally notifying the general public of the compelling research involving nitrite inhalants and their obvious role in the causation of AIDS.

Studies with mice proved and supported earlier studies that nitrite inhalants caused immune suppression as a result of injection or inhalation. Also evidenced were bronchial and lung damage, weight loss, and reversed T-Cell ratios as well as depleted T-Cell numbers, which parallels the symptoms experienced by AIDS patients. The researchers conclude, "Our studies do show that chronic inhalation of amyl nitrite can lead to an altered T-Cell helper/suppresser ratios, the same phenomenon which occurs in AIDS victims. It does look then that there seems to be a link between amyl nitrite inhalation and cellular immunity depression (Ortiz, 1985)[103]."

The association of Kaposi's Sarcoma (KS), and volatile nitrite inhalant abuse, by homosexual, AIDS patients, relative to the total number of days of abuse was established. Inhalation of nitrites was found to be the most common factor in the genesis of KS, the skin Cancer most frequently diagnosed in AIDS patients. Ninety-seven percent of the patients with KS and pneumocystis carinii pneumonia in an early CDC study were found to be abusing volatile nitrite inhalant. The quantities of nitrite abuse also paralleled sexual activity. The strong association of KS with increased income, in one study, is consistent with the argument that a drug is more likely to be the co-factor than a sexually transmitted agent (Haverkos, 1985b)[104].

An AIDS study of gay men was begun in 1983, at the University of California at San Francisco. Of the patients studied, 158 developed AIDS while 108 progressed to Kaposi's Sarcoma. The patients with Kaposi's Sarcoma were found to report the highest nitrite abuse compared to the patients that had only developed opportunistic illnesses (Osmond et al, 1985).[105]

In a study done with mice, after exposure to four varied nitrite inhalant compounds, low body weights, as well as liver and spleen damage were found in the control group (McFadden et al, 1985).[106]

In 1985 the final report was in, regarding the nitrite inhalant research that had begun in 1983. This was the study where early press releases seemed to exonerate nitrite inhalants as a cause of AIDS, which were used by the "room odorizer" manufacturers to weasel out of legal attempts to close them down. This study found no immunotoxic reactions in mice exposed to nitrites. This study was co-sponsored by the Occupational Safety and Health Department (OSHA), which partially explains the shortcomings in detecting any serious immunologic dysfunction derived from nitrite inhalants. The level of exposure to nitrite inhalant was similar to the level one might encounter as a worker in an industrial manufacturing plant. This study came nowhere close to the strength of exposure to nitrites that recreational abusers would come in contact with. The study included a disclaimer acknowledging the awareness of the inferior dosage which sounded like an apology (Lewis et al, 1985).[107]

It is amazing that anyone would give any credence to this study, especially when study after study found adverse reactions to nitrite inhalant abuse. While government sponsored studies were exonerating nitrite inhalants, independent studies were proving different (Watson, 1982) (Neefe, 1983) (Lotzova, 1984) (Ortiz, 1985) (Gangadharam, 1985) (Mathur-Wagh, 1985) (Lynch, 1985) (Gerelich, 1984) (Mayer, 1984) (Newell, 1984) (Hersh, 1983) (Jacobs, 1983) (Marmer, 1982) (Maickel, 1982) (Goedert, 1982) (Romeril, 1981) (Holt, 1979) (Maigetter, 1978) (Gardner, 1977) (Dewy, 1973). At least 21 very expensive research studies, done by hundreds of researchers, have established the immunotoxic properties of volatile nitrite inhalants, while the CDC has failed to issue a public warning as to the dangerous aspects of abusing these chemicals.

Hank Wilson, head of the committee to monitor poppers, wrote Dr. James Curran at the Center for disease Control (CDC) in 1985. In this letter, he requested the CDC to issue a statement condemning the use of poppers.

I quote from Wilson's letter: "There should be no question that popper use is quite extensive among gay males. Inhalant nitrites continue to be marketed and promoted to the gay male community as if they had no harmful health effects, nor any role in the development of AIDS!"

"The CDC should issue an alert to popper users. Popper users need to know that initial research indicates that poppers may be immunosuppressive. Users need to know that epidemiological research links poppers to KS. Users need to know that inhaling nitrites may result in cellular changes which make them vulnerable to an AIDS virus infection. A warning can be issued with the qualification that more research is needed, and the least the CDC can do is alert popper users about what is already known. Better to err on the side of caution than to say nothing."

A point to be made is that not only gay homosexuals were inhaling these dangerous inhalants, but adolescent children, high school students, as well as heterosexual adults are inhaling poppers!

From 1971, when the Pacific Western Company first came on the market with their "nitrite inhalant", a.k.a. poppers, to the date that Hank Wilson wrote his pleading letter in 1985, almost begging the CDC to make a public statement, 14 years have passed. For 14 years, the CDC has allowed our society to purchase legally and consume "the most cancer causing, immune suppressing substance known to man" (McGee and Barnes, 1956)[19] (Bogovski et al, 1981)[60] (Jorgensen et al, 1982)[71]. Not one major public statement has come out of the CDC.

(It's now the year 2000 and 29 years has elapsed, and still the CDC has not issued a public warning, acknowledging the dangers of inhaling nitrites.)

Dr. Curran's reply to Hank Wilson's letter follows:

May 6, 1985

Dear Mr. Wilson:

Thank you for your letter of April 21, and the enclosures.

Some of the studies you cite are outdated and some are quite current. You have edited and amalgamated them skillfully. The data presented by Haverkos and Moss and their respective collaborators at the recent International Conference on AIDS are intriguing and deserving of further attention. The issues they raised warrant further investigation into the whole field of co-factors and their role in AIDS causation. It is possible that heavy use of nitrites, or another factor correlated with such use, may contribute in some as yet undefined way to the development of Kaposi's Sarcoma in those already infected with HTLV-111 or who have AIDS.

I agree that this information should be disseminated, and I acknowledge the active role you have played in this effort. On the other hand, the present data does not justify an absolute "anti-popper" campaign.

We certainly wish to point out that no data exists to indicate that using nitrites is a safe, risk-free practice. Gay men should consider decreasing use of this substance until more data are available to assess those risks that may exist.

Thank you for your interest in this issue.

Sincerely yours,

James W. Curran, M.D. M.P.H.
Chief AIDS Branch
Division of Viral Diseases
Center for Infectious Diseases

From the statements that Dr. Curran has made in his letter, he presents himself as being totally out of touch with the fact that almost pure nitrite is being abused by ever increasing numbers of society in general. An epidemic of nitrite inhalant abuse is underway! He also seems to present a lackadaisical attitude to the problem of   nitrite inhalant abuse by suggesting that the gay community decrease their use of nitrites, instead of outright halting the practice of inhaling the most cancer causing, immune destructive substance known to man.

How many more irrefutable, research studies, indicting nitrites as a major player in the causation of AIDS, does Dr. Curran and the CDC need to formulate a conclusion with regards to the nitrite/AIDS connection?

As you, the reader, are witnessing, it has taken many years of high tech research costing millions of dollars to prove nitrite inhalants, aggressively abused over 4 to 6 years, can cause AIDS. Not only has research proven nitrites can cause AIDS, but also the mechanism by which nitrites destroy the immune system.

Dr. Gallo and the research team that claimed to have discovered HIV did their research in less than a year after they received the famous tainted blood sample from the Louis Pasteur Institute in France. This team has stated that HIV is the sole cause of AIDS, even though the mechanism by which HIV causes KS or any of the 25 indicator illnesses associated with AIDS, has never been proven. Not only has this not been explained, HIV when injected into chimpanzees has not caused AIDS in these animals.   Whereas inhalation of nitrite has been shown to be able to cause all of the AIDS illnesses in study after study.

The state of Wisconsin in 1985 took action to move against the "room odorizer" industry to make their products illegal by classifying them as hazardous substances. Joseph Miller, President of one of the largest manufacturers of "room odorizers", Great Lakes Products in Indianapolis, Indiana, provided the legal defense as well as the expert medical/scientific witness. The strategy was the same that the   "odorizer industry" used to slip out of the grasp of legal restraint time after time. By shifting the focus from the real purpose for which consumers purchase   "room odorizers", that being a sexual accessory drug, to the big lie, that consumers use them as room fresheners, Joseph Miller and his band of henchmen tried to win their case. One of the expert witnesses was the founder and co-director of the National Gay Task Force, Bruce Voeller. Voeller claimed that   "all studies linking AIDS and butyl nitrite were utterly flawed and without foundation."

The State of Wisconsin did not buy the "room odorizer" defense, and nitrite inhalants ostensibly marketed as "room odorizers" were formerly banned.

The irony here is that here we have a person who is supposed to be looking out for the best interests of the gay community, joining forces with a company who is trying to sell the most dangerous immune suppressing, cancer causing substance known to man, to the gay community!

The Gay Task Force was playing a major role in contributing to the abuse of nitrites, and now, that abuse of these drugs is killing their members in large numbers, the Gay Task Force is screaming for performance in the medical community as well as millions in research money to deal with the problem. Statements like Voeller made, expressing the fact that nitrite studies are flawed and trying to give the green light to nitrite abuse, may have helped to shift the government mindset from the nitrite theory to the HIV virus theory. To compound the problem, once all the AIDS cases began to build, the organized Gay Task Force pressured the government to bring the drug trial failure and killer cancer drug, AZT, out of moth balls.

The real tragedy will be realized when the gay community finally realizes that their voracious appetite for nitrites caused their AIDS, and subsequently the rush to AZT eventually killed them in the thousands.

1986

Overwhelming research, by 1986, proved "beyond a shadow of a doubt, to a prudent thinker, that nitrite inhalants were causing the Kaposi's Sarcoma (KS) that AIDS patients were presenting." The gay media picked up on the obvious connection of AIDS/KS and subsequently alerted and educated the gay community. The awareness of the massive research implicating inhalants with AIDS/KS, is responsible for the decline in "popper" sales to the gay community. Due to the decline of "popper" abuse, the percentage of cases of KS among the gay community also began to decline. For the most part, the majority of alerted gay men had stopped abusing nitrite inhalants from 1982 to 1986.

After HIV was said to be the sole cause of AIDS in 1984, the medical questionnaires utilized in AIDS research in some studies became quite inferior with regards to questions of inhalant abuse.

The questionnaires began to be more directed towards a virus, rather than a chemical cause of AIDS.

Inferior questionnaires, coupled with the fact that AIDS patients were no longer abusing poppers, and adding to this, a possible bias towards HIV, were the reasons that some studies did not favor a nitrite inhalant connection with AIDS/KS.

For example, one such study (Goedert et al, 1986)[108] asked only about inhalant abuse during the previous year and the intensity (number of sniffs per occasion) during the past 6 months. If a patient who developed AIDS/KS during a nitrite abuse period from, for example, 1978 to 1983 and then asked about inhalant abuse during the past year, in a study commencing in 1985, the patient would have answered no to the question of nitrite abuse in the past year and a half, thus creating an inaccurate, misleading picture. The aforementioned study concluded that AIDS/KS was not associated with nitrite inhalant abuse and that oral sex, enemas, and rectal douches were possible variables which suggested a viral contagion.

Other studies, such as the San Francisco Hepatitis B Cohort Study — CDC (Darrow et al, 1986-87)[109,110], as well as the multi-center AIDS Cohort Study (MACS) (Polk et al, 1987)[111] also did not favor a nitrite inhalant connection. A careful look at the questionnaires in these studies also proved to be inferior and poorly constructed.

These studies, along with the discovery of HIV, were primary players responsible for the move by the Center for Disease Control (CDC) and the National Institute of Health (NIH) to switch the focus on the causation of AIDS from the chemical theory (nitrite inhalants and IV drugs) to the viral theory, namely HIV.

With the discovery of HIV in 1984, only the mere presence of HIV antibodies in the blood was proven. No one, to this day, has shown that HIV is toxic enough to cause AIDS related illnesses. This researcher believes that the CDC and NIH made a major blunder in vacating the chemical theory as the cause of AIDS in favor of HIV.

The reaction of nitrite and cholesterol resulting in the production of free radicals, which is directly associated with the promotion stage of cancer as well as tumors, was established by researchers (Kensler, T.W. and Taffe, B.G., 1986)[112].

The State of New York banned "nitrite room odorizer" products in 1986. Also, the very same year, San Francisco and Los Angeles acted to ban these products.

This researcher believes that the early move to ban "room odorizers" in San Francisco and Los Angeles was instrumental in slowing down the AIDS statistics that would soon be showing up in 1994.

A major literary work, published in 1986 and entitled, *"Death Rush: Poppers & AIDS"*, written by John Lauritsen and Hank Wilson, was a tremendous factor in the educational exposure of volatile nitrites associated with AIDS (John Lauritzen and Hank Wilson, 1986)[113].

Death Rush will play a major role in contributing to the nitrite/AIDS educational process in San Francisco that will be instrumental in the decline in popper sales, and subsequently the decline in brand new AIDS cases in San Francisco. In 1994, the San Francisco Department of Health will make a projection, that by 1997, new AIDS cases will drop to an all time low. This researcher believes that the drop in brand new AIDS cases that will show up in 1997 is directly attributed to *"Death Rush: Poppers & AIDS"*.

Nitrite use among gay males began to drop drastically in 1986 due to underground gay newspapers publishing the massive ongoing nitrite inhalant research, implicating volatile nitrite inhalants as being directly related to KS in AIDS patients.

1987

Acute inhalation toxicity of volatile nitrite was established in rat studies done by Klonne (Klonne et al, 1987)[114].

The capability of amyl nitrite to react with cholesteryl in the body to form nitrosamine, which is the most potent carcinogenic substance known to man, was demonstrated by Mirivish (Mirivish et al, 1987)[115].

In 1986, approximately nine percent of 3,000 heterosexual high school seniors stated they had purchased volatile nitrites for the specific purpose of getting high. This was an increase of 200 percent over the 3.6 percent found inhaling nitrites in 1983. (Johnson et al, 1987)[116]

Prominent Scientist Finds HIV Not Sufficient Enough to Cause AIDS!

Soon after LAV/HIV was acknowledged in 1983/1984, respectively, the National Cancer Institute (NCI) sponsored a research study to ascertain if there was any association between cancer, HIV and AIDS. Professor Peter Duesberg from the Department of Molecular Biology and Virus Laboratory at the University of California at Berkeley was chosen to receive the grant (Duesberg, 1987)[117].

Only the nation's most brilliant research scientists are selected to receive outstanding investigator grant status. Not only is Professor Duesberg a member of this prestigious group, but he is also a world renowned pioneer in the field of retrovirus technology. Duesberg's outstanding work in the retrovirus field got him elected into the U.S. National Academy of Sciences.

Since HIV is considered to be classified as a retrovirus, you would expect Duesberg's research conclusions to be highly respected in the scientific community, regarding the study of HIV.

When Professor Duesberg's study (Duesberg, 1987)[117] was published, it was totally contrary to the establishment's accepted HIV theory. A multi-billion dollar industry in virology research is fundamentally supported by the HIV hypothesis as the cause of AIDS. When Duesberg's study poked holes in the HIV theory, he literally shocked the medical and scientific world of virologists who are getting rich as a result of research grants. Consequently, Dr. Duesberg's most favored research status has been injured, and he is being shunned by the proponents who have blindly accepted the HIV theory.

I would like to remind the reader that since 1984, thousands of research studies attempting to prove the mechanism by which HIV causes KS or any of the 30 AIDS indicator diseases have failed miserably. Whereas, the nitrite inhalant research that I have already documented has proven, beyond any doubt, that nitrites cause KS as well as AIDS.

In putting together his study of the relationship between HIV, cancer and AIDS[117], Professor Duesberg utilized the application of strict guidelines associated with investigating the cause of a specific disease. By applying what is known of the properties of HIV to a set of rules, known as the Koch Postulates, Duesberg presented some

126

very interesting facts that painted a somewhat benign picture of HIV. He concluded that HIV was not as harmful as the HIV proponents claim it to be. Many of the beliefs of HIV and how it causes AIDS, which is mostly conjecture at best, appears to be on very shaky ground when HIV is scrutinized by applying the Koch Postulates.

I believe that early HIV researchers, who ignored the fact that HIV does not stand up to all three Koch Postulates, are at the foundation of the most tragic and costly medical blunder the world has ever known.

Koch Postulates

In tracking down the cause of disease, scientists use an international standard of rules or criterion originated by a German bacteriologist, Robert Koch (1843-1910). The three Koch Postulates, as they are referred to, essentially state: One, the microorganism in question must be regularly found in lesions of the disease. Two, the subject organism should be able to be cultured from exposure of the lesions to a growing medium, in a Petri dish. Three, when introduced into a laboratory test animal, the organism must be able to reproduce the disease in the animal, and at the same time, the organism should be able to be found in the subjected animal.

If all the aforementioned criteria are not met, the subject organism is assumed not to be the cause of the disease. Strict adherence to these postulates has stood the test of time. Circumventing these three postulates in the search for the cause of a disease is not only bad science. It can be a death sentence if wrongful causes of diseases are assumed.

The research team in 1984, who claimed that HIV caused AIDS, violated the third postulate by not proving that HIV caused AIDS in test animals, thus the most diabolical tragedy imposed on mankind in the most recent past had begun.

I've said it before, and I can't say it enough, no virus causes AIDS, not even HIV.

Duesberg's Conclusions

• HIV is biochemically inactive in patients during the latent stage (asymptomatic) as well as the full blown AIDS (symptomatic) period. HIV is not chemically antagonistic at any time, which is characteristic of a retrovirus that HIV is classified as. Because HIV is a biochemically inactive virus, it is highly unlikely that HIV kills T-cells, as HIV propaganda implies.

• HIV is found in as few as 1 in 10,000 white blood cells of patients suffering from AIDS, which adds to the insignificant part that HIV plays in AIDS illnesses.

• HIV, when injected into eight chimpanzees, did not, after three years, cause these animals to develop the symptoms of AIDS! Actually, these chimps developed antibodies to the HIV virus, which basically presents a condition of antiviral immunity to HIV!

Now, 16 years have passed since the aforementioned chimps were injected with HIV, and they still have not developed AIDS. This is a blatant failure of Koch's third postulate and should put to rest the myth that AIDS originated in green monkeys in Africa.

• Because HIV is not bioactive and is expressed in so few numbers, Duesberg concludes: HIV is not sufficient enough to cause AIDS or any illness it is associated with! This suggests either a co-factor or another cause of AIDS.

Here we have one of the nation's foremost authorities in the field of virology stating, on the record, that HIV could not be the sole cause of AIDS or any of the AIDS indicator illnesses.

HIV is a type of virus that is classified as a retrovirus. Retroviruses, in general, are found to inhabit the bloodstream uneventfully for years. In fact, virology theory contradicts itself where HIV is concerned.

The foundation of the theory of how HIV causes AIDS is supported 100 percent by the conclusion that HIV kills T-cells! If HIV can't be demonstrated to kill T-cells, the telltale drop in T-cells that full blown AIDS patients experience can't be explained, using HIV theory. Thus, HIV theory, blaming HIV as the cause of AIDS, falls apart.

The primary contradiction to retrovirus, HIV killing T-cells, lies in the alleged theory of how HIV reproduces itself. According to virus theory, T-cells are necessary in order for HIV to proliferate. HIV is said to inject itself into T-cells and uses the internal mechanism of the T-cell to reproduce itself.

So, establishment virologists are grasping for straws by insisting that HIV simultaneously kills T-cells and also uses the T-cell as a host in order to reproduce itself.

If this quandary is not enough, there is one more problem with the HIV theory as the cause of AIDS. Thirty to fifty percent of AIDS patients exhibited the cancer, Kaposi's Sarcoma (KS). HIV must be shown to cause KS in order to help prove HIV theory as the cause of AIDS.

Retroviruses are not new. Billions of dollars in cancer research were spent in the search of retroviruses as the cause of cancer in any form. To this day, there is no evidence in scientific literature, anywhere in the world, that connects any virus, retro or other, with the cause of any cancer. HIV is a retrovirus; therefore, HIV does not cause cancer. It cannot be explained any simpler than that.

Along with the fact that retroviruses, as a result of massive cancer research, have been proven not to cause cancer, retro-viruses have also been proven not to kill or be lethal to cells. Since HIV is a retrovirus, HIV does not kill cells. It cannot be explained in a more logical, simpler method.

Utilizing proven, irrefutable cancer research and logical thought progression, HIV is presented as nothing more than a benign, harmless virus that just happens to be found in the blood of people, with or without symptoms of AIDS, and then in only approximately 15 percent of patients suspected as having HIV. The HIV test finds only antibodies, to the HIV virus, in up to 85 percent of patients tested.

The problem in trying to convince a brainwashed, steadfast virologist in simple, logical terms, utilizing sound scientific fact that AIDS, or any of the 30 AIDS indicator disease, are not caused by any virus, including HIV, is due to their use of illogical thought process.

HIV is a Failed Hypothesis

- HIV fails to be proved as toxic to T-cells in vivo.

- HIV fails to exhibit any capability of causing KS.

- HIV fails to cause AIDS in test animals.

Chemical Abuse Causes AIDS

Nitrite inhalants have been proven to be toxic to T-cells.

Nitrite inhalants have been proven to cause cancer.

Nitrite inhalants have been proven to cause immunosuppression in test animals.

If the NIH will fund studies testing aggressive insult of chimpanzees with nitrite inhalant, it will be proven that nitrite inhalant all alone is all that is necessary to cause AIDS in these animals.

The NIH should fund Dr. Peter Duesberg's grant request for this study.

Why the NIH will not provide grant money to prove nitrite inhalants, solely, can cause AIDS in chimpanzees, is due to the fact that this would be one more nail in the coffin of the HIV theory as the cause of AIDS.

The government powers that control the annual seven billion dollar a year in AIDS research monies are virologists who stand to lose, as well as the pharmaceutical industry. These interests do not want to face the reality that AIDS is caused solely by chemical abuse.

Nitrite inhalants, a.k.a. "poppers", a.k.a. "room odorizers" and IV drugs are the major cause of AIDS in the U.S. and other industrial nations where "poppers" have been distributed, while other recreational drugs only contribute to immune dysfunction.

Industrial solvent inhalants, along with other drugs of abuse as well as malnutrition in the third world countries, are responsible for the demise of inhabitants of these countries who are suffering from AIDS.

It is the rush to prescribe chronic abuse of antibiotics, chemotherapy, AZT and all alleged antiviral drugs to already chemically toxic persons who were abusing chemicals (prescribed and recreational) that causes a person suffering from immune dysfunction to progress to full blown AIDS and death.

All antibiotic drugs, chemotherapy, AZT and all present "drug cocktails", when prescribed chronically, are extremely destructive of the immune system, and create a no win solution in surviving AIDS. It is time the medical profession quit killing people with hopeless drug regimens.

The only hope of beating immune disorders is practicing a healthy life style, free of all drugs.

<u>Gay Drug Habits Changing</u>

In studying a sample of homosexual men who abused nitrites within a relatively small area, taking in Baltimore and Washington, D.C., the following was presented:

The data from this sample suggests that homosexual males have decreased their use of nitrite inhalants. This appears to be a result of a greater awareness of AIDS risk in this population and a subsequent trend to modify their high risk behavior. Whereas, heterosexual drug users in the same area, do not appear to have modified their nitrite use in recent years (Lang et al, 1988).[118]

The above scenario is the reason that the percentages of heterosexual AIDS cases are rising while the percentages of homosexual AIDS cases began dropping.

The Los Angeles Times published a story on 6 Dec "89" reporting that AZT being manufactured by Burroughs Welcome, was found to cause cancer in animal tests.

AZT has long been known as the failed cancer drug of the 60's, due to its highly toxic nature. AZT's adverse effects can be so severe that half of the patients put on 1,200-1,500 mg per day cannot tolerate it. Suppression of bone marrow activity, together with major adverse effects on the nervous system and muscles, can have debilitating and potentially life-threatening consequences. AZT can cause white blood cell counts to drop, as well as other side effects such as confusion, loss of sharpness, headache, neck pain, muscle spasms, nausea, rectal bleeding and tremors. AZT, when taken without liquids, has been found to contribute to ulcer formation.

<u>AZT Kimberly Bergalis</u>

In December, 1989, a 21-year-old college student had checked into a hospital suffering with a bout of pneumonia. As a result of her doctor's suspicions, and subsequent testing, it was found that his patient had tested positive for antibodies to the HIV virus. The young lady was Kimberly Bergalis from Stuart, Florida.

Kimberly had asserted that she had not used IV drugs, had never had a blood transfusion, and was a virgin, thus eliminating the possibility of being exposed to HIV by sexual contact.

Kimberly stated, on the "Oprah Winfrey Show," that she had suffered from upper respiratory illnesses most of her life. I find it highly possible that aggressive abuse of antibiotics for the illnesses that she mentioned, may have contributed to her demise. I would also ask Kimberly's friends, if Kimberly had ever inhaled "poppers," as thousands of other young school aged children testified to in the 70's and 80's (Johnson, 1979)[49]. I find it highly unlikely that Kimberly died as a result of acquiring HIV from her dentist.

HIV propaganda dictates that it takes four to seven years to incubate AIDS in HIV positive individuals.

The appointment with Dr. David Acer, that was said to be the date that Kimberly was exposed to HIV, was in 1987, only two years before she checked into the University of Miami Hospital with the pneumonia that prompted her doctor to do an HIV test.

Kimberly was prescribed the killer drug, AZT, and in a very short two years, her health deteriorated drastically. Finally, in December, 1991, Kimberly Bergalis died at 23 years of age. From onset of alleged exposure to HIV, to mortality, only four years had transpired. I believe AZT accelerated Kimberly's death.

1994

AIDS Declining in San Francisco

In 1994, the San Francisco Department of Public Health published a report entitled, "Projections of the AIDS Epidemic in San Francisco: 1994-1997". This report presented some startling evidence that the AIDS epidemic in San Francisco is beginning to decline!

The annual number of new AIDS cases is estimated to have peaked at 3,326 in 1992 and is expected to decline to 1,204 annually by 1997. The number of persons living with AIDS has also peaked, according to these projections and is expected to decline gradually from a high of 9,109 persons living with AIDS in 1992 to 6,460 living with AIDS by the end of 1997.

The projections show that there will be a decrease in the proportion of AIDS cases among gay and bisexual men and an increase in the proportion of cases of injection drug users. However, the majority of persons living with AIDS will continue to be gay and bisexual men. The number of gay and bisexual men living with AIDS is expected to decline gradually from a peak of 8,264 persons at the end of 1992 to 5,553 by the end of 1997. However, the number of heterosexual injection drug users living with AIDS is expected to increase from 571 in 1992 to 660 by the end of 1997.

The number of men living with AIDS is expected to decline, gradually, from a peak of 8,851 at the end of 1992 to 6,183 by the end of 1997. However, the number of women living with AIDS is expected to increase from 230 in 1992 to 249 by the end of 1997.

Proponents of HIV theory would like the public to believe that safe sex and using clean needles is the reason for the decline in the AIDS statistics. I believe, that educated abstinence of primarily nitrite inhalants, a.k.a. "room odorizers"/"poppers", as well as IV drugs, is the real reason for the decline in these AIDS statistics. AIDS statistics have been slowing down in the gay community since 1982, due to nitrite inhalant education in the underground gay press. Finally, nitrite inhalants were deemed to be illegal in 1991, by an Act of Congress. Whereas, San Francisco was ahead of the federal government by a few years in the state ban on the sale or possession of nitrite inhalants. It stands to reason that new AIDS cases in San Francisco would slow down slightly ahead of the rest of the country. As I stated earlier, I predicted that new AIDS cases would begin to peak with the removal of nitrite inhalants from the market place.

I also predicted that heterosexual AIDS cases would rise due to the lack of nitrite inhalant education that the gay community was privy to.

High Level AIDS Meeting

A high level meeting of toxicologists and AIDS researchers convened on the 23rd of May, 1994 in Galtersburg, Maryland, at the request of the National Institute on Drug Abuse (NIDA). The purpose of the discussion was to review nitrite inhalant research and discuss the connection between nitrite inhalants, a.k.a. "poppers" and AIDS related Kaposi's Sarcoma (KS).

Present at the meeting was: Dr. Harry Haverkos from NIDA, who chaired the gathering, and who has also been a major player in the ongoing educational process elucidating the relationship between "nitrite inhalants" ("poppers"), and AIDS related KS since 1985; Dr. Robert Gallo from the National Institute of Health, who was a member of the research team, who originally announced that HIV was the sole cause of AIDS in 1984; Dr. Peter Duesberg who published his research paper in 1987, which concluded that HIV could not cause AIDS and whose application for a grant to study chronic exposure of nitrite inhalants has been consistently turned down by the NIH.

This is 1994, 10 years since the discovery of HIV and the origin of the National Institute of Health (NIH) conclusion that HIV is the sole cause of AIDS. In the past ten years, hundreds of thousands of human beings have died while being treated with highly dangerous anti-viral drugs, based on the HIV theory, as the sole cause of AIDS! Now that research is proving that HIV is more than likely, not the sole cause of AIDS, and possibly not even toxic enough to cause AIDS at all, a major quandary is surfacing! The fact that these high level government researchers are even discussing other contributing factors that possibly cause AIDS, poses a major problem. The tragic possibility that AIDS patients have been incorrectly treated for over 10 years, with the incorrect treatment contributing to their mortality, is a haunting thought.

Hard facts that were brought out at the high level meeting:

Problems with HIV/AIDS theory is prompting high level researchers to re-think the AIDS syndrome. No scientist, to this day, has signed his name to any study that proves HIV kills T-cells, other than the original paper authored by Dr. Gallo.

The willingness of the public health officials to re-think the role that nitrite inhalants play in AIDS, and possibly fund Dr. Peter Duesberg's experiments regarding the chronic exposure of animals with nitrite inhalant, is testimonial to the fact that HIV is no longer considered as the sole cause of AIDS.

Just a reminder: In 1983, over 10 years ago, the French team that originally sent the first sample of HIV tainted blood to the U.S., stated that HIV was harmless and nitrite inhalants were more likely to cause AIDS! This was all brought out at the medical conference in Connecticut in 1984 by Dr. Cherman from the Pasteur Institute in Paris.

Dr. Peter Duesberg essentially stated the same conclusion in his paper published in 1987. For over six years, Dr. Duesberg has been turned down by the NIH in his pursuit of grant money to study his nitrite inhalant theory.

Finally, Dr. Gallo, who was present at the final discussion session, agreed that Dr. Duesberg's animal studies investigating nitrite inhalants be funded.

Dr. Gallo was the first staunch supporter of HIV being the sole cause of AIDS. For Dr. Gallo to offer support to Dr. Duesberg in his request to study the nitrite inhalant/AIDS connection, he is espousing the fact that there is more to the cause of AIDS than HIV alone! This is a credit to Dr. Gallo, as a researcher, to admit that his first hypotheses may not be entirely correct.

There is a horrendous tragedy associated with the possibility that HIV does not cause AIDS. If HIV does not cause AIDS, as I believe it doesn't, the treatment will have been wrong, and the possibility that chemotherapy and/or AZT may have contributed to AIDS patient death prevails.

I believe that government health officials will never admit the error. Instead, once they realize that chemotherapy and/or AZT was the primary cause of death in AIDS patients, doctors will replace chemo and AZT with a nontoxic pill, similar to a sugar pill. While giving the credit to the miraculous sugar pill, the real credit will go to abstaining from chemo and/or AZT, along with embarking on a healthy lifestyle, in reversing an AIDS diagnosis.

Chapter IX

What is the Real Care to be Given in Treating AIDS

First of all, get rid of the notion that AIDS is caused by viruses. Admit it, and do not lie to your physician as to all the chemicals that you have been abusing. Immediately, stop abusing all chemicals!! Do not accept chemotherapy or AZT. Stop smoking and drinking alcohol and caffeine. Pure nicotine, alcohol, and caffeine can kill you. Cigarettes, coffee, and alcoholic beverages, when taken in by a chemically toxic person, will only slow down the ability to regain one's immune system.

All the bacteria that causes AIDS associated upper respiratory illnesses are classified as saprophytes. The only food that these bacterial organisms live on is dead organic matter. Any raw food that is heated above 90 degrees is considered dead organic matter. So, if you eat cooked or steamed food while you have saprophytic bacterial organisms inhabiting your lungs and sinuses, you will only prolong their existence. All the bacteria that cause most all of our upper respiratory illnesses (URI's), for the most part, are normal residing bacterial organisms that dwell in our lungs and sinus all our lives because we eat cooked food. What keeps these normal residing bacteria under control is a healthy immune system producing a sufficient number of T-cells. However, when a person stunts T-cell production by abusing their body with chemicals, the normal residing bacterial organisms are allowed to grow unchecked, which is the cause of all upper respiratory illnesses.

There are two ways of combating bacterial organisms that cause upper respiratory illnesses. Only eat fresh, raw fruit and vegetables, thus starving these organisms by taking away the dead organic (cooked) food that they need to survive or by toxic antibacterial drugs. An already chemically toxic AIDS patient cannot afford the latter.

The optimum diet, for an AIDS patient to be on, to get rid of dead food-eating bacteria, is living food. What is living food? Fresh vegetables and fresh fruits. It is best to juice raw vegetables in order to avoid salad dressings and oils that upper respiratory bacteria thrive on.

By changing to a lifestyle of eating approximately 80 percent of your diet being fresh raw fruits and fruit juices and about 20 percent fresh raw vegetables and raw vegetable juices (no pasteurized bottled juices), your energy level will increase, you will feel better and most of all, your immune system will regain its strength.

Avoid all dairy products, including cheese. Avoid all meat, including beef, pork, chicken, turkey and fish. Avoid all pastries, bread, and candy. In other words, nothing but fresh, raw fruits and vegetables and their raw juices should be taken in.

This is what is called a natural hygiene diet, which, when practiced, will eliminate most all upper respiratory illnesses without ever needing to rely on toxic antibacterial drugs.

In severe cases of upper respiratory illnesses, fasting while only taking in pure distilled water for a period of time, will get rid of upper respiratory illnesses at warp speed (from one to four weeks). Essentially, you are starving these pathological organisms to death. You will find that therapeutic fasting (not starving) is easy and not harmful with a little bit of education by purchasing the book titled, *"Fasting Can Save Your Life"* by Dr. Shelton, found at most health food stores.

Chemical treatment for AIDS is not the answer.

Halting all chemicals stops the real cause of AIDS in the first place (chemical poisoning of the thymus). Embarking on a natural hygiene diet helps rid the body of the upper respiratory illness, bacterial organisms. The real benefits of a natural hygiene lifestyle becomes a little more complex. A natural hygiene diet builds the immune system, not only for AIDS patients, but for anyone who embraces this lifestyle.

When all food is eaten, it must be broken down into its simplest forms: simple sugar, water, vitamins, minerals and nutrients that are able to be assimilated by every cell in the body. Food is broken down into its simplest form by substances called enzymes. Enzymes are submicroscopic and are found in all living foods that are not destroyed by heating above 90 degrees. It is this enzyme activity that brings unripened fruits and vegetables to the ripened state. When raw fruits and vegetables are eaten, most all of this food is broken down into its simplest useable form by the enzyme action that is already present in the raw fruit or vegetable. This eliminates the need for the person or animal that ate the food to have to manufacture the enzymes to convert this raw food, thus conserving body energy.

However, if food is cooked, and the enzymes are destroyed, the person or animal who eats cooked food has to manufacture the necessary enzymes in the body to be able to break down the food into useable simple form, thus wasting much body energy. A good example is presented when a large meal of meat and potatoes is eaten, the need to siesta for a couple of hours occurs.

So, what I have just described is the awareness of the fact that there are two ways that the necessary enzymes for the purpose of converting our food, can be gotten. One is from outside the body, which is referred too as exogenous and found in all raw food that is not heated above 90 degrees. The other is manufactured inside the body and called endogenous.

When vegetables and fruit are eaten in a raw state, the digestion and conversion of the food occurs very easily with a minimum of time and no harmful end products of digestion. All the simple sugars, water, minerals and nutrients are very efficiently used up.

However, when the same cooked food is eaten, problems occur. First of all, the human body is highly inefficient in the manufacturing of endogenous enzymes. As a result, the body cannot produce enzymes, at a sufficient enough rate, to convert all the cooked food we eat. Besides our pets, humans are the only animals on the planet that normally eat cooked food. Humans have inefficiently evolved over thousands of years to be able to produce enzymes in order to eat cooked food.

Once food is eaten, it has to be gotten rid of as soon as possible in order not to spoil in our stomach or intestine. Due to the inefficient production of digestive enzymes, humans and other animals (our pets) maintain from five to seven pounds of saprophytic bacteria in our stomach and intestinal tract in order to help break down our food.

We can only use a limited amount of the cooked food that we eat due to our inefficient enzyme production. The rest of our food that is broken down by the saprophytic bacteria is useless and downright toxic and harmful. End products of bacterial digestion can include ptomaine, putrescence, leukocidins, ammonia, phosphoric acid, sulfuric acid, and uric acid, just to name a few.

When cooked food is predominately eaten and five to seven pounds of these poisonous bacteria are dumping their toxins, every day of your life into the blood stream, you are, essentially, causing a constant insult to the blood stream, which is a perpetual insult to the immune system. This is evidenced by the observation that persons who maintain a predominantly cooked food diet also maintain a white blood cell count between ten to twenty thousand per cubic milliliter, while maintaining a body temperature of 98.6 degrees.

When a person practices a diet, mainly consisting of raw fruit and vegetables, his or her white blood cell count drops to around three thousand per cubic milliliter and body temperature drops to 97.6 degrees.

To explain why this difference prevails, one must understand that the body produces a white blood cell count according to a fundamental law of physiology, utilizing the "law of Adaptive Secretion." This law states that the immune system expends the disease fighting white blood cells in a direct relationship to the degree of toxicity in the blood stream.

So, the lower white blood count and body temperature of a person maintaining a natural hygiene diet, in this case, presents a much healthier picture than a person who utilizes a cooked food diet. A person suffering from AIDS would greatly benefit from a natural hygiene diet.

Please do not mistake the lowered white blood cell count of a person on a natural hygiene diet as an earmark for an AIDS diagnosis. The difference between a lowered white blood cell count, associated with AIDS and a natural hygienist, is that when a toxic insult occurs, the natural hygienist's white blood cell count will shoot up, very responsibly, while the AIDS patient's white blood cell count will not. Many unsuspecting doctors have erred in requesting an AIDS test when finding a natural hygienist with a low white blood cell count. Natural hygienists are very healthy and are rarely seen by a doctor.

The major argument against a natural hygiene diet that is constantly mustered, is, what about protein? You do not have to worry about protein because fruit contains five to eight percent of calories as protein, which is almost identical to the amount of protein as found in mother's milk, fresh from the breast. Mother Nature deems it necessary to provide breast milk with only five to seven percent of calories as protein, at a time in a human's life when protein requirement is at its greatest, and growth rate is the fastest. The protein content of raw vegetables ranges from 13 to 20 percent of calories as protein.

As you can see, a diet of raw fruit and vegetables more than meets the protein requirements of humans.

Society has been formally mis-educated by our nation's traditional dieticians and nutritionists, regarding protein requirements for over a hundred years. Nutritionists have been utilizing outdated rat studies, done by Osborn and Mendel dating back to 1914, in order to pattern our protein requirements.

It was found that rats thrive on 49 percent of calories as protein, as found in the makeup of a mother rat's milk. Based on these results, nutritionists developed the Class A Protein Theory that they are still using to misinform the public.

The protein content of human breast milk was not known until 1952, when researcher William Rose published his results. He found that human milk contains only 5 percent of calories as protein, whereas cow's milk maintains 20 percent of calories as protein. The World Health Organization, today, accepts the fact that human beings only need five to eight percent of calories as protein in the diet.

Our consumption of protein, beyond five to eight percent of calories as protein, is actually harmful, especially where animal protein is concerned. Animal protein (beef, fish, chicken, pork) ranging around 30 to 80 percent of calories as protein, is extremely high in phosphorus and sulfur. Since most high protein foods are eaten in a cooked state, most of these foods are digested by the bacteria in the stomach and intestines. It is the phosphorus and sulfur content of high protein digestion by these bacteria that causes most of the toxic poison that insults the blood stream on a daily routine. Phosphorus and sulfur end products of digestion also maintain a high degree of acid in the body fluids, which is also extremely harmful.

The toxic bacterial end products of protein digestion, relative to the over-consumption of protein in this country, is responsible for nervous stress, irritability and tension, due to too much acid being dumped into the blood stream. This is also the cause of attention deficit disorder (ADD) in children. All you physicians who are poisoning your young patients with Prozac, wake up! Look into their protein intake.

This researcher believes that the perpetual poisoning of the blood stream with toxic end products of bacterial digestion of cooked foods is the major cause of degenerative diseases in human beings and their pets. Diseases of humans came into vogue with the process of cooking, thus causing most all of our food to be digested by bacteria.

I believe, onset leukemia, in the early years of life in children, is caused initially as a result of bacterial digestion of formula, cereal and pasteurized dairy products. The toxic end products of these foodstuffs poisons the blood stream, causing the vibrant immune system of young children to overproduce white blood cells, which is the symptom leading up to a diagnosis of leukemia. I believe leukemia to be 100 percent cured by a change to a natural hygiene diet.

The bacterial digestion of cooked food produces toxic poisons that a person, weakened with AIDS, cannot tolerate. Pure foods, namely fresh raw fruit and vegetables, along with pure distilled water, along with plenty of rest and sunshine and getting off all drugs are the only answer to surviving an AIDS diagnosis.

Again, this information has been passed on to you as a nutritional consultation only. Please consult with your own health care provider. I do advise, however, that an alternative health care practitioner be consulted, preferably in the practice of teaching natural hygiene.

The allopathic medical internist has a near 100 percent failure rate in treating AIDS patients with chemicals, so let your conscience be your guide.

A list of alternative healthcare professionals can be received by contacting the American Natural Hygiene Society, P.O. Box 30630, Tampa, Florida 33630, or Fax: (813) 855-8052.

In Summary

Research has established that volatile nitrite, one of the most cancer causing, immune destructive chemicals known to man, is also able to cause immune dysfunction when aggressively abused over a four to seven year time frame, depending on the frequency, intensity and duration of abuse.

Aggressive, chronic abuse of volatile nitrite, IV drugs, as well as other immunosuppressive chemicals, are able to cause progressive deterioration of the organ that maintains a healthy T-cell count, namely the thymus. It is the progressive deterioration of the thymus that gradually causes the T-cell drop that allows the opportunistic infections that are associated with AIDS. The relative length of time that it takes to cause the atrophy of the thymus in each unique AIDS case is the mysterious latency factor that has been puzzling AIDS researchers for over 16 years. Chemical atrophy of the thymus causes AIDS and not HIV.

Nearly 100 percent of all the early AIDS cases were found to have been abusing volatile nitrite aggressively for four to seven years or more, prior to their AIDS diagnosis. Since nitrite inhalants have been shown in research to have a direct relationship to Kaposi's Sarcoma (KS), it is not surprising that these AIDS cases, who were abusing nitrites, also presented KS symptoms.

I have demonstrated:

• That the most important factor leading up to the AIDS epidemic was the entry into U.S. interstate, international commerce of Clifford Hassing's falsely represented "room odorizers," a.k.a. "Locker Room," a.k.a. "poppers," in 1971 that were formulated with almost pure butyl nitrite.

• The fact that it is necessary to abuse nitrite inhalant aggressively for a minimum of four years, and maybe seven years, before symptoms of AIDS show up, is why not all individuals who have abused nitrites exhibit AIDS symptoms.

• The fact that 1974 was established as the year that the practice of inhaling "poppers" had reached every corner of the gay community.

- That by adding a seven year immune dysfunction timeframe to the established 1974 date, 1981 would be the most logical expectation for the first nitrite related AIDS cases to show up, which is when they began to appear.

- The fact that brand new homosexual AIDS/KS cases simultaneously dropped, along with the decline of nitrite abuse in 1985, as a result of research linking nitrite inhalants to AIDS/KS, is a strong observation that is hard to ignore.

- The sheer fact that "poppers" are almost exclusively abused by the homosexual community, is why AIDS statistics have remained 80 percent to 90 percent gay.

- That finally, in 1990, by an Act of Congress, nitrite inhalants were banned, and now, seven years later, a major decline in brand new AIDS cases is being observed in the June, 1997 CDC AIDS Surveillance Report.

Most all of the first patients suffering with immune dysfunction were treated with aggressive chemotherapy, because they exhibited symptoms of KS, considered to be a cancer. Obviously, since chemotherapy did not work, when in fact 100% of these patients died in two to three years, it is obvious that chemotherapy was not a correct treatment to prescribe.

In hind sight, realization of the error in prescribing chemotherapy to patients with immune dysfunction, becomes extremely obvious when HIV positive long term survivors, who have refused chemotherapy or AZT are found to be living indefinitely.

Not all AIDS patients, in the beginning, were exhibiting (KS). As many as 50% or greater were only presenting pneumonia (PCP). These non cancer patients were still treated with chemotherapy on the anticipation that they might develop (KS).

Not only were non-cancer AIDS patients (those who had advanced PCP and had not yet progressed to KS) being treated prophylactically with chemotherapy to anticipate and prevent KS, physicians were also aggressively abusing powerful antibiotics such as Bactrim and Septra in the same prophylactic mode in order to anticipate and prevent PCP from occurring in persons who were worried about their lifestyle practices. While these people were not sick they ultimately did get sick from the antibiotic abuse. How many of these individuals developed PCP from the antibiotics and then were prescribed with chemotherapy prophylactically to prevent KS and consequently died as a result of all the compounding drug regimens, when they were never sick in the first place, is a scary thought. If these individuals survived into the AZT era and ultimately were prescribed AZT, we should all know, by now, how their prognosis ended.

The truth in reality, was, that the chemotherapy that physicians were imposing on these immune deficient patients was the primary cause of death in these early AIDS patients.

Shortly after the failure of chemotherapy was realized, the discovery of HIV occurred. Since AIDS was now being blamed on a virus, an anti-viral drug was needed. You wouldn't prescribe a killer cancer drug for a viral infection. But, that's exactly what happened when AZT was brought on the market.

AZT was a failed cancer drug, that was so toxic, that the doctor who invented it did not bother to patent it. Burrough's Wellcome, a major pharmaceutical manufacturer, took the failed drug and re-classified it as an anti-viral drug, even though it was still a systemic cancer drug that also kills the majority of the patient's T-cells. All that occurred with the AZT replacement was one cancer drug for another. Chemotherapeutic/cancer drugs were proven failures. Changing the name of a cancer drug to an anti-viral drug (AZT) still left AIDS patients being treated with a cancer drug. Again, I repeat cancer drugs were proven failures.

All the drugs AZT, DDI, DDC, D4T and 3TC are all chemotherapy drugs disguised as anti-viral drugs. All of these types of drugs are proving to be failures. It seems that persistence in prescribing systemic killer drugs that perpetually weaken the thymus and subsequently the body's ability to fight bacterial infection, borders on the side of stupidity.

The only success stories in long term AIDS survival, involves alternative health care, utilizing nutritional science and abstinence from drugs.

Unfortunately, most medical doctors do not have the proper knowledge in non drug therapy that is essential to cure immune dysfunction. It is obvious that frequent bouts of bacterial infection are able to be cured with antibiotics, but there is a limit to a person's ability to withstand chronic use of antibiotics, as well as all immuno-suppressive drugs either prescribed or recreational. Full blown AIDS is essentially the saturation point where a person's thymus is chemically exhausted.

The need to reduce chemical exposure from prescribed, as well as recreational chemicals, is of utmost importance. A 100% death rate of AIDS patients being treated with chemotherapy and or AZT by medical doctors is proof that these medical doctors are not able successfully to treat an AIDS patient, whereas alternative health care, utilizing non-drug therapy, is the only mode of treatment that is working with long-term survivors.

Onset immune dysfunction is brought on by chemical abuse, recreational or prescribed. However, full blown AIDS for the most part in the majority of AIDS patients occurs as a result of compounding chemical abuse with killer chemotherapeutic cancer drugs and AZT which are the true, real, ultimate cause of death in AIDS patients.

After HIV was discovered, persons who were not yet sick, were put on AZT very early, based on their only having antibodies to HIV. Having, antibodies to a virus, in the field of virology has always meant that you are immune to the virus. In the majority of HIV anti-body positive individuals, the HIV virus can't even be found. Yet, killer chemotherapy/AZT has been prescribed aggressively the minute someone has tested positive to an antibody test. Early detection of a potential AIDS patient, using the HIV test, found many patients HIV positive with their immune system still vibrant. It is understandable, that prescribing immunosuppressive drugs, to healthier patients would exhibit a longer latency period (the length of time from suspected exposure to HIV to full blown AIDS).

The AIDS patients prior to the discovery of HIV and subsequent HIV antibody test, had already developed full blown AIDS symptoms and thus were very sick when they were put on chemotherapy. Consequently, they exhibited a short latency period to full blown AIDS and death.

So, early intervention as well as varying degrees of prescription dose of, the ostensibly referred to anti-viral drugs, are responsible for the long latency period that occurs in some AIDS patients. It is obvious that full blown AIDS, leading to death is directly related to not only the patients prior drug abuse, but also the prescribed drug regimen that the physician is utilizing.

146

You would also expect the longest latency period to occur in the unfortunate individuals, who were never sick in the first place, who had tested false positive with faulty HIV test kits, and were aggressively treated with AZT. These AIDS death statistics, may very well be the AIDS cases, who were not showing drug abuse in their history.

When you read about the criminally fraudulent, clinical trial utilized to license AZT in the back of this book, the pharmaceutical genocide that has been going on for the past thirteen years will become readily apparent.

The control group, taking AZT, had to be kept alive with multiple blood transfusions due to the deleterious effect of AZT on the bone marrow. The fact that this situation was hidden from the licensing board is grounds for extreme criminal prosecution. The licensing procedure and fraudulent clinical trail of AZT demands a congressional investigation.

As unbelievable as it may seem, this researcher believes that the majority of AIDS deaths in the U.S. are the result of death caused iatrogenically (at the hands of the physician utilizing a universal treatment of choice that incorporates pharmaceutical genocide).

The primary reason substantiating the aforementioned statement is the fact that there are thousands of HIV positive individuals living indefinitely, who are refusing traditional medical treatment with chemotherapy or AZT.

While I have highlighted volatile nitrite inhalants, as what I believe to be the primary cause of immune dysfunction symptoms leading to a doctor's visit, it is obvious that inhalants are not the only factor. All aggressive chemical abuse, that is immunosuppressive when aggressively abused, are also possible factors. Others in the spotlight more than likely include IV recreational drugs and benzene derivative lubricants, primarily due to their direct insult to the bloodstream, therefore bypassing the body's protective organs such as the kidneys, etc.

The relatively exclusive use by homosexual community of volatile nitrite inhalants and benzene derivative lubricants are foremost factors of all the chemicals having been mentioned with regards to developing immune dysfunction, to warrant a doctors visit. Once again it is the misdiagnosis of a virus namely, HIV, as being the cause of the suspected immune disorder that leads to the wrongfully prescribed use of chemotherapy/AZT, that is the ultimate cause of death in AIDS statistics.

I believe, had the FDA acted aggressively against the "room odorizer" industry in the first place, by defining their products as drugs and banning them, the majority of AIDS cases would not have occurred in the U.S. and other countries where they were marketed.

Finally, the only hope of treating persons with immune deficiencies, lies in a nutritional science approach, while advising the patient on the importance of practicing a healthy lifestyle without drugs.

What we are witnessing is the beginning of the end of the AIDS epidemic, in the United States as we know it. Brand new AIDS cases are dropping by more than 20%. Now, if the "room odorizer" manufacturers, who are still selling their products illegally, and the companies who have just reformulated their products are shut down, new AIDS cases will drop even faster. If the manufacturers of sexual lubricants remove their benzene derivatives as Project AIDS International suggests, that will also aid in the reduction of new AIDS cases. If the NIH would wake up and educate, not only our society, but the rest of the world about the dangers of the aforementioned products and their potential to cause immune dysfunction leading to AIDS, that will help reduce new AIDS cases.

To add to that, if the people who are developing AIDS as a result of chronic abuse of IV, recreational drugs, would stop their chemical abuse, brand new AIDS cases would only be left to physicians who are causing AIDS with their over-prescribed immunosuppressive drugs such as chemotherapy, AZT, antiviral, anti-inflammatory (arthritic) and aggressive abuse of antibiotics.

Toxicology, as well as epidemiology, research has irrefutably proven that aggressive chemical abuse, is able to cause AIDS, whereas no one, not one scientist, has signed his name to any research paper that describes the mechanism by which HIV is able to cause AIDS or any illness, for that matter, with the exception of the paper authored by Dr. Gallo.

I believe that HIV is only residual, fragmented, cellular debris that only serves as an indicator of toxic chemical poisoning of the bloodstream in persons who abuse chemicals. The only exception is people transfused with tainted blood products, and babies born to HIV positive mothers.

In this book I have presented the untold facts behind the scenes of medical research going on, regarding the AIDS epidemic while describing the true co-factors of this monstrous tragedy.

- I have described the recreational chemical abuse with immuneosuppressive drugs that caused the immune dysfunction in the earliest AIDS patients that prompted these patients to go to a doctor's office in the beginning of the AIDS epidemic.

- I have shown how the very first AIDS patients were abusing nitrite inhalants that presented KS a rare cancer not found in otherwise healthy young men that compelled the first doctor who treated these patients to prescribe aggressive chemotherapy to these already toxic individuals which abruptly caused their death.

- I have made you aware of the fact that physicians were prescribing antibiotics and chemotherapy to individuals prophylactically who were not sick, anticipating that they would get sick due to their high risk lifestyles. They never would have gotten sick had they not gone to a doctor who was practicing knee-jerk medicine.

- I have demonstrated that the foundation supporting HIV as the cause of AIDS is extremely weak due to the fact that no other scientific research study in the whole world has duplicated Dr. Gallo's original hypothesis concluding that HIV is a direct or, for that matter, even an indirect killer of T-cells.

- The fact that thousands of HIV positive persons have been surviving for over 16 years with many of them reverting to HIV negative status without any antiviral therapy would be enough proof to a logical thinker that HIV is not the killer that the NIH/CDC/HIV/AIDS medical branch claims it to be.

- The fact that 100% of the AIDS patients who accepted chemotherapy or aggressive AZT therapy, have died, supports the more logical belief that the treatments imposed on AIDS patients for the past 16 years have been wrong considering thousands of people who have refused these treatments are surviving.

- The fact that AZT is nothing more than a failed chemotherapy cancer drug that has been shown to "cause cancer at any dose", "cause bone marrow failure", and was presented to be "1000 times more toxic than presented at the clinical licensing board", highly portrays this drug as a probable cause of death in anyone who was prescribed with it.

- In the pre HIV era, antibiotics compounded with aggressive chemotherapy is suspected as the cause of death in not only sick people but healthy people as well who were scared into being prophylactically treated with antibiotics and chemo that is highly suspected in the cause of their demise.

- In the post HIV era, once a person was diagnosed with HIV, the only treatment that was accepted as "the universal treatment of choice" in the medical community was AZT. Now that the true toxic effects of AZT are being exposed, it is no wonder why over 400,000 U.S. citizens who were prescribed with AZT did not survive.

- A side bar tragedy is that hundreds and maybe thousands of people may have suffered the consequences of AZT as a result of a false positive HIV test.

The whole gamut of every major medical blunder has been played out in the twisted complex of treating AIDS patients as well as healthy patients. It is not surprising that it has taken over 19 years to sort this out and affix a sense of sanity and discovery as to how this all happened in the first place.

I hope after all this you don't still believe the silly Hollywood version about the monkey who bit a native who hitched a ride to Florida and had sex with a flight attendant who, like little Johnny Appleseed, spread AIDS over hill and dale.

This researcher believes that in 100% of all persons who <u>develop</u> immune deficiencies their illness was a result of chronic abuse of toxic chemicals (recreational and prescribed) focusing on direct insults to the blood stream, mainly inhalants and IV drugs. It is also only commonsense that malnutrition plays an important role in the progression of immune deficiencies. In developing countries industrial solvent inhalants (ISI) along with malnutrition is at the forefront of blame in AIDS causation. While each individual is responsible for the onset of their own immune deficiency, it is the misdiagnosis of HIV as the cause of AIDS and the subsequent treatment of toxic alleged antiviral drugs that are not antiviral and are actually life terminating poisons. It is the treatment of AIDS patients with these life ending drugs by blindly ignorant physicians that is the true primary cause of death in otherwise remedial AIDS patients.

The primary argument that proponents of the HIV/AIDS establishment has used for years to support their arguments against the chemical/AIDS hypothesis is the fact that thousands of AIDS patients attested to no inhalant, IV drug or any recreational chemical abuse at all. Until I discovered people who weren't sick rushing to doctors for aggressive antibiotic and chemo abuse along with the discovery that faulty AIDS test kits may have caused thousands of people to start terminal AZT therapy as a result of a false positive HIV antibody test, the mystery of non-drug using people developing AIDS was a puzzlement. The aforementioned scenario closes the door to that mystery.

As I stated earlier the cause of AIDS that has been defined for decades in the Merck medical manual is immuneosuppressive drugs (foremost being antibiotics, chemo, and radiation). When a full understanding of the real toxicity of AZT is realized, AZT will probably be categorized as one of the most toxic immuneo-suppressive drugs ever imposed on man. <u>It is extremely absurd that thousands of people who were not sick rushed to a doctor to engage aggressive drug therapy for the prevention of AIDS, with drugs that are defined as the primary cause of AIDS</u>. What is worse than the ignorant, embarking on this perilous journey is the fact that trained physicians accommodated these misguided unfortunates. Malpractice suits have already been settled out of court regarding this stupid practice on the part of these physicians.

So, the above scenarios solving the mystery of AIDS patients who claimed no drug use completely closes the door on the only arguments that the HIV AIDS establishment could muster in order to counter the chemical/AIDS hypothesis.

In brief, the AIDS epidemic encompasses, recreational chemical abuse, commercial greed on the part of the "room odorizer"/nitrite inhalant industry, government medical, research errors in supporting a failed HIV/AIDS hypothesis in the first place, doctors blindly following harmful government treatment directives, doctors engaged in malpractice by treating persons who were not sick with antibiotic/chemo drugs, false positive HIV tests, and the criminally, fraudulent licensing of AZT that was not meant for human consumption, which caused pharmaceutical genocide.

This has been an all American tragedy! <u>AIDS is easily reversible once all drugs are halted and a natural hygiene dietary lifestyle is practiced.</u> <u>AIDS IS NOT A DEATH SENTENCE.</u>

Blaming HIV as the cause of AIDS is the most diabolical medical blunder of modern times, and almost 400,000 individuals have probably died due to the wrongful diagnosis of the real cause of AIDS, as well as the wrongful prescribing of potent killer chemo-therapy/AZT that already toxic AIDS patients cannot possibly endure. Why else would you suspect that no AIDS patients that have submitted themselves to traditional AIDS treatment in the past 18 years have lived? Do 400,000 more U.S. citizens have to die before the medical community wakes up to the fact that HIV/AIDS is a failed hypothesis and an all American tragedy?

Let this be a notice to all allopathic, medical, care givers who have blindly followed the CDC/HIV/AIDS hypothesis in the diagnosis and subsequent treatment of AIDS patients. The CDC/HIV/AIDS branch, is not going to cover your legal expenses in your individual malpractice suits, that are inevitable, once society sees the light.

Blindly following a universal treatment of choice, as dictated by government medical science, that is being proven, everyday, to be wrong, does not insulate an individual health care giver from legal responsibility.

The hypothesis that HIV causes AIDS is presumed and, to this day, not proven by scientific study or paper, authored by anyone. Since HIV has never been proven to be able to cause any illness, let alone any of the AIDS indicator illnesses, the foundation supporting the treatment of AIDS patients with alleged antiviral drug therapy, does not exist.

All HIV positive persons, treated with aggressive chemo/AZT, have died, whereas all HIV positive persons who are surviving over 14 years, and, indefinitely, have refused chemo/AZT and all alleged antiviral drugs, which proves that HIV does not cause full blown AIDS, whereas abstinence from chemo/AZT/alleged antiviral drugs, plays a primary role in the failure to progress to full blown AIDS.

152

The CDC/HIV/AIDS hypothesis regarding the cause and treatment of AIDS, has been dead wrong from the beginning and associated with the true cause of death in over 400,000 U.S. citizens. I suggest that all physicians whose patients have died while being treated aggressively with chemo/AZT or any antiviral drug, start looking for a good attorney.

Where Do We Go From Here?

There needs to be a major policy change at the CDC/AIDS branch, in that an open minded approach regarding AIDS research needs to be implemented. The dogma that the CDC/AIDS branch has been espousing contains two major problems.

First of all, the treatment strategy and philosophy, founded on the HIV hypothesis for 15 long years, has been a miserable failure.

Secondarily, I think 20 years of research, without one, true, scientific, paper establishing proof that HIV is able to cause AIDS by explaining the mechanism by which it does so, intensifies the need to re-appraise the HIV/AIDS hypothesis.

If it was left up to the virologists, in the SMON, epidemic research project, they would still be searching for the elusive SMON virus, which would be a real tragedy, needless to say the countless lives that would have continued to be lost. Even worse, is the fact, that thousands of people died as a result of the time wasted on viral obsession by researchers with closed minds and blinders on. There is no room for research scientists who are plagued with a closed mind. Keeping an open mind is one of the most important principles that a person learns when embarking on a career in scientific research.

The SMON episode should be an eye-opener, as well as a good reason for the present CDC/AIDS branch policy makers to open their minds and join the now, totaling, over 1,000 scientists, Nobel prize winners and professional people who have formed The Group for the Scientific Re-appraisal of the HIV/AIDS Hypothesis.

I wouldn't want to be the person to be responsible for anyone loosing their job, but if a corporate president was in charge of a failing corporation, for going on 20 years, I don't think he would still have a job. I think 20 years is more than enough time to give a failing policy. If the present department heads at NIH, CDC, AIDS, policy level are not able to open their minds and try a somewhat fresher approach, maybe it's time to clean house.

For the past 15 years, the NIH, CDC, AIDS branch has not disbursed one dime of AIDS research money to any research project, other than the HIV viral theory. That sounds to me like obsessive, viral compulsion and, considering all the dissention taking place in the scientific community, at home and around the world, I wouldn't put much confidence in anyone hanging on to their job who is not able to develop an open mind regarding the cause of AIDS in the near future.

The primary reasons why I can state emphatically that changes are in the wind, is due to the fact that it is widely known, now, that the longest known HIV positive survivors (14 years plus) are still living because they have refused antiviral therapy with chemo-therapy, AZT as well as the drug cocktails. This leaves absolutely no doubt that chemotherapy and AZT have been a primary player in the cause of death of thousands of otherwise remedial persons suffering with immune deficiencies. This is concrete proof HIV does not cause AIDS.

Funding Dr. Peter Duesberg's grant request to study chronic nitrite inhalant exposure with chimpanzees, would put to rest the question of whether or not nitrite inhalants in themselves are able to cause immune dysfunction in chimps (it has already been proven in mice).

The chimpanzee study is only necessary for obsessed virologists who can't see "the forest through the trees," regarding the chemical/AIDS connection.

The CDC who has been censoring open debate regarding the HIV/AIDS hypothesis vs. the chemical/AIDS hypothesis, needs to open up and allow open scientific debate. This isn't Russia. Scientific oppression is not healthy for scientific advancement.

Bibliography

1. Gottlieb MS, Schanker HM, Fan PT, Saxon A, Weisman JD, Polaski I, Pneumocystis Pneumonia, Los Angeles Morbid Mortal Weekly Rep. 1981; 30: 250-52

2. Hymes KB, Cheung T, Greene, JB et al. Kaposi's Sarcoma in Homosexual Men: A Report of Eight Cases. Lancet 1981; ii: 589-600

3. Friedman-Klien A, Laubenstein L, Marmor M, et al. Kaposi's Sarcoma and Pneumocystis Pneumonia Among Homosexual Men, New York City and California. Morbid Mortal Weekly Rep. 1981; 30: 305-08

4. Friedman SM, Felman YM, Rothbberg R et al. Follow Up On Kaposi's Sarcoma and Pneumocystis Pneumonia Morbid Mortal Weekly Rep. 1981; 30: 409-10

5. Editorial. Immuno-compromised Homosexuals Lancet 1981; ii: 1325-26

6. Gottlieb MS, Schroffer, Schanker HM et al. Pneumocystis Carinii Pneumonia and Mucosal Candidiasis In Previously Healthy Homosexual Men: Evidence of a New Acquired Cellular Immunodeficiency. N Eng J Med 1981; 305: 1425-31

7. Masur H, Michals MA, Greene JB et al. An Outbreak of Community Acquired Pneumocystis Carinii Pneumonia; Initial Manifestation of Cellular Immune Dysfunction. N Eng J Med 1981 305: 1431-38

8. Siegal FP, Lopez C, Hammer GS, et al. Severe Acquired Immunodeficiency In Male Homosexuals Manifest by Chronic Perianal Ulcerative Herpes Simplex Lesions. N Engl J Med 1981; 305 1439-44

9. Waltzer PD, Perl DP, Krongstad DJ, Rawson PG, Schultz M.G. Pneumocystitis Carini Pneumonia In the United States: Epidemiologic, Diagnostic and Clinical Features. Ann Intern Med 1974; 80: 83-93

10. Klepp O, Dahl O, Stenwig JY. Association of Kaposi's Sarcoma and Prior Immunosuppressive Therapy: A 5-Year Material of Kaposi's Sarcoma in Norway. Cancer 1978; 42: 2626-30

11. Gange RW, Jones EW. Kaposi's Sarcoma and Immuno-suppressive Therapy: An Appraisal Clin Exp Dermatol 1978; 3: 135-46

12. Safai B. Good RA. Kaposi's Sarcoma: A Review and Recent Developments CA 1981; 31: 1-112

13. Bruenton, T. On the Use of Nitrite Of Amyl In Angina Pectoris. Lancet 2: 97-98, 1867

14. Brunton, T. Lectures On the Action Of Medicines. New York: McMillian Co., 1897. pp 332-343

15. Wilkins, RW; Haynes, FW; and Weiss, S. The Role of the Venous System in Circulatory Collapse Induced by Sodium Nitrite. J Clin Invest 16: 85-91, 1937

16. Darling, RC, and Roughton, FJW. The Effects of Methemoglobin on the Equilibrium Between Oxygen and Hemoglobin. Am J Physiol 137: 56-68, 1942

17. Lester, D, and Greenburg, LA. The Comparative Effects From Carbon Monoxide and Methemoglobin. J Pharmacol Exp Ther 81: 182-188, 1944.

18. Finch, C: Methemoglobinemia and Sulfhemoglobinemia N Engl J Med 239: 470-478, 1948

19. Magee, PN, and Barnes, JM. The Production of Malignant Primary Hepatic Tumors in the Rat by Feeding Dimethylnitrosamine. Br. J. Cancer 10: 114-122, 1956

20. Israelstam, S; Lambert, S; and Oki, G. Poppers: A New Recreational Drug Craze. Can Psychiatry Assoc J 23: 493-495, 1978

21. Sutton, WL. Aliphatic Nitro Compounds, Nitrates, Nitrites, Alky Nitrites. In: Fassett, DW, and Irish, D, eds Industrial Hygiene and Toxicology. Vol. II New York: Interscience, 1963. pp 414-438

22. Lubell, I.   Correspondence With Burroughs Wellcome Co., 1964;

23. Smith, PAS. The Chemistry of Open-Chain Organic Nitrogen Compounds. Vol. 2. New York: WA Benjamin, 1966. p. 466

24. Louria, DB. Sexual Use of Amyl Nitrite. Med Aspects Hum Sex 4: 89, 1970

25. Pearlman, JT, and Adams, GL. Amyl Nitrite Inhalation Fad JAMA 212: 160, 1970

26. Fverett, G. Effects of Amyl Nitrite on Sexual Experience. Medical Aspects of Human Sexuality, December 1972, pp 146-151

27. Gay, GR, and Sheppard, CW. "Sex In the Drug Culture." Med Aspects Hum Sex 6: 28-47, 1972

28. Fenter, JD; Findlay JD; Port, CD; Ehrlech, R, and Coffin, DL. Chronic Exposure to Nitrogen Dioxide.   Arch Environ Health 27: 85-89, 1973

29. Harwood, AR, Osoba, D, Hofsteader SL, et al.   Kaposi's Sarcoma in Recipients of Renal Transplants. Am J Med; 1979; 67: 759-65

30. Stribling, J, Weitzner S, Smith, GV. Kaposi's Sarcoma in Renal Allograft Recipients. Arch Intern Med 1974; 133: 307-11

31. Myers, BD, Kessler, E, Levi J, Pick, A, Rosenfeld, JB. Kaposi's Sarcoma in Kidney Transplant Recipients. Arch Inten Med. 1974; 133: 307-11

32. Penn, I. Kaposi's Sarcoma in Organ Transplant Recipients: Report of 20 Cases. Transplantation. 1979; 27: 8-11

33. Hoshaw, RA, Schwartz, RA.   Kaposi's Sarcoma After Immunosuppressive Therapy with Prednisone.   Arch Dermatol. 1980; 116: 1280-2

34. Brown, SM, Stimmel, B, Tavb, RN, Kochwa, S, Rosenfield, RE. Immunologic Dysfunction in Heroin Addicts. Arch Intern Med. 1974 134: 1001-6

35. Mayer, KH.   Medical Consequences of the Inhalation of Volatile Nitrites. In: Ostrow, DG, Sandholzer, TA; Feldman, YM, eds. Sexually Transmitted Diseases in Homosexual Men.   New York: Plenum Medical Book Co., 1983 pp 237-242

36. Reed D. The Multi-million Dollar Mystery High. Christopher Street 2: 21-27, 1979

37. Everett, GM. Amyl Nitrite ("Poppers") as an Aphrodisiac. In: Sandler, M, and Gessa, GL, eds. Sexual Behavior: Pharmacology and Biochemistry, New York: Raven Press, 1975. pp. 97-98

38. Labataille, L.   Amyl Nitrites Employed in Homosexual Relations. Med Aspects Hum Sexuality 9: 122, 1975

39. Bruckner, JV, and Peterson, RG. Review of the Alipiatic and Aromatic Hydrocarbons. In: Sharpp, CW, and Brehm, ML, eds. Review of Inhalants: Euphoria to Dysfunction National Institute on Drug Abuse Research Monograph 15.   Dhew Pub. No (ADM) 77-553. Washington, D.C. U.S. Govt. Print. Off., 1977. pp 124-163

40. Couri, D.   "Introduction to Preclinical Pharmacology and Toxicology" in Review of Inhalants: Euphoria to Dysfunction, eds. Sharp, CW and Brehm, ML. Rockville, MD.: 1977 pp 100

41. Sigell, LT; Kapp, FT; Fusaro, GA; Nelson, ED; Falck, RS. Popping and Snorting Volatile Nitrites: A Current Fad for Getting High. Am J Psychiatry 135: 1216-1218, 1978.

42. Margetter, RZ; Fenters, JD; Findlay, JC; Ehrlich, R; and Gardner, DE. Effect of Exposure to Nitrogen Dioxide on T and B cells in Mouse Spleens. Toxicol Lett 2: 157-161, 1978.

43. Dimijian, GG. Contemporary Drug Abuse. In: Goth, A, ed. Medical Pharmacology. St. Louis: C.V. Mosby, 1978. pp. 279-330.

44. Israelstam, S; Lambert, S; Lambert, S, and Oki, G. Use of Isobutyl Nitrite as a Recreational Drug. Br J Addict 73 (3): 319-320 1978

45. Nickerson, Mark; Parker, John, O; Lowry, Thomas; Swenson, Edward, W. "Isobutyl Nitrite and Related Compounds." Published by Pharmex LTD 1978.

46. McClung, MD, Spyker, DA. Abuse of Butyl Nitrite. Program for the Annual Meeting of the American Academy of Clinical Toxicology, pp. 43 October 1978.

47. Maickel, RP, and McFadden, DP. Acute Toxicology of Butyl Nitrites and Butyl Alcohols. Res Commun Chem Pathol Pharmocol 26 (1): 75-83, 1979.

48. Holt. PG; Finlay-Jones, LM; Keast, D; and Papadimitrous JM. Immunological Function of Mice, Chronically Exposed to Nitrogen Dioxide (No 2.) Evion Res 19: 154-162, 1979.

49. Johnson BL; Bachman, J; O'Malley, P. 1979 Highlights: Drugs and the Nation's High School Students: Five-year National Trend. National Institute On Drug Abuse.

50. Werner, M. "Inhalant Abuse," The Pharmchem Newsletter, 8 (September/October, 1979,) 4-5 Sharp and Korman, "Volatile Substances."

51. Horne, MK 3D; Waterman, MR; Simon, LM; Garriot, JC and Foerster, EH. Methemoglobinemia From Sniffing Butyl Nitrite. Ann Intern Med 91 (3): 417-418, 1979.

52. NIDA Capsules; Butyl Nitrite; Press Office of the National Institute On Drug Abuse 5600 Fishers Lane, Rockville Maryland, 20857 (April 1979)

53. Lowry, T.P. The Volatile Nitrites As Sexual Drugs: A User Survey. J Sex Educ Ther 5: 8-10, 1979

54. Haley, T.J. Review of the Philological Effects of Amyl, Butyl, and Isobutyl Nitrites. Clin Toxicol 16 (3): 317-329, 1980.

55. Pryor, G.T.; Howd, R.A.; Bingham, L.R.; Rebert, C.S.; and Jenson, R.A. Biomedical Studies On the Effects of Abused Inhalant Mixtures. Sri International Project LSU-5956. Final Report. National Institute On Drug Abuse Contract No. 271-77-3402. Feb. 4, 1980. pp 36-59

56. Lowry, T.P. Neurophysiological Aspects of Amyl Nitrite. J. Psychedilic Drugs 12: 73-74, 1980.

57. Mirvish, S.S.; Babcock, D.M.; Deshpanade, A.D. and Nagel, D.L. Identification of Cholesterol As A Mouse Skin Lipid That Reacts With Nitrogen Dioxide to Yield A Nitrosating Agent (NSA,) and of Cholesterol Nitrite As the NSA Produced In A Chemical System From Cholesterol Cancer. Lett 31: 97-104, 1980.

58. NIDA Capsules; Inhalants; Press Office of the National Institute On Drug Abuse; 5600 Fishers Lane, Rockville, Maryland; 20857 October, 1980.

59. Quinto, I. Mutagenicity of Alkylnitrites In the Salmonella Test. Boll Soc Ital Biol Sper 56: 816-820, 1980.

60. Bogovski, P., and Bogovoski, S. Animal Species In Which N-Nitroso Compounds Induce Cancer. Int J Cancer 27: 471-474, 1981.

61. Dixon, D.S.; reich, R.F.; and Santinga, P.H. Fatal Methemoglobinemia Resulting From Ingestion of Isobutyl Nitrite, A "Room Odorizer" Wildly Used For Recreational Purposes. J Forensic Sci 26: 593-597, 1981.

62. Fisher, A,A.; Brancaccio, R.R.; and Jelenek, J.E. Facial Dermatitis In Men Due To Inhalation of Butyl Nitrite. Cutis 27: 146, 152-153, 1981

63. Covalla, J.R.; Strimlan, C.V.; and Lech, J.G. Sever Tracheo-bronchitis From Inhalation of an Isobutyl Nitrite Preparation. Drug Intell Clin Pharm 15: 51-52, 1981.

64. Romeril, K.R., and Concannon, A.J. Heinz Body Haemolytic Anemia After Sniffing Volatile Nitrites. Med J Aust 1 (6): 302-303, 1981.

65. Hamilton, R.L. Report On Inhalant Abuse In Maryland; Maryland Department of Health and Mental Hygiene; Drug Abuse Administration Jan 9, 1981.

66. Shesser, R.; Mitchel, J., Edelstein, S: Methemoglo-binemia From Isobutyl Nitrite Preparations. Ann Emerg Med 10: 262-264 May, 1981.

67. Digovana, J.J., and Safai, B. Kaposi's Sarcoma: Retrospective Study of 90 Cases With Particular Emphasis On the

Familiar Occurrence, Ethnic Background and Prevalence of Other Diseases. Am J Med 71: 779-783, 1981.

68. Centers For Disease Control. Kaposi's Sarcoma and Pneumocystitis Pneumonia Among Homosexual Men-New York City and California. MMWR 30: 305-308, 1981.

69. Durach, D.T. Opportunistic Infections and Kaposi's Sarcoma In Homosexual Men. N Engl J Med 306: 1465-1467, 1981

70. Wood, R.W.; Cox, C. Acute Oral Toxicity of Butyl Nitrite J Appl Toxicol 1 (1): 30-31, 1981.

71. Jorgenson, K.A.; Lawesson, S-O. Amyl Nitrite and Kaposi's Sarcoma In Homosexual Men. N Engl J Med 307: 893-894, 1982.

72. Goedert, J.J.; Neuland, C.Y.; Wallen, W.C.; Green, M.H.; Mann, D.L.; Murray, C.; Strong, D.M.; Fraumenti, J.F.; and Blattner, W.A. Amyl Nitrite May Alter T Lymphocytes In Homosexual Men. Lancet 1: 412-416, 1982.

73. Marmer, D.J.; Jacobs, R.F. and Steele, R.W. "Invitro Immunotoxicity of Amyl Nitrite. Clinical Research P. 5, vol. 30, no. 5, 1982.

74. Marmor, M.; Friedman-Kien, A.E.; Laubenstein, L.; Byrum, R.D.; William, D.C.; Donofrio, S.; and Dubin, N. Risk Factors For Kaposi's Sarcoma in Homosexual Men. Lancet 1: 1083-1087, 1982.

75. Centers For Disease Control. Epidemiologic Aspects of the Current Outbreak of Kaposi's Sarcoma and Opportunistic Infections. N Engl J Med 306: 248-252, 1982.

76. Lowry, T.P. Psychosexual Aspects of the Volatile Nitrites. J Psychoactive Drugs 14: 77-79, 1982.

77. McManus, T.J.; Starrett, L.A.; Harris, J.R.W. Amyl Nitrite Use By Homosexuals. Lancet 2: 503, 1982

78. Goedert, J.J.; Wallen, W.C.; Mann, D.L.; Strong, D.M.; Neuland, C.Y.; Greene, M.H.; Murray, C.; Fraumeni, J.F., Jr.; and Blattner, W.A. Amyl Nitrite May Alter T Lymphocytes In Homosexual Men. Lancet 1: 412-416, 1982.

79. Watson, E. Sue; Murphy, James C. "Use of amyl nitrite may be linked to current epidemic of immunodeficiency syndrome." Unpublished letter sent to the Journal of the American Medical Association, October, 1982. (Gleaned from "Death Rush" written by John Lauritsen and Hank Wilson)

80. Quaglirello, Vincent; The Acquired immunodeficience syndrome: Current Status. Yale Journal of Biology and Medicine, pp 443-52, 1982

81. Prussman, R. Public Health Significance of Environmental N-Nitroso Compounds. In: Egan, H., ed. Environmental Carcinogens: Selected Methods of Analysis. Vol. 6, N-Nitroso Compounds. Iarc Scientific Publication no. 45. Lyon, France: International Agency For Research On Cancer, 1983 pp. 3-17.

82. Hersh, E.M.; Reuben, J.M.; Bogerd, H; Rosenblum, M.; Bielski, M; Mansell, P.W.A.; Rios, A.; Newell, G.R.; and Sonnenfield, G. Effect On the Recreational Agent Isobutyl Nitrite On Human Peripheral Blood Leukocytes and on In-vitro Interferon Production, Cancer. Res 43: 1365-1371, 1983

83. Jacobs, R.F.; Marmer, D.J.; Steele, R.W.; and Houge, T.R. Cellular immunotoxicity of Amyl Nitrite. J Toxico 20 (5): 421-449, 1983.

84. Neefe,J.R.; Ganjii, A.; Goedert, J.G. "Daily amyl nitrite inhalation decreases mouse splenocyte response to concanavalin A." (abstract 3850) Federation proceedings 42 (4): 949, 5 March 1983.

85. Centers For Disease Control "An Evaluation of the Immunotoxic Potential of Isobutal Nitrite" pp 457-458, 64 9 Sep. 83.

86. Barre-Sinoussi F.; Chermann, J.C.; Rey, F.; et al. Isolation of A T-lymphotropic Retrovirous From A Patient At Risk For Acquired Immune Deficiency Syndrome (AIDS.) science 220: 868-871 (1983)

87. Lotzovia, E.; Savary, C.A.; Hersh, E.M.; Khan, A.A.; and Rosenblum, M. Depression of Murine Natural Killer Cell Cytotoxicity by Isobutyl Nitrite. Cancer Immunol Immunother 17 (2): 130-134, 1984.

88. Osterloh, J., and Goldfield, D. Butyl Nitrite Trans-formation In-vitro, Chemical Nitrosation Reactions, and Mutagens. J Analtoxicol 8: 164-169, 1984.

89. Mayer, K.H. Inhalation Induced Immunosuppression Sniffing Out the Volatile Nitrate-AIDS Connection. Pharmaco-therapy 4: 235-236, 1984.

90. Fisher, A.A. "Poppers" or "Spappers" Dermatitis In Homosexual Men. Cutis 34 (2): 118-122, 1984.

91. Newell, G.R.; Adams, S.C.; Mansell, P.W.A. and Hersh, E.M. Toxicity, Immunosuppressive Effects and Carcinogenic Potential of Volatile Nitrites: Possible Relationship To Kaposi's Sarcoma. Pharmacotherapy 4: 284-291, 1984.

92. Popovic, M.; Sarngadharan, M.G.; Read, E.; Gallo, R.C.; Detection, Isolation, and Continuous Production of Cytopathic Retroviruses (HTLV-III) From Patient with AIDS and Pre-AIDS. Science 224: 497-500, 1984, April.

93. Curran, J.W.; Lawrence, D.N.; Jaffe, H.W.; Kaplan, J.E.; Zyla, L.D.; Chamberland, M.; Weinstein, R.; Kung-Jong, L.; Schonberger, L.B.; Spira, T.J.; Alexander, W.S.; Swinger, G.; Ammann, A.; Soloman, S; Auerbach, D.; Midvan, D.; Stoneburner, R.; Jason, J.M.; Haverkos, H.W.; and Evatt, B.L. Acquired Immunodeficiency Syndrome (AIDS) associated with transfusions. N Engl J Med 310: 69-75, 1984.

94. Averbach, D.M.; Darrow, W.W.; Jaffe, H.W.; and curran, J.W. Cluster of cases of the acquired immune deficiency syndrome: Patients linked by sexual contact. Am J Med 76: 487-492, 1984.

95. Newell, G.R.; Mansell, P.W.A.; Spitz, M.R.; Reuben, J.M.; Hersh, E.M. Volatile Nitrites: Use and Adverse Effects Related To the Current Epidemic of the Acquired Immune Deficiency Syndrome. Am J Med 78: 811-816, 1985a.

96. Newell, G.R.; Mansell, P.W.A.; Wilson, M.B.; Lynch, H.I.; Spitz, M.R.; and Hersch, E.M. Risk factor analysis among men referred for possible acquired immune deficiency syndrome. Prev Med 14: 81-91, 1985 b.

97. Lewis, D.M.; Koller, W.A.; Lynch, D.W.; and Spira, T.J. Subchronic Inhalation Toxicity of Isobutyl Nitrite In Balb/C Mice. II. Immunotoxicity Studies. J Toxicol Environ Health 15: 823-833, 1985.

98. Lynch, D.W.; Moorman, W.J.; Burg, J.R.; Phipps, F.C.; Lewis, T.R.; Khan, A.; Lewis, D.M.; Chandler, F.W.; Kimbrough, R.D.; and Spira, T.J. Subchronic Inhalation Toxicity of Isobutyl Nitrite in Balb/C Mice. I. Systemic Toxicity Studies. J Toxicol Environ Health 15: 823-833, 1985.

99. Mathur-Wagh, U.; Enlow, R.W.; Spigland, I.; Winchester, R.J.; Sacks, H.S.; Rorat, E.; Yankovitz, S.R.; Klein, M.J.; William, D.C.; and Mildvan, D. Longitudinal Study of Persistent Generalized Lymphadenopathy in Homosexual Men: Relation to Acquired Immunodeficiency Syndrome. Lance 1: 1033-1038, 1984.

100. Mathur-Wagh, U.; Mildvan, D.; and Senie, R.T. Follow up at four and one half years on homosexual men with generalized Lymphadenopathy. N Engl J Med 313: 1542-1543, 1985.

101. Osmond, D.; Moss, A.R.; Bachetti, P.; Volberding, P.; Barre-Sinoussi, F.; and Chernan, J.C. A case control study of risk factors for AIDS in San Francisco. In: International Conference of Acquired Immunodeficiency Syndrome (AIDS,) Atlanta, GA, April 14-17, 1983.

102. Gangadharam, P.R.J.; Peruman, V.K.; et al "Immuno-suppressive Action of Isobutyl Nitrite" (Presentation to the International Congress on immunopharmacology, Florence, Italy, May 1985)

103. Ortiz, J.S.; Rnera, V.L. "The Effect of Amyl Nitrite on T-cell Function In Mice." (Presentation to the American Public Health Association Convention, November, 1985.

104. Haverkos, HS; Pinsky, PF; Drotman, DP; and Bregman, DJ. Disease Manifestation Among Homosexual Men with Acquired Immunodeficiency Syndrome: A Possible Role of Nitrites in Kaposi's Sarcoma. Sex Transm Dis 12:203-208, 1985b.

105. Osmond, D; Moss, AR; Bachetti, P; Volberberding, P; Barre-Sinoussi, F; and Chermann, JC. A Case-Control Study of Risk Factors for AIDS in San Francisco. In: International Conference on Acquired Immunodeficiency Syndrome (AIDS), Atlanta, GA. April 14-17, 1985.

166

106. McFadden, DP, and Maickel, RP. Subchronic Toxicology of Butyl Nitrites in Mice by Inhalation. J. Appl Toxicol 5:134-139, 1985.

107. Lewis, DM; Koller, WA, and Lynch, DW and Spira, TJ. Subchronic Inhalation Toxicity of Isobutyl Nitrite in Balbic Mice. II Immunotoxicity Studies J Tosicol Environ Health 15:835-846, 1985.

108. Goedert, JJ; Biggar, RJ; Melbye, M; Mann, DL; Wilson, S; Gail, MH; Grossman, RJ; Digioia, RA; Sanchez, WC; Weiss, SH and Blattner, WA. Effect of T_4 Count and Cofactors on Incidence of AIDS in Homosexual Men Infected With Human Immunodeficiency Virus. JAMA 257:331-334, 1986.

109. Darrow, WW; Byers, RH; Jaffe, HW; O'Malley, PM; Rutherford, GW; and Echenberg, DF. Cofactors in the Development of AIDS and AIDS-Related Conditions. Abstract presented at the Second International Conference on AIDS, Paris, France, June 1986 p. 99.

110. Darrow, WW; Echenberg, DF; Jaffe, HW; O'Malley, PM; Byers, RH; Getchell, JP; and Curan, JW. Risk Factors For Human Immunodeficiency Virus Infections in Homosexual Men. Am J Public Health 77:479-483, 1987.

111. Polk, F; Fox, R; Brookmeyer, R; Kanchanaraksa, S; Kaslow, R; Visscher, B; Rinaldo, C; and Phair, J. Predictors of the Acquired Immunodeficiency Syndrome Developing in a Cohort of Seropositive Men. N Engl J Med 316:62-66, 1987.

112. Kensler, TW, and Taffe, BG. Free Radicals in Tumor Promotion. Adv Free Radical Biol Med 2:347-387, 1986.

113. Lauritzen, J, and Wilson, H. Death Rush: Poppers and AIDS. New York: Pagan Press, 1986 64 pp.

114. Klonne, DR; Ulrich, CE; Weismann, J; and Morgan, AK. Acute Inhalation Toxicity of Aliphatic (C_1-C_5) Nitrites in Rats. Fundam Appl Toxicol 8:101-106, 1987.

115. Mirvish, SS, and Ramm, MD. Demonstration of In Vivo Formation of the Nitrosamine N-Nitroso-N-Methylaniline from Amyl Nitrite Cancer Left 36:125-129, 1987.

116. Johnston, L; Bachman, J; O'Malley, P. Use of Licit and Illicit Drugs for American's High School Students 1975-1986. National Institute on Drug Abuse. DHH Pub No (ADM) 85-1394. Washington, D.C.: Supt of Docs., U.S. Govt. Print. Off., 1987. 159 pp.

117. Duesberg, PH. Retroviruses as Carcinogens and Pathogens: Expectations and Reality. Cancer Res. 47 (1987:1199-1220).

ADDITIONAL READING AND CORRESPONDENCE

REAPPRAISING
AIDS

MAINE MOTHER WINS COURT FIGHT
AGAINST HIV DOCTORS

This researcher belongs to, "'The Group' For The Scientific Reappraisal of AIDS". I would like to report on a major milestone, court battle and the instrumental part that "The Group" played in helping a Maine mother win her court case against the state of Maine's Department of Human Services (DHS) and the HIV AIDS establishment.

A twenty-seven year old Mother, Valerie Emerson, her son, Nicholas and daughter, Tia from Bangor, Maine had tested positive for HIV antibodies and were prescribed Zidovudine (AZT). All three had begun to experience severe headaches, muscle pain, appetite suppression and in general, symptoms associated with AZT poisoning.

Finally, during the next 12 months following the onset of AZT therapy while Valerie's and her children's health greatly diminished, her daughter, Tia died in her arms. Soon after Tia died, Valerie and Nicholas could no longer tolerate AZT and halted the drug, while almost immediately, their condition began to improve. As a result of this observation, Valerie began to question the effectiveness of AZT, as well as the theory of HIV as the cause of AIDS.

After reading about the work of Reappraising AIDS (RA) member, Professor Peter Duesberg at the University of California at Berkley, Valerie realized that HIV status was not causing her and her son's deteriorating health, rather it was the AZT. As a result, Valerie decided that she and Nicholas would stop all antiviral drug therapy permanently including the most recently touted "drug cocktail" therapies.

When attending physicians were informed of Valerie's decision, they reported her to the state of Maine Department of Human Services (DHS), citing, "serious parental neglect". The DHS officials filed a suit to take Nicholas into state custody.

Valerie, a single mother, being indigent, qualified her for assistance along with help from family and a supporter who read about the case, managed to hire a local attorney, Hilary Billings.

Billings hired two expert witnesses who sit on the RA board of directors: Protease inhibitor expert Dr. David Rasnick and physician Dr. Roberto Giraldo. Rasnick and Giraldo testified that HIV is harmless and that anti-HIV drugs provide no benefits and actually cause a variety of serious illnesses, some of them deadly, and some that even fit the description of AIDS, the very conditions they are prescribed to prevent. They also testified that Nicholas would surely die if he followed the doctor's recommendations, but had an excellent chance to live a long healthy life, if he stayed off the HIV drugs.

On September 14, 1998 Judge Douglas A. Clapp issued forth a landmark decision in favor of Valerie Emerson's right to withhold all anti-HIV drug therapy from Nicholas. He stated that the DHS "has not sufficiently proved what the benefit will likely be and that no significant injury or harm may ultimately befall the child if that therapy is now commenced. The mono (AZT) therapy, which the best doctors told Ms. Emerson was appropriate for her daughter many months ago failed fatally and is now not recommended by the same experts. Instead, they have recommended a more aggressive and powerful therapy. They may be right in this advice. Current statistics can be interpreted that they may also, just as likely be wrong . . . . . . She has discontinued her own treatment with no apparent present ill-effects. She has observed an outward improvement in her sick son's condition with a discontinuance of drug therapy. The state of Maine is now in no position to tell her in face of her unique experience that she is wrong in her current judgement . . . . The current body of information available to any mother in her situation is limited or conflicting.

He concluded that Valerie's decision to reject the HIV drugs was "rational and reasoned" and did not "place Nicholas' health or welfare in jeopardy".

The DHS declined to appeal the case, however the court appointed Guardian Ad Litem – a Maine attorney with a history of representing pharmaceutical interests – appealed to the state's Supreme Court. On November 18th "the court unanimously upheld" the earlier ruling as reported by the Associated Press.

The previous case is an excerpt from the news letter Rethinking AIDS formally titled Reappraising AIDS, the October 1998 edition. Instructions on how to subscribe to the Rethinking AIDS news letter is in the back of this book.

The Emerson vs the state of Maine case is going to be considered as a turning point in the public awareness of the pharmaceutical genocide that has been going on since AZT was first prescribed to persons suffering with AIDS. I have already informed you in this book of thousands of HIV positive persons who have been living normal lives, beating AIDS mortality statistics and even reverting to HIV negative status by refusing all antiviral durg therapy. My question to you is, why is this still a secret to the general public and why is the medical establishment still trying to cram AZT as well as all alleged antiviral drugs down people's throats? Just as Nicholas would surely die if he took any anti-HIV drug, the over 400,000 U.S. AIDS mortality statistics who have already died of AZT poisoning are not going to live long healthy lives, as Nicholas is, solely because the over 400,000 U.S. AIDS mortality statistics took AZT and Nicholas' mother has refused AZT. GOOD FOR YOU VALERIE EMERSON!

Just as the NIH/CDC/HIV AIDS branch has failed to alert the general public as well as high risk groups about the dangers of nitrite inhalants and their potential to cause AIDS, they are not informing AIDS patients that the only patients that are surviving AIDS, long term, are those who are refusing antiviral drugs.

Professor Peter Duesberg at the University of California at Berkley, has been trying for many long years to debate the chemical theory as the cause of AIDS in a public forum. The NIH/CDC/HIV AIDS branch has been censoring Dr. Duesberg by preventing him from appearing on at least 6 major network TV programs by envoking FCC pressure. Programs like Mac Neil-Lehrer News Hour; Good Morning America; CNN; Larry King; Day One; Night Line; Dr. Fauci has mysteriously appeared in Dr. Duesberg's place while the program's producers informed Professor Duesberg, in many instances, only hours before the programs were to Air that he was canceled.

It is not a matter of whether or not all of the universal treatments of choice that have been prescribed to AIDS patients since 1981 have killed the patient (chemotherapy, aggressive use of antibiotics like Bactrim or Septra, AZT, protease inhibitors, present cocktail regimens), it's only a matter of time until society finds out the truth. My answer to the NIH/CDC/HIV AIDS branch is that you can't hide the truth forever and ladies and gentleman the blood of hundreds of thousands is on your hands as well as every physician who has blindly doled out these death potions.

Dr. Peter Duesberg has been trying to tell the world medical community since 1987 that HIV was harmless and AIDS was directly related to chemical abuse. Think about it for a moment . . . how many lives would have been saved since then had all the HIV positive individuals been provided the same course that Nicholas is taking, who is going to survive an HIV positive diagnosis and live a long healthy life. The NIH/CDC/HIV AIDS branch has censored scientific debate and generated billions of tax payer's money down an HIV rat hole since 1984.

The Valerie Emerson case is extremely important for many reasons.

I

It provided public exposure to the war going on between the growing number of dissidents in the scientific community who no longer believe that HIV causes AIDS and the government HIV/AIDS establishment.

II

The case actually demonstrated a contrasting realife medical experiment rarely observed. It is very depressing that the little girl, Tia had to give her life in order to alert her mother that the antiviral drugs that they were all taking were dead wrong and would have killed all three of them had Valerie not halted the drug regimen that they were prescribed. Tia's death has not been in vain. In death, she saved her mother and brother by exposing the toxic, death dibilating effects of the antiviral drugs that were being imposed on her. On the opposite side when Tia's death prompted Valerie to halt their AZT therapy, immediately improving their health, the self evident proof that AZT was killing them became blatantly obvious. Now, that Valerie and Nicholas are getting healthier everyday, it demonstrates that HIV is not the problem that the HIV/AIDS establishment has been assuming it to be for over sixteen years. While Professor Duesberg proved in 1987, that HIV was harmless Valerie and Nicholas along with thousands of other HIV positive individuals in the U. S. who are living indefinately without antiviral drugs, are proving today in realife that HIV is able to be lived with and more than likely harmless. This interaction created a public awareness causing one to search for the answers to three primary questions. Does HIV really cause AIDS? Do anti-HIV medications help HIV positive persons? Do anti-HIV drugs actually cause full blown AIDS?

173

III

The Emerson case also supported legal precedent giving parents informed concent which allows a parent the right to choose medical treatments where questionable, conflicting prognosis prevails, especially where AIDS treatment is concerned. The verdict evidenced a maturing attitude in the courts that seemed to convey a lack of confidence in present day AIDS treatment, and rightly so.

The following Public Information Dossier was authored by Jeremy Selvey, President of International Educational Development, Inc. and Project AIDS International. The Dossier was presented to the United Nations Commission on Human rights, Geneva, Switzerland.

Permission to publish the forementioned Dossier has been granted by Jeremy Selvey.

Project AIDS International and International Educational Development, Inc., headed up by Jeremy Selvey should be commended for their work in AIDS research and their dissemination of AIDS information to the masses.

Project AIDS International can be contacted at:

Project AIDS International
8033 Sunset Boulevard #2640
Los Angeles, CA 90046-2427

PROJECT A.I.D.S., INTERNATIONAL

PUBLIC INFORMATION DOSSIER

AN URGENT APPEAL FOR ACTION

PRESENTED TO:

THE UNITED NATIONS
COMMISION ON HUMAN RIGHTS
GENEVA, SWITZERLAND
AND
MR. LUIS VARELA QUIROS
SPECIAL RAPPORTEUR

BY:

INTERNATIONAL EDUCATIONAL DEVELOPMENT, INC.
AND
PROJECT AIDS, INTERNATIONAL (PAI)

REGARDING:

AIDS, HIV AND HUMAN RIGHTS

SUMMARY

We maintain that the introduction of the chemical substance zidovudine (AZT) into HIV-positive but otherwise healthy persons – based on unproven theories that human immunodeficiency virus (HIV) is, in and of itself, the direct cause of acquired immune deficiency syndrome (AIDS) – will ultimately <u>result in their premature deaths</u>. This direction, if continued, will result in the needless deaths of millions of people worldwide. This paper will outline our findings.

Since 1984, it has been assumed that the human immunodeficiency virus (HIV) is the sole and direct cause of the acquired immune deficiency syndrome (AIDS). This assumption is based on the postulation of Dr. Robert C. Gallo (formerly a cancer researcher from the U.S. National Cancer Institute, NCI) the alleged discoverer of HIV who is currently working for the U.S. national Institutes of Health (NIH) as their leading AIDS researcher.

In December, 1992 <u>Dr. Gallo was convicted of science fraud</u> by the Office of Research Integrity – an oversight department of the NIH – based on his declaration that he had discovered HIV. In fact, the discovery of HIV had been accredited to Dr. Luc Montagnier of the Institutes de Pasteur in France. Dr. Montagnier has stated on numerous occasions, *"I do not believe that HIV is, in and of itself, the cause of AIDS. I believe we should place as much emphasis on potential co-factors as we have on HIV"*.

Dr. Gallo is currently under investigation by the U.S. Congress on various other charges of scientific fraud, which by their very accusation, cast doubts on the validity of any of Dr. Gallo's work pertaining to AIDS. In addition, Dr. Gallo has received, and continues to receive, millions of dollars in royalties based on the test he created for HIV.

Based on Dr. Gallo's unproven hypothesis that HIV is the sole and direct cause of AIDS, the U.S. Public Health Service[1] has embarked on a campaign of implied terror and misinformation that has continued to state that *"HIV, the virus that causes AIDS"* can be

---

[1] Consisting of the Center for Disease Control (CDC), National Institutes of Health (NIH), Food and Drug Administration (FDA) and other governmental health care agencies.

controlled by getting tested for the "AIDS virus" and starting early intervention in the event of a positive test result. Early intervention is defined as starting "treatment" with the drug zidovudine, also known as AZT – a nonselective nucleoside analogue, DNA chain terminating chemotherapy manufactured by Wellcome, Ltd. AZT is cytotoxic, in that it <u>kills all cells</u> indiscriminately, not just those cells infected by HIV.

In addition, promoters of this false hypothesis state that the "proper monitoring of your T-Cells" will assure that you will know at what stage to begin AZT treatment. The current primary measure for early intervention with AZT is when your T-Cells (specifically CD4+ helper Cells) "fall to 500 or below on two consecutive blood tests". The CDC states (without benefit of scientific reference) that the "normal" range for CD4+ helper cells in HIV-negative "healthy" person is 600 to 1,200. However, based on PAI's research, given the published information in accredited medical journals[2] the normal range of CD4+ helper cells for healthy HIV-negative adults is 237 0 1,817.

Further, in tests completed on U.S. Olympic athletes in 1984, the average range of CD4+ helper cells was between 400 and 600. Certainly, the U.S. athletes were not considered to be unhealthy; yet these are the markers used in instill fear and manipulate HIV-positive persons into taking a toxic chemotherapy when they are otherwise healthy.

Project AIDS International charges that this dogmatic hypothesis based on the findings of a person <u>convicted of science fraud</u>, and the perpetration of this information by the United States government who continues employing Dr. Gallo is either directly or indirectly responsible for the premature deaths of hundreds of thousands of people worldwide.

In the following pages, we will explain – with properly cited scientific data from some of the world's most respected and renowned scientists and medical professionals – the basis for our charges concerning the violation of the most basic human right – <u>the right to life</u> – by the practice of financial profit over human life.

---

[2] Journal of the American medical Association (JAMA) Denny, et al. 1992, vol. 267; 1484-1488.

Project AIDS International and International Educational Development, Inc. <u>strongly</u> urge the United Nations to:

1. Intervene in the dissemination of propaganda with regard to the unfounded hypothesis that HIV is the direct cause of AIDS.

2. Ban the use of AZT and all nonselective nucleoside analogue – DNA chain terminating drugs, which have been falsely identified as "antivirals", in treating HIV-positive persons who otherwise show no signs of clinical illness. We propose that the ban be in effect until such time as they have been irrefutably proven to be effective, viable treatments against acquired immune deficiency syndrome.

The urgency of this matter cannot be over emphasized. Millions of lives are at stake. Your intervention is of the utmost importance.

OUTLINE IN DETAIL

Human immunodeficiency virus (HIV) is said to be the virus that causes acquired immune deficiency syndrome (AIDS). This virus is inappropriately named, as it has never been proven to cause immunodeficiency in either animals or humans. Further, it is not even found in all cases of AIDS[3]. Koch's Postulates which are the most widely accepted criteria for the definition of a disease state that three factors must exist in order *"to prove that a microorganism is the cause of a disease"*.

1. *"....it must be present in all cases of a specific disease...."*
   Note: HIV is not present in all cases of AIDS.

2. *"....inoculations of its pure culture must produce the same disease in animals...."*
   Note: efforts to produce AIDS by inoculation in animals have been unsuccessful.

3. *"....and from these it must be obtained in pure cultures and propagated."*
   Note: this has yet to be accomplished.

Therefore, <u>HIV cannot be the direct cause of AIDS</u>. This may also explain why we have "long term survivors" who are HIV-positive and without symptoms in excess of fourteen (14) years[4].

A paper published in 1990 by Beverly E. Griffin[5] quotes two London microbiologists who say, *"It would be irresponsible to produce guidelines on AIDS until an infectious microorganism is identified and the means by which it caused disease are understood. It is only now becoming obvious that infection with HIV does not usually give rise to AIDS"*.

---

[3] U.S. CDC Report of AIDS cases without the presence of HIV – December 1992
[4] UCSF – Buchbinder, et. Al. "HIV + Long Term Survivor Study" – October 1992
[5] Director and Professor of Virology, Royal Postgraduate Medical School, London – Nature, May 1990

HIV-FREE AIDS

On July 1992 the CDC reported unexplained CD4+ T-lymphocyte depletion in persons without the presence of HIV. This occurred after it was unexpectedly announced at the Eighth Annual International Conference on AIDS in Amsterdam that these cases had been observed and documented. In its report CDC originally defined these cases as having the human intracesternal retrovirus (HICRV), but changed the definition to read idiopathic CD4+ T-lymphocytopenia (ICL). Thus, <u>cases of AIDS exist without the presence of HIV.</u>

PAI contacted the CDC several times and found that they disavowed any knowledge of cases of HICRV or ICL. After speaking with several physicians and scientists working in conjunction with various government offices it was reported[6] there exists over two thousand cases of HIV-free AIDS; however, we were cautioned that, even though this is a public health issue, this <u>information was (and is) embargoed.</u>

After much pressure from PAI, CDC sent documentation of at least *thirty (30)* cases of HIV-free AIDS. Subsequently, as of December 31, 1992, CDC reported *ninety-seven (97)* such cases. Since 1985 there have been cases of HIV-free AIDS reported and <u>confirmed</u> by the serology of p24 antigen expression, polymearse chain reaction (PCR) and viral culture tests. In light of the incidence of HIV-free AIDS and HIV-positive long term survivors without progression to AIDS, how can we permit the dominant notion that HIV is "the virus that caused AIDS" to be perpetuated?

This single-minded approach to AIDS research *<u>has not saved one life,</u>* and precludes any other form of potentially viable research into the actual cause(s), or treatment option(s), of the condition termed AIDS.

Robert Root-Berstein, an Associate Professor of Physiology at Michigan State University states, *"On the existence of HIV-free AIDS, if non-HIV immunosuppressive agents can cause AIDS in HIV-free people, they can also cause AIDS in HIV-infected people. It's time to re-evaluate the HIV/AIDS hypothesis".*

---

[6] P.H. Duesberg, Science, September 1992

LIFE THREATENING PROPAGANDA

In pursuit of answers, PAI contacted the CDC in January 1993 for scientific citation as to their claim that HIV was, in fact, the cause of AIDS. An unidentified person at CDC stated that "it was just known" that HIV causes AIDS; but was <u>unable to cite any scientific reference</u>. In response to our demand for documentation, three weeks later we received an information packet citing Dr. Gallo's published paper[7] on the cause of AIDS that stated, unequivocally, HIV was the sole and direct cause of AIDS. Since receiving this document it was reported that Dr. Gallo was convicted of one count of science fraud for <u>falsifying official scientific documentation</u> with other charges pending.

PAI questions why the CDC spends so much money in marketing this false hypothesis via the media and in print. By misinforming the medical profession and the general public, and creating a climate of fear and despair, CDC is not only acting irresponsibly, but also is <u>intentionally inflicting undue mental duress</u> on its citizens.

It is with grave concern that PAI recognizes that the scientific and medical practices of the United States are accepted without question as an authority in most developing countries, with the same faith that U.S. citizens placed in Dr. Gallo. If we have been deceived it has surely <u>cost hundreds of thousands of lives</u> and will ultimately result in the <u>needless loss of millions of lives worldwide</u>.

In what appears to be a conspiracy of profit over life, we wish to call attention to the propaganda of various AIDS educational publications; especially those documents published by the CDC in conjunction with the Pharmaceutical Manufacturer's Assocation[8] [which is also endorsed by the U.S. FDA] and includes the sharing of letterhead with the Pharmaceutical Advertising Counsel[9]. This appears to indicate an implication of impropriety based on the fact that the U.S. FDA is an enforcement agency charged with the regulation of all legal drugs and, therefore, should maintain a professional distance from private pharmaceutical interests so as to remain an impartial, unbiased oversight agency.

This has resulted in a monopoly of manipulation based on an unproven HIV hypothesis which is being actively marketed to the people by both private and government sectors for the sake of financial gain at the expense of human life.

---

[7] Journal of Acquired Immune Deficiency Syndromes 1:521-535 / 1988
[8] A private sector trade union of which Wellcome is a member
[9] Document Number A6 / PAI Archives 1992

AZT: AIDS BY PRESCRIPTION

The drug zidovudine, known as AZT under the brand name Retrovir(, is a nucleoside analogue DNA chain terminator: it <u>kills human cells indiscriminately</u> by terminating DNA synthesis, which is the central molecule of life.

AZT was claimed by the manufacturer (Wellcome, Ltd. UK) to be the only drug of the AIDS crisis, at a time when desperate AIDS patients had lost all hope. Burroughs-Wellcome Company[10] alleged that they were the creators of AZT – only after realizing that a very profitable market existed for "long term" treatment with the drug.

Burroughs-Wellcome's statement contradicts the assertion of Dr. Jerome Horowitz[11] who claims that he created AZT in 1964. This was followed by an onslaught of scandals alleging bribes, payoffs and cover-ups regarding the initial clinical trials of the toxicity and effectiveness of AZT. Despite the previous claims of discovery, it was uncovered by PAI that AZT was originally created by Dr. Richard Beltz in 1961 during his research of nucleoside analogues dating back to 1951[12].

According to Dr. Beltz the reasons that AZT was abandoned were: 1) its extreme toxicity made it unsuitable for any chemotherapy – even short term. and 2) it was carcinogenic (cancer causing) at any dose.

IN a quote by Dr. Peter H. Duesberg[13], *"Since AZT cannot distinguish HIV infected cells from uninfected cells, and only one in one thousand CD4 cells (1/1000) is ever infected, AZT must kill nine hundred and ninety-nine healthy cells for every one cell infected (999/1). AZT suppresses HIV by suppressing the manufacturing of CD4 cells, predictably causing anemia, immunodeficiency and other degenerative diseases; thus AZT is AIDS by prescription".*

---

[10] A U.S. subsidiary of Wellcome, Ltd.
[11] A researcher for NIH
[12] R. Walters Thesis, Lorna Linda University – 1972 / PAI Archives
[13] Profession of Molecular Cell Biology, UC Berkeley and a distinguished member of the National Academy of Science

BABIES ARE DYING...
AND THEY'RE NOT EVEN SICK!

An eighteen month study consisting of three dozen pediatric physicians in ten European cities[14] states that of 372 infants born to HIV-positive mothers, only _13%_ of the infants ever acquired the HIV virus. Thus, _87%_ of the infants who showed to be HIV-positive, either by presumption or serology, seroconverted to HIV-negative within eighteen months without therapeutic intervention.

In the United States, this has been further documented[15] in a study demonstrating that approximately _two thirds_ of infants born to HIV-positive mothers also seroconverted to HIV-negative within eighteen months; again, without therapeutic intervention.

From this, one could conclude that the practice of treating HIV-positive infants with AZT – based on 1) tests with questionable accuracy such as the ELISA and Western Blot, and/or 2) presumptive diagnosis when no clinical illness is present – is **murder**. Murder as used here means _"the introduction of a known toxic substance that ultimately results in the infant's premature death"_. The fact that prescribing AZT is considered a "majority practice" is no defense for the violation of the basic human right to life.

Physicians in the United States are under an oath to "…..do no harm". The 18th World Medical Assembly in Hellsinki, Finland in June of 1964 binds physicians with the words "…the health of my patient shall be my first consideration". The American Medical Association (AMA) is a signature to this declaration. Why then, do physicians worldwide dispense the toxin AZT to otherwise healthy persons when they know its effects?

---

[14] Peckham, et. Al. Infant Seroconversion Profile London - 1990
[15] New York University Medical Center Pediatric Department - 1990

AZT: DEFENSES BY WELLCOME

Wellcome, Ltd. Cites numerous studies to substantiate their claims that AZT both "prolongs life" and "enhances its quality". An analysis shows an overwhelming concern of impropriety of data based on one simple fact: <u>all studies that tout AZT's benefits are made possible, either directly or indirectly, by grant money from Burroughs-Wellcome Foundation</u>. Studies that show impartial data are done so without the influence of Wellcome, Ltd. And indicate that AZT <u>neither</u> prolongs life or enhances its quality[16,17]. The U.S. original Phase I and II clinical trials of the safety and efficacy of AZT were patently fraudulent and criminal in their application[18]. This information clearly demonstrates that the U.S. FDA is <u>criminally liable</u> for <u>violating the very laws that they are entrusted to enforce</u>.

WELLCOME'S DECEPTION

The Failure of Burroughs-Wellcome and the U.S. FDA to disclose the facts that the use of AZT <u>will result in the patient's premature death</u> is not just restricted to the U.S. Throughout the United Kingdom Wellcome's propaganda continues to cite unfounded promises of hope in an outlandish breach of truth in advertising. According to Wellcome's information pamphlet, "Positive Benefits", there are *"no life threatening side effects associated with zidovudine".*

Meditel, a London based medical television production company, filed criminal complaints against Wellcome with the Medicines Control Agency (MCA) in England. This action was based on the breach of Section 93 of the Medicines Control Act by misleading claims of the benefits of AZT in Wellcome's advertising in the UK[19]. As a result, Wellcome filed a complaint against Meditel for libel with the Broadcast Complaints Commission. However, they ceased their action when Meditel demanded clinical registry information on persons who have lived longer than three years on AZT. Since Wellcome was <u>unable to provide the required data</u> they retracted their complaint against Meditel. Still the MCA has taken no satisfactory actions against Wellcome for reasons not as yet made clear.

16,17 Hamilton, et. Al. VA Study 1990 / CDC Unreleased Study 1990
18 U.S. Freedom of Information Act documents - 1986
19 Wellcome, Ltd. Brochure – "Positive Benefits"

Meditel's complaint addressed to Professor William Asscher[20] states: *"We are particularly concerned about four claims and one omission in Wellcome's literature about AZT. These matters are very serious, in deed, as we believe that Wellcome's ëPositive Benefits' brochure and leaflet on AZT produced together with the Terrence Higgins Trust should be withdrawn immediately whilst these matters are being investigated".*

In a quote from Dr. Joseph Sonnabend, a renowned AIDS researcher in the U.S., regarding AZT: *"It is beyond belief, I don't know what to do, I'm ashamed of my colleagues. I'm embarrassed. This is such shoddy science, it's hard to believe nobody's protesting. Damned cowards! The name of the game is to protect your grants. Don't open your mouth. It's all about money. It's ground for just following the party line and not being critical when there are obvious financial and political forces that are driving this".*

Dr. Sonnabend filed a report[21] questioning the basis for the licensing of AZT. He was never even given a reply from either the U.S. FDA or Burroughs-Wellcome.

Dr. Harvey Bialy, a molecular biologist and science editor of BIO/TECHNOLOGY states, *"I'm stunned by the low quality of science surrounding AIDS research. I'm horrified by the widespread use of AZT. Not just because it is toxic, but because <u>the claims of efficacy are false</u>. I can't see how this drug can be doing anything other than <u>making people very sick</u>".* [PAI emphasis]

AZT: NOT TOXIC?

Here is a list of the effects of AZT that Wellcome says *"improves the quality of life":*

Anemia requiring blood transfusions – cancer – bone marrow depletion – granulocytopenia – nose bleeds – hemtologic toxicity – fever – malaise – loss of mental acuity – paresthesia – atrophy – diarrhea – diaphoresis – dyspnea – headaches – taste perversion – insomnia – confusion – anorexia – ambloypia – vomiting – neuropathy – skin rash – asthenia -anxiety – nausea – dizziness –

---

20 Committee on Safety of Medicines, St. George's Medical School, London
21 J.A. Sonnabend Report on MultiCenter Study of AZT to FDA - 1987

somnolence – dyspepsia – myalgia – impotence – depression – vertigo – hearing loss – photophobia – nervousness – seizures – leukocytopenia (which is the immunodeficiency of white cells).

In addition to the above, studies indicated that the original toxicity profile[22] of AZT was fraudulently reported and is actually **1,000 times** more toxic to human cells than what was originally claimed[23]; therefore, the drug is <u>more harmful than beneficial</u> with no therapeutic window.

The pharmaceutical industry's and U.S. government's joint endorsement of "early intervention" (the prescribed use of AZT in persons who are otherwise clinically free of illness) suggests a form of criminally negligent homicide. People who are not clinically ill are becoming sick based on a toxic treatment given for an unproven hypothesis. Wellcome and the U.S. government fund most U.S.-based nonprofit organizations who perpetuate this myth and recommend the use of AZT "as soon as you get your positive test result".

CONCLUSION

If action is not taken **immediately** against those who are directly or indirectly responsible for these crimes against humanity through the practice of profit over life, the drug-induced AIDS deaths will, most certainly, reach proportions <u>unparalleled by any natural catastrophe in human history</u>. Even one case of deprivation of this most basic human right – the right to life – should be the concern of all mankind.

[22] Chernov, 1986; Elwell et al., 1987; Yarchoan and Broder, 1987b; Smothers, 1991; Yarchoan et al. 1991
[23] P.H. Duesberg, Pharmac.Ther.. Vol. 55, pp201-277 / Alvramis et al. 1989 / Balzarini et al. 1989 / Ho and Hitchcock, 1989 / Hitchcock, 1991

PRESS STATEMENT
08 March 1993

I). Changing The Hypothesis. HIV-AIDS=Death

1981 - Clinical description of increased frequency of Kaposi's sarcoma (KS) and Pneumocystis Carininii Pneumonia (PCP) in gay males in the United States reported to Centers for Disease Control (CDC) by Dr. Michael Gottlieb of the University of California at Los Angeles (UCLA).

1983 – Dr. Luc Montagnier, et al. Describes retrovirus termed LAV in lymphocytes in AIDS patient.

1984 – (1) **Dr. Robert Gallo**, et al. Publish experimental findings that the human immunodeficiency virus [HIV] (identical to the French LAV) destroys lymphocytes (T-4 immune cells by "directly killing" them in *vitro.*

(2) HIV infection declared to be the single cause of Acquired Immune Deficiency Syndrome [AIDS].

(3) Dr. Gallo receives patent rights for HIV-antibody test ("AIDS test") worldwide.

(4) CDC definition of AIDS in gay males and hemophiliacs in the United States reads as those with T4 cells $\leq 200/$ µl with HIV antibody presence. *(Morbidity and Mortality Weekly Report [MMWR] 1984)*

1986 – In a sworn statement given in the patent interference case Dr. Gallo maintains he *"saw no evidence"* that LAV was the cause of AIDS *"up through the allowance of the Gallo patent"*. *(Crewdson – Chicago Tribune, November 1989 – received through the Freedom Of Information Act).*

1987 – Dr. Peter H. Duesberg questions destruction of T-cells *in viro* and states "no direct killing" of T-cells by HIV.

1988 – Dr. Gallo retracts his hypothesis of the "direct killing" of T4 immune cells by HIV and suggests perhaps more important indirect mechanisms other then HIV are contributing to T4 cell depletion. *(Journal of Acquired Immune Deficiency Syndromes, vol. 1, #6 1988, page 525).*

1990 – Dr. Montagnier, et al. Posts experimental evidence that HIV does **not** kit T-cells. *(Science, May 1990) / (Research in Virology, March 1990)*

1992 – Several scientists and medical professionals of the international group rethinking AIDS propose the reappraisal of the HIV=AIDS=DEATH hypothesis.

1993 – (1) fifteen years after the alleged beginning of HIV infection in the western world, published evidence indicates that the majority of people with HIV are not getting AIDS, with numerous documentation that AIDS conditions exist without the presence of HIV. *(WHO Weekly Epidemic Report #42, 1992 / P.H. Duesberg, Science, September 1992).*

None of the hypotheses of Gallo (HIV=AIDS=DEATH), Montagnier (HIV+co-factor M. Incognito = AIDS), Duesberg (Drugs=AIDS) or any other scientist of direct, or indirect killing of T4 cells has been proven.

II). Use Of AZT As A Consequence Of The HIV=AIDS Hypothesis

(1) AZT is a synthetically manufactured molecule that is being integrated into the genes of all human cells; therefore, it blocks the replication of the genes; thus causing a deficit in new cells. Sooner or later these exists a lack of newly produced immune cells which causes the condition that is called AIDS.

(2) The effect of AZT to inhibit the new maturation of cells also includes, temporarily, all microbes that are present in the body (i.e.: virus', vacteria's and so on).

This temporary inhibition of microbes will result in, sooner or later, the lack of newly moderated necessary body cells such as red and white blood cells, stomach mucosa, immune cells, etc. The organism that is so weakened now has to cope with the resistant (by mutation) microbes.

Thus, the patient is dying of AIDS because not only the one of the one thousand T4 cells infected with HIV is damaged or killed, but, so too, are the nine hundred and ninety-nine cells that are not infected.

III). Conclusion

The patient is not dying of the unproven destruction of human cells by HIV, but by the proven effect of AZT.

Therefore, we state that the use of AZT is both (a) cruel treatment and (b) fulfills the fact of clean torture. We state **"cruel treatment"** because the patient has been given a death sentence based on the unproven hypothesis of HIV=AIDS=DEATH and the patient cannot escape the physician's authority (also know as a "fear trap") that the patient must take AZT.

We state **"clean torture"** because the death caused by AZT will be said that it was the prognosed death caused by HIV infection. The result is a "self-fulfilling prophesy". The cause of death will be called HIV infection rather than the treatment prescribed through the physicians. While the patient is dead, the physicians are left clean.

UNITED NATIONS HUMAN RIGHTS COMMISSION (UNHRC)
Geneva, Switzerland
March 1993

PRESS RELEASE HR/3358
08 March 1993 (afternoon) page 13
Children's Issues – Agenda Item 24

"KAREN PARKER (International Educational Development) said that children in the United States suffered the most governmental disregard of any in the developed world. The United states had a relatively high percentage of children born to HIV-positive mothers. Studies showed that between two thirds to 87 percent of those infants would seroconvert to HIV-negative within 18 months without any therapeutic interventions. Unfortunately, many infants were treated with AZT, a drug whose extreme toxicity had been bringing it under scrutiny. According to many researchers, there was no rational reasons to give HIV-positive babies that drug – the drug itself would surely kill them. The international community, and especially developing countries where AIDS was a crisis situation, needed to have all appropriate mechanisms such as adequate drug monitoring in order to ensure compliance with the most basic right – the right to life".

PRESS RELEASE HR/3360
09 March 1993 (afternoon) page 14
Science and Technology – Agenda Item 14

"KAREN PARKER (International Educational Development) said the introduction of the chemical substance AZT into HIV-positive but otherwise healthy persons was based on unproven theories that human immunodeficiency virus (HIV) was the direct cause of acquired immune deficiency syndrome (AIDS). It, not AIDS, ultimately resulted in their premature deaths. Based on Dr. Robert C. Gallo's unproven hypothesis that HIV was the sole and direct cause of AIDS, the United States Public Service had embarked on a campaign that had continued to state that HIV would be controlled by getting tested for the "AIDS virus" and staring early intervention in

194

the event of a positive test result. This dogmatic hypothesis based on a person convicted of science fraud and the perpetration of this information by the United States Government was either directly or indirectly responsible for the premature deaths of hundreds of thousands of people worldwide. She urged the United Nations to intervene in the dissemination of propaganda with regard to the unfounded hypothesis that HIV was the direct cause of AIDS and urge a ban on the use of AZT".

EXCERPT FROM

The Daily Telegraph
London – 03 April 1993

**HIV Carriers
Advised To Stop Their Treatment**

By Peter Pallot
Health Services Staff

A LEADING specialists told 13,000 apparently healthy people infected with the AIDS virus yesterday that would be better off without drug therapy.

Professor Tony Pinching, director of immunology at St. Bartholomew's Hospital, London, urged symptomless HIV-positive individuals to "hang around" after publication of research showing the drug AZT failed to stop the development of AIDS.

Thousands of people are taking AZT, manufactured by Wellcome, in the hope of delaying development of the disease, which occurs on average about 10 years after exposure to the virus.

Prof. Pinching said: "The necessity to do something should not be presumed. There may be people who remain well indefinitely; that is still a possibility".

"The situation before the trial was that preliminary data, certainly not conclusive, suggested we could intervene with treatment in symptomless individuals. But we also said it was perfectly appropriate to wait until they became ill before intervening with AZT.

195

It is now clear that AZT is not the answer, and people should hang around until other trials are concluded".

Prof. Pinching added that the latest three-year international study, involving 1,749 people, had "brought us back to earth".

Patricia Wilson in Washington writes: American health officials reacted cautiously to Anglo-French research showing that AZT provides little, if any, benefit. The findings of the European trial run counter to the practice among American AIDS experts of recommending patients infected with the HIV virus to begin taking AZT long before the onset of fully-fledged AIDS.

WHERE DO WE GO FROM HERE......

Our continuous action at the United Nations is to call other's attention that what was, and is being done for AIDS research and treatment has not shown to be viable – clearly indicating that the need exists to pursue "new options" that do not, in and of themselves, pose such a serious health risk as conventional approaches have shown, as well as research into other potential causes of AIDS that do not follow the HIV model.

Our purpose is to continue our research into other possible factors as to the cause(s) and treatment(s) of the condition AIDS. We will be providing periodic Public Awareness meetings that will offer a clear, unbiased forum for both the conventional and the alternative sectors of AIDS research. It is the position of Project AIDS, International that in order for persons affected by AIDS to make *informed* decisions regarding treatment options – if any are warranted – they must first be aware of as much information as is available on the treatment in questions.

For conventional physicians to discount or discredit alternative approaches that have shown scientific viability – based on ego, ignorance, or simple refusal without scientific basis – is wholly irresponsible and clearly indicates a lack of concern for the patient. The same holds true of alternative practitioners who discount the viability of all orthodox treatment approaches – again, either out of ignorance, ego or simple refusal.

We are in this for the long haul. Still, our greatest hope is that we may see the day when our services are no longer required. When the threat of AIDS has been reduced to historical reference and truth in science and medicine has been restored, we will then have accomplished what we originally set out to do.

Help us reach this day – today.

The following Curriculum Vitae of the late Dr. Robert Willner M.D., Ph.D. and author of the AIDS book title "DEADLY DECEPTION", is printed here to establish Dr. Wilner's credentials in the process of presenting additional support for the AIDS/chemical hypothesis as the true and only cause of immune dysfunction that leads to AIDS. Following Dr. Willner's Vitae, is printed with his permission, a white paper titled, "A Call For Truth", along with an open letter to fellow colleagues in the medical profession. The forementioned, are excerpts from the book "Deadly Deception" published by Peltic Publishing in Bacoa Raton Fla.

As you will see, Dr. Willner's beliefs and approach to the AIDS crisis are similar to this author's as well as hundreds of other research scientists, Noble Prize winners, doctors and professional persons who are presently re-appraising the AIDS/HIV hypothesis.

Curriculum Vitae – Robert E. Willner, M.D., Ph.D.

EDUCATIONAL BACKGROUND

1987   University for Humanistic Studies (accredited)
Las Vegas, Nevada
Degree: Doctor of Human Letters (Ph.D., In Nutrition)

1951-1955   New York Medical College
New York City, New York
Degree: Doctor of Medicine

1948-1951   New York University College of Arts and Sciences,
University Heights
New York City, New York
Degree: Bachelor of Arts
(Major: Psychology, Minor: Biochemistry, Music)

1947-1948   University of Southern California
Los Angeles, California
Freshman Year Toward B.A. Degree

1943-1947   Music and Art High School
New York City, New York
Degree: High School Diploma, Music Major

POSTGRADUATE ACTIVITIES

1987   American Board of Pain Management Specialties
Fellow (FABPMS-C)

American Academy of Neurologic and Orthopedic
Medicine and Surgery, Fellow (FAANaOS-Cm)

American Board of Legal Analysis In Medicine and
Surgery, Fellow (FABLAAMS)

1983   Chelation Therapy Workshop
The American Academy of Medical Preventics Reno,
Nevada

1979   The American Board of Family Physicians Recertification

1976	Postgraduate Institute for Emergency Medical Care University of California, San Diego "Our Inner Conflicts" CE208 School of Continuing Studies University of Miami, Miami Florida
1974	Second World Symposium on Acupuncture and Chinese Medicine The American Society of Chinese Medicine
1973	The American Association of Sex Educators and Counsel American University Certificate In Sex Education
1972	American Board of Family Medicine Diplomate (ABFMD)
1961	Arroyo Academy of Advanced Hypnosis Certification
1959	Florida Board of Medical Examiners Certification
1956	School of Aviation Medicine – Basic Certification
1955	National Board of Medical Examiners

POSTGRADUATE PROFESSIONAL CAREER

1959-1989	Private Practice of Medicine, North Miami Beach, Florida
1955-1959	United Sates Air Force, General Medical Officer, Chief of Emergency Service, Chief of Obstetrical Service, Base Psychiatric Officer
1955-1956	Memorial Hospital, Phoenix, Arizona – Internship
1954-1955	Flower and Fifth Avenue Hospital New York, New York - Internship Bird S. Coler Hospital For Physical Medicine and Rehabilitation - Internship

SOCIETY MEMBERSHIPS

1989-1991   American Physicians Associations

1985-1991   American College of Advancement In Medicine

1984-1991   American Academy of Neurological and Orthopedic Medicine and Surgery

1962-1987   Southern Medical Association

1983   International Association for the Study of Pain

1983   International Laser Research Academy

1979   German Academy of Auricular Medicine

1979   American Society of Bariatric Physicians

1975   South Florida Council of Medical Staffs

1972   American Institute of Hypnosis

1960   American Medical Association
Florida Medical Association Dade County Medical Assoc.
American Academy of Family Physicians
Florida Academy of Family Physicians
Dade County Academy of Family Physicians

1952   Phi Delta Epsilon Medical Fraternity

HOSPITAL ASSOCIATIONS

1960-1989   Parkway Regional Medical Center, North Miami Beach Florida – Senior Attending Physician

HONORS AND SPECIAL ACTIVITIES

1990-1991   American College of Advancement In Medicine Sergeant At Arms

1989-1991	American Physicians Association Executive Secretary
1988-1991	American Academy of Advancement In Medicine Board of Directors
1987-1991	American Board of Pain Management Specialties Professor and Chairman
1983-1984	International Laser Research Academy President
	Linda Georgian Television Show Medical Advisor
1982-1984	Conference of Holistic Medicine – Walter Reed Hospital, Washington D.C. Lecturer
1977-1984	Concept House Drug Rehabilitation – Miami Florida Medical Director
1981-1982	Medical Research Laboratories – Chicago, Illinois Medical Director
1980-1982	Oleda, Inc. – New York City, New York Medical Director
1980	The Funhouse Motion Company – "The Funhouse" Medical Consultant
	McGill University Medical School Preceptor
1978-1980	Florida International University Lecturer
	University of Miami School of Medicine Lecturer
1979	Paramount Pictures Corporation – "Spanner's Key" Medical Consultant

1962-1979   Dade County Medical Association
Lecturer

1978   Truman Van Dyke Company Medical – "Woman In White"
Consultant

1978   Nurse Practitioner Program – University of Miami
Preceptor

1977-1978   National Acupuncture Research Society
Board of Directors

1974-1977   National Acupuncture Research Society Faculty

1977   Motion Picture "The Champ"
Medical Consultant

1972-1976   Spectrum House Rehabilitation Center – Miami Florida
Medical Director

1975   South Florida Council of Medical Staffs
Secretary

1974   Florida Academy of Family Physicians
Vice President

American Medical Association Physician,
Recognition Award

American Academy of Family Physicians,
Award Certificate

1968-1974   Dade County Academy of Family Physicians
Board of Directors

1968-1974   Florida Academy of Family Physicians
Board of Directors

1973   American Academy of Family Physicians
Charter Fellow

1972   Parkway General Hospital – Certificate of Appreciation
Chief of Staff

1971	Parkway General Hospital – Dept. of Family Practice Chairman
1970-1971	Dade County Academy of Family Practice President
1966	City of North Miami Beach – Certificate of Recognition and Appreciation
1955	Cor et Manus New York Medical College Award of Distinction
1951	National Student Association New York University Senior Delegate
	Perstare et Praestare New York University Honor Society
	Student Council New York University

POSTGRADUATE EDUCATION

1976-1987	Parkway Regional Medical Center Continuing Education Seminars – Forty Credits Per Annum
1986	American Academy of Neurologic and Orthopedic Medicine and Surgery "Communication Skills Workshops" Fifty Hours, Las Vegas, Nevada
1986	"Allergy In Practice" Roche Biomedical Laboratories – Miami Florida
1975	Advanced Acupuncture Workshop National Acupuncture Research Society
1974	Intermediate Acupuncture Workshop National Acupuncture Research Society
1972	Family Practice Review Course University of Alabama, School of Medicine

PUBLICATIONS

1993	Deadly Deception, Peltec Publications, Ltd.

The Cancer Solution, Peltec Publications, Ltd.

1984   *The Pleasure Principle Diet*, Prentice-Hall, May 1985
ISBN O-13-683442-6 (225 pages).

The Effect Of Low Power On Osteoarthritis Of The Hands, IV World Pain Congress
Seattle, Washington 1978

Communicating With The Depress Elderly Patients
Co-author: Marcia Willner
Continuing Education, November 1978

1974   *Acupuncture Desk Reference*

Touching Is.....

Acupuncture Wall Charts

Professional Acupuncture Seminar Workbook

LECTURES

Over 250 presentations have been given to the profession and the public. Many radio and television appearances have been taped. A list of most of the lectures is available on request. Some audio and video tapes are also available.

PERSONAL DATA

Date of Birth: June 21, 1929
Place of Birth: New York City, New York

RECENT ACTIVITIES

1989-1993   Retired from the practice of medicine to pursue research in Cancer, AIDS, Chronic Degenerative Diseases and solutions to ecological problems.

Productos Ecologicos De Mexico, S.A. de C.V., Medical
Ecological Director

1993   Cydel medical Center for Advanced Therapies, Consulting Executive Medical Director to update and expand Therapeutic program.

Life-Line Consultants
Executive Director
Independent Guidance to the Availability of Therapeutic Solutions to Cancer, AIDS and Chronic Degenerative Diseases

A CALL FOR THE TRUTH
(A White Paper On The Viral-AIDS Hypothesis)
Robert E. Willner, M.D., Ph.D.

The history of medicine contains a plethora of instances in which physicians have acted tragically under "consensus of opinion" rather than relying on substantial scientific evidence. This practice has its origins in the long-held concept that medicine is an "art" rather than a science. In recent decades, the major advances in technology have allowed us to emerge from the "dark ages" of diagnostic and therapeutic doctrines that were often based on personal prejudice and "medical politics". Unfortunately, we have also fallen victim to fraudulent scientific papers because of the inherent trust we place in our colleagues engaged in arcane areas of medical research. In the early 1980's, physicians became aware of what appeared to be an emerging epidemic which is now known throughout the world as AIDS. Along with all of my colleagues, I eagerly followed the releases from the "authorities" about the progress of the disease and the involved explanations related to behavior of the new retrovirus which was given the designation HIV. In spite of my relative ignorance about retroviruses, I became suspicious that something was awry when retrovirologists, who had spent twenty years and in excess of twenty billion dollars in research on viruses, became involved in extensive apologetics with reference to HIV. They began to use terms such as "mysterious" and "intelligent" in the ever growing number of additional hypo-thetical explanations needed in the attempt to clear up the contradictions arising with reference to the original virus — AIDS **HYPOTHESIS**. I underscore the work hypothesis to remind my colleagues that the so-called AIDS virus has never been proven scientifically to cause any disease, let along AIDS. Every scientific pronouncement is without laboratory proof and is mere supposition.

Allow me to be presumptive enough to speak on behalf of some of our most respected colleagues in the area of research on AIDS; Dr. Peter Duesberg, Professor Molecular Biology, University of California at Berkeley, the world's foremost retrovirologist; Dr. Charles A. Thomas, Professor of Microbiology, Harvard; Dr. Kary Mullis, six-time Nobel Candidate, Nobel Laureate, 1993 and discoverer of the Polymer Chain Reaction. These are just a few of the hundreds of prominent scientists who have banded together to form "The Group For The Reevaluation Of The AIDS Hypothesis". I have spent five years in researching as many scientific papers and lay periodicals as possible in order to try to fully understand the enigma of the phenomena called AIDS. Everything I have read and verified has confirmed the suspicions which grew out of the obvious contradictions of the "hypothesis" and the practical experience from treating AIDS victims. AIDS is not an enigma, our medical texts have clearly defined the causes of acquired immune deficiencies for over fifty years. What appeared to be an emerging epidemic amongst homosexuals, occurred as a result of three coincidental phenomena; the advent of the "drug culture" of the sixties, the use of amyl nitrite ("poppers") and the visibility of the "gays" as a group when they "came out of the closet". If we add two other obvious factors, starvation in Africa (long recognized as the major cause of immune deficiency) and the use of AZT, the enigma of AIDS becomes crystal clear. The "mysterious" and the "intelligent" virus suddenly becomes the uneventful, ordinary, inanimate piece of dead tissue that it is.

I present to you just a fraction of the facts that cry out for an immediate investigation and re-evaluation of what I **now** know to be the "Deadly Deception" – The Viral-AIDS Hypothesis.

WHY HIV CANNOT CAUSE AIDS

None of the proposed explanations, of which there are more than forty, as to the *modus operandi* of HIV, nor the virus-AIDS hypothesis itself, are based on scientifically acceptable evidence or proof. The available laboratory evidence speaks against the hypothesis. The remainder of the evidence is epidemiological, and even that, when scrutinized and truthfully presented without first being selectively screened, proves that HIV is innocent of any involvement in AIDS.

EPIDEMIOLOGY

We are asked to believe that a single virus is the cause of both cell-destructive diseases, i.e. Pneumocystis pneumonia, and cellproliferative diseases, i.e. Kaposi's sarcoma!

Worse, we are asked to believe that a single virus can cause two distinctly different complexes, and do so on the basis of geographical distribution, sexual preferences and gender.

In Africa, AIDS is virtually 100% fever, diarrhea and wasting. In the United States and Europe, AIDS is 25 to 35 distinct diseases, depending on how they are classified.

There are no uniform or significant genetic differences between the isolated HIV or any of its mutants found in the U.S.A., Europe or Africa to account for the wide discrepancies in disease occurrences.

The incidence of HIV in Africa differs from one country to another and correlates only with malnutrition and starvation. Elsewhere it correlates with drugs, the male gender, sexual preference and crosses all national boundaries.

In Europe and the United States, 86% to 90% of AIDS cases are males. In Africa, AIDS occurs evenly between the sexes.

The predicted epidemic has not occurred. In the past 10 years (since 1984), 204,000 individuals in the U.S.A. have developed AIDS. 602,000 were predicted. In Africa, 129,000 have developed AIDS. 3,063,000 were predicted. If these figures were corrected for the normal incidence of all of the acquired immune deficiency diseases, as well as starvation and drugs (AZT included), none would be left to blame on HIV.

The predicted AIDS **epidemic** in Thailand produced only 123 AIDS cases in 8 years.

Laboratory rats treated with antibiotics and cortisone, both immunosuppressive, developed Pneumocystis pneumonia which is the most common disease of AIDS.

In Europe and America approximately 1/3 of the AIDS cases are diseases which are not truly immune deficient, i.e. Kaposi's sarcoma, lymphoma, wasting disease and dementia.

83% of American AIDS babies are "crack babies" (born to drug addicted mothers) or hemophiliac (congenital).

In Africa, the virus has little or no affinity for sexual or behavioral risk groups.

In spite of the ubiquitous presence of Pneumocystis and Candida, these diseases do not occur in AIDS in Africa.

50% of American AIDS patients are **presumptively diagnosed-** without a positive test.

AIDS occurs mostly in the 20 to 45 year-olds, our healthiest and armed forces-recruitable years.

The virus prefers males (90%), but the diseases it supposedly causes are not male specific.

THE VIRUS CALLED HIV

HIV has never been present in AIDS cases in amounts large enough to cause disease, and yet it supposedly kills the victim. Only 1 virus per 100,000 lymphocytes can be found in only 20% of AIDS cases, even when death is imminent.

The presence of the virus is often 40 times greater in healthy HIV-positive individuals than in fatal AIDS cases, where many times it can't be found at all.

The virus cannot be found in the lesions of Kaposi's sarcoma.

The virus cannot be found in the brain in dementia.

In order to isolate the virus from the blood of an AIDS victim, you have to culture at lease 5 million leucocytes and it may take 15 separate attempts to do so.

The incidence of AIDS is 1/3 lower in health care workers, caring for AIDS patients, than in the general population.

AIDS hypothesis supporters claim incredulously, without any proof, that the failure of the unproven HIV to meet Koch's Postulates, invalidates that 100 year-old standard for etiological proof!

The HIV test for the presence of antibodies, not the virus, AIDS is the first disease in the history of medicine in which immunity indicates the patient will die of the disease! Of course, there are at latent viruses which, under opportune situations of debilitation, replicate in sufficient numbers to cause clinical infection and even death.

This has never occurred with HIV, and has only been postulated and proclaimed a fact without any proof whatsoever.

The Centers For Disease Control in the U.S.A. never report the incidence of HIV in its HIV/AIDS Surveillance Report.   To do so would expose the fraud.

HIV correlates only 50% with AIDS. **Cytomegalovirus** correlates 100% with AIDS, as do **drugs** and the **Epstein-Barr virus.** There are also significantly higher correlations with **Hepatitis A, Hepatitis B, HSV**, the **number of blood transfusions, malnutrition** and **starvation.**

DISCREPANCIES ABOUND

Since HIV came onto the scene the median age of hemophiliacs has increased by 5 years!

The risk of AIDS in HIV-positive non-hemophiliacs is twice that of HIV-positive hemophiliacs.

The incidence of AIDS in the wives of HIV-positive hemophiliacs is 1/5 of the number predicted by the AIDS hypothesis.

The incidence of AIDS hemophiliac children **tripled** two years **after** the virus was filtered out of blood transfusions.

According to official statistics AIDS had not spread for 7 years – until they added 5 more diseases (1985-1992).

We are constantly being warned of the coming catastrophic epidemic. Yet, there is undeniable evidence that HIV has existed for a least 50 years and probably millions of years.

HIV in non-drug using prostitutes is virtually non-existent.

Venereal disease and unwanted pregnancies have **increased** in the past 8-10 years, but **not** HIV.

Only 1 provirus (not the virus) was found out of 1 million cells in only 1 out of 25 HIV-positive males.

Statistics indicate that if you want to "get AIDS" from an HIV-positive male you have to be on drugs for a long time.

In the U.S.A. and Africa the evidence is conclusive that there is no difference in the incidence of AIDS diseases between HIV-positive and HIV-negative babies.

If AIDS was sexually transmitted, the perinatal transmission would make it a pediatric disease – the incubation period is supposedly two years. **It is not a pediatric disease.**

A report released by the U.S. Job Corps and the U.S. Army, which was based on millions of tests, indicated that HIV was **evenly distributed between males and females** in the age group from 17 to 24. However, the Center for Disease Control in the U.S. reports that 85% of the AIDS cases in the same age group are **males**.

A proportionality exists between HIV and AIDS only if starvation, transfusions and drugs, including AZT are involved. Otherwise, being HIV-positive is meaningless.

10% of male and female **heterosexuals** prefer **anal** intercourse. The incidence of HIV and AIDS in those women is the same as compared to women who prefer vaginal intercourse. Yet, the incidence of AIDS is 90% male.

The AIDS virus has been demonstrated in blood samples from 50 years ago, at the same time that Masters and Johnson confirmed a high incidence of anal intercourse amongst **heterosexuals**.

Statistics show that in Africa it has to take an average of 10,000 acts of intercourse to transmit AIDS as compared to the U.S.A. and Europe's 1,000. That's 20 times a week!

HIV **in vivo,** when present, is rare and neutralized by antibodies (HIV-positive) and therefore non-infectious. **In vitro** (in the laboratory) they are infectious because there are no antibodies present.

AIDS amongst laboratory workers is the same as the general population even though their exposure is many millions of times greater.

More than a dozen co-factors have been **proposed** as necessary to cause AIDS along with HIV. HIV is usually **not** even present (80% of the time) and it is always dormant.

AIDS diseases are claimed to be the result of the immune deficiency or autoimmunity caused by HIV. However, four of the major diseases, Kaposi's sarcoma, lymphoma, dementia and wasting disease are not caused by immune deficiency.

Hoffman in 1990, in defense of his **theory** involving auto-immunity, wrote that all of "Duesberg's paradoxes" could be understood in the light of his (Hoffman's) "model" (Now there's a brilliant scientist; let's make Duesberg responsible rather that the Virus-AIDS hypothesis).

The autoimmune **theory** of Hoffman fails to explain: Kaposi's sarcoma, lymphoma, dementia and wasting disease; the specific diseases related to specific behavior (i.e. "poppers" and Kaposi's sarcoma); the incredible differences in the types of diseases between the HIV-infected groups; the bias for males; and the 80% (U.S.A) to 98% (Africa) HIV-positives who haven't developed AIDS since 1984.

One really bright group of scientists, Shaw et al., argued for the concept (never demonstrated) of the formation of antibodies against the HIV antibodies. If we accept their theory, then all viruses should cause AIDS.

Gallo, whose memory lapse about having stolen Montaigner's virus, for which he was declared guilty of "scientific misconduct" by his peers, claims to have observed HIV killing primarily T-cells. Montaigner, his "co-discoverer", published a paper declaring the exact opposite the same year, 1984.

Gallo **without any scientific evidence** and in direct contradiction to the 20 years of knowledge gained from the intensive and conclusive 20 billion dollar study of retroviruses during Nixon's "war on cancer", claims that HIV retrovirus **kills** its host cell which it absolutely needs in order to reproduce. The conversion of RNA to DNA requires the mitosis of the host cell, not its death!

The very reason that retroviruses were investigated as a probable cause of cancer, was their **non**cytocidal replication.

Gallo patented a technique of indefinitely reproducing T-cells in culture and **hypothesizes** that the T-cell line has developed a resistance to being killed by HIV. However, this has always been basically true of every T-cell line.

It is claimed that 50% of HIV infected individuals are supposed to die over a ten-year period. In Africa only 0.3% die each year which means we will have to wait 150 years for 50% to die! In the first 10 years of AIDS, the prediction for the United States and Europe was overestimated 300%.

After four years of on-site intensive study, investigators in Tanzania (Krynen, Phillipe and Evelyne, Directors of the Partage mission and reported by Neville Hodgekinson for the *Sunday Times* in the United Kingdom on 3 October 1993), state that there is no AIDS epidemic.

The Annual Conversion Rate from HIV-positive to AIDS is published each year by the World Health Organization. The figures indicate that if you are HIV-positive, your chances for survival are up to 300 times better if you live in Zaire rather than in Europe or the United States of America!

All claims for pathogenicity of HIV by virtue of mutation have never been observed or demonstrated and are contrary to all established facts.

HIV is claimed to have unique genes and toxins that destroy nerve tissue. Again, none of these claims are substantiated or demonstrated. The RNA information, structure and function of HIV do not distinguish it from other retroviruses.

The Simian Immunodeficiency Virus (SIV) which is claimed to cause "AIDS-like" diseases in macaques is being cited to argue support for the Virus-AIDS Hypothesis. However, SIV is only 40% similar to HIV; causes disease 15 times more effectively in 1/10 the time; does not stimulate antiviral antibodies; does not deplete T-cells; produces an entirely different spectrum of diseases; and only does so in laboratory macaques, and not naturally in the wild species. So much for a supposed analogy.

THE REAL CAUSES OF AIDS

The first edition (1952) of the *Merck Manual* listed the causes of acquired immune deficiencies in the order of occurrence: **malnutrition, drugs, radiation....**

The incidence of AIDS in Africa, which is completely different from the 25-odd diseases Europe and the United States of America and is characterized as **diarrhea, fever and wasting,** correlates virtually 100% with **malnutrition, starvation and parasitic disease.**

The incidence of drug use, i.e. **street drugs** (used orally or intravenously) all types, **amyl nitrite** (poppers) and other immune suppressive **medical drugs, particularly AZT, correlate virtually 100% with the development of AIDS in Europe and the United States! These factors have been proven sufficient to cause the diseases of AIDS. HIV is a sometimes present, innocent bystander that has yet to be proven necessary for anything that is occurring.**

Research by a respected group of Australian scientists have declared the test for HIV as scientifically invalid. They found that **malnutrition, multiple infections, malaria, multiple sclerosis, tuberculosis, the "flu" and measles can result in a positive test**. In Russia, screening with the Elisa test resulted in 30,000 positive tests. Yet, only 66 could be confirmed with the Western Blot.

Imagine the medical carnage being caused when individuals, because they once had measles or the "flu", are falsely diagnosed as having a virus which has never been proven to cause any disease, are given a drug which will kill them!

The incidence of AIDS in hemophiliacs drops dramatically when the protein contaminants in the added Factor VIII is refined three times.

Rare anecdotal cases of AIDS that were supposedly outside the risk groups, had been sensationalized in the press throughout the world. The cause of death was cited as AIDS due to HIV infection, but a closer look tells a different story:

An 18-year-old hemophiliac, Ryan White died of internal bleeding and **have been treated extensively with AZT** which causes AIDS (see package insert).

Paul Gann, a 77-year-old blood transfusion recipient died in 1989. Although the transfusion which was given in 1982 was not demonstrated to have HIV, it was blamed for his death. Gann had a **5-vessel bypass surgery** in 1982, **bypass surgery again** in 1983 and in 1989 was hospitalized for a **fractured hip, developed**

pneumonia and dies. How many times has this happened in virtually every doctor's practice before AIDS? Yet, his death was blamed on AIDS.

Kimberly Bergalis, who supposedly contracted AIDS from her dentist during a tooth extraction (the mode of transmission was never established) was tested for HIV after the dentist disclosed he was homosexual. **Kimberly was given AZT.** The incidence of HIV-positives amongst the dentist's patients was 0.4%, the **same** as it is for all Americans!

The increase in the annual death rate of American males between the ages of 25 to 44 rose by 10,000 during the 1980's. They were assumed to be due to AIDS. During the same period, however, the deaths from intravenous drug use rose 400%.

Male homosexuals comprise 60% of American AIDS patients. One study involving 170 of them produced the following breakdown of drug use, usually in multiple combinations:

nitrite inhalants – 96%   ethyl chloride inhalants – 42%
lysergic acid – 50%   cocaine – 55%
amphetamines – 60%   phenylcyclidine – 40%
methaqualone – 50%   marijuana – 90%
barbiturates – 25%   heroin – 10%
prescription drugs – 50%

Many other studies involving thousands confirm these figures.

AIDS victims had twice the lifetime drug dose that HIV carriers!

When amyl nitrite ("poppers") was outlawed in the State of Massachusetts, the incidence of Kaposi's sarcoma dropped 7-fold (700% difference). Wherever its use has been charted, the incidence of the disease parallels the use of the drug. This is also true of all other AIDS diseases. The incidence of multiple diseases, which usually results in the frequent use of antibiotics was as follows:

Gonorrhea – 80%   Hepatitis B – 50%   syphilis – 55%
Mononucleosis – 15%   parasitic diarrhea – 30%

AZT, A CAUSE OF AIDS

AZT is toxic to all cells; it is a DNA chain terminator. An independent laboratory found AZT to be 1,000 times more toxic than shown in the studies performed by the National Institutes of Health and the manufacturer (Burroughs-Wellcome).

180,000 HIV carriers worldwide are currently taking AZT. The drug insert clearly states that **AZT causes acquired immune deficiency.** Studies indicate that AZT does not effect the downward progression of CD-4+ cells.

Human and animal tests indicate that AZT causes severe depression (potentially fatal) in the production of red and white blood cells, muscle atrophy, plymyositis, lymphomas, hepatitis, dementia, mania, ataxia, encephalopathy, seizures and impotence. It is carcinogenic in mice.

Although it is well known that disease from drug use is dose related, this fact has been largely ignored in epidemiological research.

The only controlled study on AZT (FISCHL, et al., 1987) was discontinued after four months, supposedly because the beneficial effects were obvious. This study is a prime example of medical corruption:

- ➤ **The AZT group received transfusions 6 to 1 over the control group.**

- ➤ **The two groups were not matched or staged.**

- ➤ **Other "concomitant medications" were used.**

- ➤ **Drug sharing occurred between the AZT and placebo groups.**

- ➤ **The AZT group had 56 side effects and the placebo group had 31 side effects. This could only occur if the code had been broken, thus making the study useless.**

The code was broken the first week.

The ultimate outcome of the study and others performed since, indicated that AZT actually triples disease risk. The administration of AZT adds new serious and fatal disease risks. These include serious anemias requiring life-saving transfusions, leukopenia and death (20% in 9 months on AZT).

Studies clearly indicate that AZT accelerates progression to death, increases the incidence of lymphoma **3,000%** and does not prolong life.

Several studies have revealed recovery of cellular immunity and general improvement when AZT was discontinued.

IN SPITE OF THESE FACTS, THE FDA HAS NOT RECALLED AZT

The AIDS virus has been called mysterious, intelligent, strange, not ordinary, unpredictable and inconsistent. Compared to the unpredictability of the Virus-AIDS hypothesis, the Drug-AIDS hypothesis accurately predicts drug-specific diseases distinctly to the type of drug. AIDS diseases occur in HIV-free individuals, but are simply reported under their old names instead of being called AIDS.

Physicians have been victimized by less-than-scientific, self-serving researchers and politicians who mouth hypotheses as though they were truth and present half-truths which convey misleading conclusions. As a result, other scientists continue their expensive and fruitless search for "sharks in the desert". Meanwhile, hundreds of thousands, and eventually millions, will continue to die from lack of knowledge as to the true causes of AIDS and iatrogenic death from AZT.

It is time for physicians to remove the "art of medicine" mask of protection from criticism and boldly show their faces as true scientists. We must demand an immediate re-evaluation of the Virus-AIDS hypothesis in the interest of our patients and our sacred obligation to "above all do no harm".

Robert E. Willner, M.D., Ph.D.*

*Author of *Deadly Deception*
Peltec Publishing Co., Inc.
4400 North Federal Highway
Suite 210
Boca Raton, FL 33431

An Open Letter To Colleagues
Of
The Medical Profession

Dear Colleague,

It is my firm belief that most physicians, like myself, entered the field of medicine because of an intense desire to spend our lives in a meaningful and gratifying endeavor. I perceived medicine as a profession of science, compassion, and dignity, which would bring the honestly earned rewards of respect, honor and a relatively comfortable life. I believed that it was a profession that fostered independent though, creativeness and innovation, deeply rooted in integrity. I naively trusted medicine rose above avarice, politics, fraud and vindictiveness. During the thirty-five years that I practiced medicine, I have been privileged to work with many dedicated physicians and was honored by the opportunity to serve the profession as lecturer, president of medical associations, societies, boards and hospital staffs.

I made the decision to leave practice, so I could write, do research, actively fight for informed freedom of choice for patients, I wished also to help achieve for physicians, the freedom to include in the practice of medicine, homeopathics, herbs, vitamins and supplements in the prevention and treatment of disease. The political forces of organized medicine are disgracing our profession by dishonorable and unethical tactics aimed at the thousands of physicians who are repulsed by the many dangerous and ineffective drugs fostered on us by an unholy alliance with the pharmaceutical industry. More patient visits were made to practitioners of alternative therapies last year, than to medical family physicians. The reason: the public is disillusioned and disappointed in our ability to treat them. Their thought processes are not hindered by the intense beliefs brought about by our allopathic indoctrination. Many of us believe that ours is the only way, that we are at the cutting edge of science. Have we lost the ability to think with an open mind as a scientist should? Have we become so arrogant that we denounce even those things about which we have little or no knowledge?

I, like many of you, have seen incredible advances in technology. The medical profession excels in its genius in dealing with emergency and surgical problems. It may astound you to know, that when dealing with the remaining ninety percent of medical problems, we are largely ineffective. In claiming sole rights to so-called state-of-the-art science, we conveniently ignore the fact that more than eight percent of our therapies have never been double-blinded. Yet we deny to our colleagues the right to practice treatments that were used by Hippocrates and the physicians of the East, which have persisted for thousands of years. We have been denied access and exposure to these therapies because "they have not been proven". Because of this hypocrisy and self-imposed imprisonment of the mind, our patients suffer and we are denied the gratification of providing successful care. For many of us, this was the main reason we became doctors!

Unfortunately, we have seen the growth of stifling bureaucracy and control, often from within our own ranks or imposed by government. The inevitable consequences of such circumstances are the loss of freedom of thought and creativity, the suppression of innovation or the tyranny of a few whose beliefs seek to hold us hostage. This, in turn, reaps even greater evils; the opportunity by the establishment to perpetrate fraud with impunity, resist inspection, defy challenge and reverse progress.

A travesty of science and medicine has occurred in the past decade, of such dimension and incredulity, that your first impulse will be to dismiss any an all criticism. This indeed, was the belief of its perpetrators and thus far, they have succeeded. Because of the inherent trust that we place in our fellow scientists; we were easily led down a deceptive path because it was decorated with primrose flowers of arcane scientific jargon with which many of us may not have been adequately familiar. Such is the case with AIDS – the so-called "Epidemic of the Century". Please read *Deadly Deception* (Why Sex And The Virus Absolutely Do Not Cause AIDS). It is fully referenced, factual and will astonish you. I implore you, do not dismiss this as something that will not be changed by your input. The names of the individuals, who seriously questions the HIV-AIDS theories, read like a "Who's Who" in science. They include:

Dr. Peter H. Duesberg, Professor of Molecular Biology, University of California, Berkeley, CA; international authority on retroviruses; member of the National Academy of Sciences and recipient of its highest honor;

Dr. Charles A. Thomas, Jr., Harvard Biologist, founder of The Group for the Scientific Reappraisal of the HIV-AIDS Hypothesis;

Dr. Kary Mullis, Biochemist; 1993 Nobel Laureate, inventor of PCR, the Polymerase Chain Reaction, which is the most accurate measure of the presence of viruses;

Dr. Robert Root-Bernstein, Professor of Physiology, Michigan State University, leading authority on AIDS;

Dr. Gordon Steward, Emeritus Professor of Public Health, University of Glasgow, World Health Organization consultant on communicable diseases;

Dr. Joseph Sonnabend, pioneer AIDS researcher, founder of the AIDS Medical Foundation – and many more!

At this writing, the number of prominent scientists exceed five hundred. The reputation of American medicine has been placed in great jeopardy by dishonest and greedy scientists who wield astonishing power because they have linked very influential government agencies into their fraud. We in medicine have been deprived of an unbiased forum because the detractors have been denied access to medical meetings. It is now up to physicians and their patients to demand a complete and open investigation by the Congress of the United States, so that the opposition can be heard. This action will serve to exonerate medicine from complicity in this contemptible affair.

Your respectful colleague,
Robert E. Willner, M.D., Ph.D.

Sample Letter (telegram) To The Congress, Senate, Parliament or Appropriate Officials and Representatives of Your Government

(you should write it in your own words if possible)

Dear _____,

    I strongly support an investigation of the possibility of a major fraud in relation to the entire so-called AIDS crisis. Many of the world's most prominent researchers have raised serious questions as to its cause, treatment and research difficulties. It appears that the epidemic may have nothing to do with a virus, but is, in reality, an expression of excessive drug use, both medically and illegally in the "street". Please read the enclosed paper which documents the major discrepancies and distortions upon which the hypothesis is based. Drs. Peter Duesberg (U of Cal., Berkeley) and Charles A. Thomas, Jr. (Harvard) head a group of over a thousand scientists who are demanding a re-evaluation. Officials in government agencies, who have a substantial financial interest in AIDS testing, have used the most disgraceful tactics to prevent an investigation into this matter. If the suspicions are true, and the evidence is overwhelming, many billions of dollars are being wasted and many individuals will die from inappropriate treatment.

                    Sincerely,

(if you wish to pass on what you have learned, send your copy of this book and add the following post-script)

P.S. – Please read the enclosed book.

ADDITIONAL READING SOURCES

The Group For The Scientific Re-Appraisal of AIDS
(Newsletter-monthly)

Editor -Paul Philpot
(734) 467-7339

Availability
Re-Appraising AIDS
7514 Girard Avenue, #1-331
La Jolla, CA 92037

Price: $25.00/Year - Make Check Payable To – The Group

Inventing The HIV Virus
Author – Peter Duesberg
Availability – Local Book Stores

Deadly Deception
Author – Dr. Robert E. Willner, M.D., Ph D.
Availability – Local Book Stores

The Great AIDS Hoax
Author – T. C. Fry

Availability – MRKCO Dist.
PO Box 32034
Chicago, IL 60632

Price: $12.95 Plus $3.00 Shipping
Illinois Residents add $1.13 Sales Tax.
Make Check Payable To - MRKCO Dist.

223

AZT Poison By Prescription
Author – John Lauritsen
Availability – Local Book Stores

AIDS, Inc.
Author – Jon Rappoport
Availability – Local Book Stores

The Secrets Behind HIV & AIDS:
Causes-Cures Contradictions and Conspiracies
Author – Jeremy F. Selvey

Availability
Project AIDS International c/o
The Levitican Empire
318 N. Carson St., Suite 214
Carson City, NV 89701
(323) 660-3381

The AIDS Indictment
Author – Marvin R Kitzerow Jr.

Availability – MRKCO DIST.
PO Box 32034
Chicago, IL 60632

Price - $14.95 includes free shipping and handling
Illinois residents add $1.31 Sales Tax.
Make check payable to MRKCO DIST.

USA
CANADA
AUSTRALIA
EUROPE
JAPAN
HONG KONG
MALAYSIA
KOREA
MEXICO

MRKCO MARKETING/DIST.

INTERNATIONAL MARKETING/DISTRIBUTING
AND BUSINESS DEVELOPMENT

ORDER FORM

Pay by check or money order drawn on U.S. bank.
Make check/money order out to MRKCO Marketing.

MAIL TO:
MRKCO MARKETING/DIST.
P.O. Box 32034
Chicago, IL 60632

Name: _____

Address: _____

City: _____ State_____

Zip: _____

Country: _____

Enclose $14.95 plus free shipping and handling in U.S.;
Illinois residents add $1.31 sales tax.
Outside U.S.A. add $3.95 shipping and handling.

CREDIT CARD PURCHASES
See
aidsindictment.com

USA
CANADA
AUSTRALIA
EUROPE
JAPAN
HONG KONG
MALAYSIA
KOREA
MEXICO

MRKCO MARKETING/DIST.

INTERNATIONAL MARKETING/DISTRIBUTING
AND BUSINESS DEVELOPMENT

ORDER FORM

Pay by check or money order drawn on U.S. bank.
Make check/money order out to MRKCO Marketing.

MAIL TO:
MRKCO MARKETING/DIST.
P.O. Box 32034
Chicago, IL 60632

Name: _____

Address: _____

City: _____ State_____

Zip: _____

Country: _____

Enclose $14.95 plus free shipping and handling in U.S.;
Illinois residents add $1.31 sales tax.
Outside U.S.A. add $3.95 shipping and handling.

CREDIT CARD PURCHASES
See
aidsindictment.com